AF696339

A Curious Intimacy

A Curious Intimacy is an innovative study into the interrelation between art and neuro-psychoanalysis which significantly narrows the divide between the humanities and the sciences.

Situating our grasp of the creative mind within the historical context of theories of sublimation, Lois Oppenheim proposes a change in paradigm for the study of the creative process, questioning the idea that creativity serves, above all, the reparation of early object relationships and the resolution of conflict. The book is divided into two parts. Part I, **Art and the brain**, introduces the field of neuro-psychoanalysis and examines the contribution it can make to the discussion of gender and art. Part II, **A new direction for interdisciplinary psychoanalysis**, draws on the verbal and visual artistry of Samuel Beckett, Paul Klee, and Martha Graham to put to the test the proposed new direction for applied psychoanalysis. Lois Oppenheim concludes by addressing the future of psychoanalysis as it becomes increasingly informed by neuroscience and raising questions about what the neurobiology of emotion and feeling has to tell us about the creative experience of an individual and what might constitute a "neuro-psychoanalytic aesthetics".

A Curious Intimacy will have great appeal for all those interested in the study of imagination and creativity. It will also be of particular interest to students across the humanities and sciences and to psychotherapists and psychoanalysts wanting to explore the contribution that neuro-psychoanalysis can make to our understanding of the creative process.

Lois Oppenheim is Distinguished Scholar, Professor of French and Chair of the Department of Modern Languages and Literatures at Montclair State University.

A Curious Intimacy

Art and Neuro-psychoanalysis

Lois Oppenheim

Routledge
Taylor & Francis Group
LONDON AND NEW YORK

First published 2005
by Routledge
27 Church Road, Hove, East Sussex BN3 2FA

Simultaneously published in the USA and Canada
by Routledge
270 Madison Avenue, New York, NY 10016

Routledge is an imprint of the Taylor & Francis Group

© 2005 Lois Oppenheim

Typeset in Times by RefineCatch Limited, Bungay, Suffolk
Printed and bound in Great Britain by MPG Books Ltd, Bodmin
Cover design by Lisa Dynan

All rights reserved. No part of this book may be reprinted or reproduced or utilized in any form or by any electronic, mechanical or other means, now known or hereafter invented, including photocopying and recording, or in any information storage or retrieval system, without permission in writing from the publishers.

This publication has been produced with paper manufactured to strict environmental standards and with pulp derived from sustainable forests.

British Library Cataloguing in Publication Data
A catalogue record for this book is available from the British Library

Library of Congress Cataloging in Publication Data
Oppenheim, Lois.
A curious intimacy: art and neuro-psychoanalysis / Lois Oppenheim.—1st ed.
p. cm.
Includes bibliographical references and index.
ISBN 1–58391–806–X (hbk)
1. Psychoanalysis and the arts. 2. Creation (Literary, artistic, etc.)
I. Title.
NX180.P7066 2005
700′.1′9—dc22 2005008648

ISBN 1–58391–806–X hbk

To Peter B. Neubauer, M.D.
A singularly wise and compassionate man

The tears stream down my cheeks from my unblinking eyes. What makes me weep so? . . . Perhaps it is liquified brain.

Samuel Beckett,
The Unnamable

Contents

Foreword

When the notion of a "neuro-psychoanalytic aesthetics" first came to my notice, it came as something of a surprise. Neuro-psychoanalysis seeks to draw psychoanalysis more securely into the family of natural sciences, thereby subjecting its hypotheses to new levels of objective scrutiny. The application of psychoanalytic hypotheses to understanding and appreciating art and artists, one might think, draws it in quite the opposite direction.

This book shows how wrong-headed such thinking is. One of the great strengths of psychoanalysis has always been its attempt to unite in a single tissue of theory such apparently disparate subjects as psychopathology and art. A basic science of the human mind must of course trench on all the "human sciences"; but what was special about psychoanalysis was that it attempted to provide a natural science of the human element in those other fields. It aspired to be nothing less than the missing link between the natural and human sciences.

There *must*, after all, be objective laws which account comprehensively for the part of nature that we call the human mind. The alternative would imply that human behaviour is somehow beyond comprehension, above and beyond the whole of the natural universe. There must, therefore, also be universals in human aesthetic experience and creativity. To the extent that neuro-psychoanalytic methods render psychoanalytic hypotheses more secure, to that extent they can only enhance our understanding of art and artists. This book represents a first step in that direction and therefore deserves the attention of anyone who values this approach to human nature.

Mark Solms
Chair of Neuropsychology, University of Cape Town
Director, Arnold Pfeffer Center for Neuro-Psychoanalysis, New York

Acknowledgements

I wish to thank a number of people who contributed, sometimes in ways unbeknownst to themselves, to the preparation of this volume. In particular, Alice W. Flaherty, M.D. and Oliver Turnbull, Ph.D. were extraordinarily generous with their time and were always at the ready as I delved deeper into neuroscience. Thomas G. Benedek, M.D. graciously lent his expertise in rheumatology to my research on scleroderma; Charles Brenner, M.D., David Milrod, M.D., Peter Dunn, M.D., and others at the New York Psychoanalytic Institute clarified matters on the psychoanalytic front, as did Irwin Badin, Ph.D. Christopher A. Bürgi gave me access to his family's extraordinary Klee collection in Bern; and Michael Molnar of the Freud Museum in London, the personnel in the Archives of the British Psychoanalytic Society in London and at the Paul Klee Stiftung in Bern, Julian Keenan, Ph.D., Michele McKee at the C.G. Jung Center in New York, and Julian A. Garforth, Ph.D. of the Beckett International Foundation were all helpful in securing materials and supplying various kinds of information. Stuart Hodes, Pearl Lang, and Marni Thomas Wood spoke to me at length about Martha Graham; Dr. George Hogle and Dr. Joseph Henderson did the same about Frances Wickes; and Tracy Boyd was very helpful with regard to Jung. Sidney Feshbach remained as he always has: enthusiastic about discussing any new idea as it occurred to me. Ellis Oppenheim is to be thanked for withstanding all a spouse inevitably endures when books are in gestation. He withstood it with his usual equanimity, for which I remain immensely grateful.

Introduction

In his celebrated paper of 1910 on Leonardo da Vinci, Freud concluded: "Instincts and their transformations are at the limit of what is discernible by psycho-analysis. From that point it gives place to biological research."[1] Already in 1895, in his unpublished "Project for a Scientific Psychology," Freud had attempted an outline of the neurological foundation of our psychic makeup, but the anatomical explanation was limited by the scientific environment in which it was conceived. Disillusioned, he abandoned the neurobiological pursuit. He never retreated, however, from the belief that neurology would one day confirm his thinking on the functioning of the mind.

Today the biology of mental processing (popularly known as the "hard problem") is among the most notable conundrums faced by scientists. Indeed, why the psyche is apprehended in two distinct forms, as a physical organ and as mental acts, is a question that has assumed a new sense of urgency in recent years. A derivative of the mind–body legacy bequeathed by Descartes, it presents a fresh challenge to neurology and psychology alike. Recognizing the mind as a sequence of functions performed by the brain, neuroscientists are increasingly joining forces with mental health practitioners to rid us of the dualistic conception once and for all.

With recent advances in biotechnology – PET scans (proton emission tomography), fMRI (functional magnetic resonance imaging), and TMS (transcranial magnetic stimulation) – we have gained considerably more knowledge of the brain than was available to Freud and his contemporaries. Neuro-psychoanalysis, a young but vital discipline, builds on that knowledge in addressing the dynamic implications of the neurophysiology of emotion and feeling, and of the mechanisms of consciousness and cognition as well. With the renewed interest of some psychoanalysts in biology – in the integration of physico-chemical structures with conscious and unconscious processes – much has already been learned about affect regulation, motivation, and other aspects of psychological function previously knowable only through clinical observation. That a need for rethinking the relation between our intrapsychic and socio-cultural realities has resulted is clear. But how might it be achieved?

Among the most conspicuous arenas in which this relation is played out is the aesthetic, whether the making or reception of art. As a point of departure, therefore, the following question might be addressed: What is meant by the "pleasure" of visual or verbal creative expression when the body – its chemical, neurological, musculo-skeletal, and visceral systems – is shown to be the basis of mental imaging and the self? Such is the impetus for this book.

It was Freud's notion of the diversion of libidinal energy known as "sublimation" that implicated the human body as a source of creativity. As self psychologists and object relations theorists[2] departed from drive theory and sought alternative contexts in which to explain the creative endeavor, the idea of creativity as a defense of the ego against unacceptable, somatically derived urges of the id has fallen into disrepute. On the very border between the intrapsychic and the environmental, however, the concept is still useful, necessary even, for our understanding of civilization as a whole. In fact, as Joel Whitebook has recently noted, indispensable in accounting for the creation of all cultural objects, it accounts for the origination of psychoanalysis itself.[3]

Sublimation, in a word, was viewed by Freud as a healthy inhibition of aim. Channeling libidinal energy into culturally acceptable (intellectual or artistic) endeavors, the sublimatory act, he claimed, diverts the discharge of sexual energy toward a non-sexual aim. In *Three Essays on the Theory of Sexuality* (1905) and *The Ego and the Id* (1923), Freud explained the concept developmentally: With the deferral of the reproductive functions of the sexual impulse, the child enters a period of latency during which the impulse is reconfigured. It is transformed from an erotic libido into a kind of narcissistic libido in which the ego itself is substituted for the love-object. From this beginning in childhood sexual latency, sublimation becomes the means whereby instinctual forces or bodily drives are redirected in creative thinking and artistic expression.

Almost 50 years later Donald Winnicott would ask, "Does the concept of sublimation really cover the whole pattern?"[4] It was his contention that Freud had not sufficiently demonstrated where, in the mind's topography of consciousness, the preconscious, and the unconscious, sublimation was to be situated. Without denying the body as the primary source of creativity, Winnicott located the origin of sublimation not in body functioning, but in body experience. His emphasis was on the infant's experiencing of an emotional environment "good enough" to allow for the development of a creative interaction with the world. In this sense, Winnicott's notion of sublimation – his situating the origin of cultural experience within the object relation, within the "potential space" between infant and reliable mother where creative living first appears as play – differed significantly from Freud's.

Others have similarly stressed the importance of object relations over drive determination in their writings on sublimation. For example, Melanie Klein and Hanna Segal, her closest associate, described the essence of the creative experience as a restorative process implicating attachment above all else. Symbol formation, requisite to the imaginative production of art, was said by both Klein and Segal to be rooted in the depressive position, the early experience of mourning the object loved, hated, and lost. Restitution, then, of what the instinctual impulses psychically destroyed, was viewed as the artist's principal aim.

In the same tradition, Ella Sharpe also focussed on the reparative function of creative expression. But Sharpe saw sublimation as based more on a "primal identification" with the parents than on a coming to terms with loss. Hostily targeted for their association with the life-and-death problem of nourishment, the introjected parental images were thought by Sharpe to be overpowered through the externalization that is art. Malevolent impulses, in other words, were what led to the artist's rendering or symbolic reshaping of an identification infused with aggression.

In France, psychoanalysis has grappled with the drive versus object relations controversy under the specter of Jacques Lacan's pervasive influence. Reappraising the Freudian legacy, Lacan retained the primacy of drive determination in the principle concepts of psychoanalysis inclusive of sublimation. But he privileged the structural relation between the unconscious and language to the detriment of the drive's integrity and organicity. Subsumed by the manifestation of fantasy on the order of linguistic symbolism, object relatedness was similarly deconstructed. Sublimation, reduced by Lacan to a play of symbols and signifying functions, thus re-presented rather than projected the desire of sexuality.

Psychoanalysts in the United States in the middle of the last century viewed the sublimatory process from a radically different perspective. Though a bird's eye view can hardly do it justice, it is worth noting that the ego psychology of Heinz Hartmann favored the notion of drive neutralization, the idea of a deinstinctualized energy, over that of the libidinally charged sublimation originally espoused by Freud. Ernst Kris sought the middle of the road: In his 1955 paper "Neutralization and Sublimation: Observations on Young Children," Kris suggested that the term "neutralization" be used to indicate the transformations of energy so as to reserve "sublimation" solely for the deflexion of goal.[5]

For his part, Hans Loewald objected to the implication that "neutralization" was altogether non-instinctual, a function of the autonomous ego. Substituting a "reconciliation" between object-oriented libidinized energy and narcissistic libido, Loewald defended the dynamic quality of the sublimatory process against the debiologizing tendency of ego psychology. At the same time, however, he refused the idea of sublimation as a purely biological force. Maintaining that it was not to be viewed as a defense against the id, he situated it on the order of internalization and ego development. In so doing, he did away with the notion that a reduction of tension, a discharge of object libido, was endemic to the sublimatory act. Instead, he stressed the faculty of object relatedness, the capacity to form new connections with the world, which developed out of the psychic matrix of the infant's symbiotic union with its mother: "Sublimations," he wrote, "are progressing differentiations that culminate in new synthetic organizations of such unitary experiences."[6] He thereby proved significantly closer, in the matter of sublimation, to Winnicott than to Freud.

To be sure, the question of the role played in sublimation by drive determination versus object relations is (as it is in all the major concepts of psychoanalysis) highly reductive. But evidence supporting the neurobiological genesis of drive theory is increasingly compelling. Should the correlation between the discharge and inhibition of libidinal drive and the interdependent subcortical structures comprising the limbic circuits of the brain continue to be successfully documented,[7] what already appears to be a renewed interest in Freudian affect theory will most certainly increase.

In the neurobiological context the question underlying the concept of sublimation and its variations – why do we make and enjoy art? – today gives rise to another, formulated by psychoanalyst Gilbert Rose as follows: "How does a work of art transform a mere visual image into one that can convey emotional expressiveness?"[8] Thinking along the same lines, but targeting literature, the critic Geoffrey Hartman has phrased it somewhat differently: "How does the primary process enter language?"[9] To the "how" as well as the "why" neuroscience, as Freud believed it would, has begun to provide answers.

In fact, evidence now exists that complex neural structures – those of the cerebral cortex, of the right and left hemispheres, and other sites of the brain as well – are responsible for what Antonio Damasio describes as "wordless storytelling," a naturally occurring inner narrative:

> The entire construction of knowledge, from simple to complex, from nonverbal imagetic to verbal literary, depends on the ability to map what happens over time, *inside* our organism, *around* our organism, *to* and *with* our organism, one thing followed by another thing, causing another thing endlessly. [. . .] The brain inherently represents the structures and states of the organism, and in the course of regulating the organism as it is mandated to do, the brain naturally weaves wordless stories about what happens to an organism immersed in an environment.[10]

It is, at least in part, from this preverbal narrative – "the imagetic representation of sequences of brain events"[11] – that visual and verbal art are made.

They also obtain, however, from the fundamental characteristic of human relatedness that finds expression in compassion, empathy, and other social emotions. These, too, are neurologically based. As Peter Neubauer and Alexander Neubauer have explained:

> A neurological system of transmission seems to exist from infancy,

> allowing for the information of social signals – smiles, frowns, cries, and laughter – to be received, understood, and re-communicated. Identification with these emotions is the next step, one which begins and matures predictably for everyone except those who have neurological defects in these emotional pathways.[12]

Another significant finding of recent studies is that the different regions of the brain, once thought to be individually responsible for any given function, work together and are crucial to making the others perform as they should. The cerebellum, for example, on which the coordination of our physical movements depends, has also been found responsible for cognitive sequencing. And it plays a role in visualization and in ordering the thinking required to create. Indeed, motor function has been shown to be intricately linked to functions once thought to be solely of the "mind." As psychiatrist John Ratey tells us, "movement is a physical expression of e-motion" insofar as feelings, triggered by thoughts, produce chemical and hormonal changes that, in turn, affect not only breathing, heart rate, and other physiological states, but laughter and crying, facial expressions, and physical stance or posture as well. Moreover, the proximity of the limbic system to the cerebellum and basal ganglia (also involved in motor regulation) explains the "close relationship between emotion and movement, and the feelings of emotional consequences of our actions." Hence the connection between some emotional changes and movement disorders like depression and Parkinson's disease.[13] What are the implications of such neuroscientific data, of the interaction of sensory and motor function, for our understanding of artistic creation and the aesthetic experience?

To the extent that the neurophysiology of emotion is rapidly becoming clear – that the neural mechanisms essential to emotional processing are increasingly being identified – we can appreciate the consequences of neuroscientific discovery for psychoanalysis. Indeed, uncovering how affective states correlate with the architecture and functioning of the brain; how repression, attention, reality testing, and other human mental processes are neurologically organized; and how aspects of personality are structurally related to human anatomy defines the confluence of psychoanalytic and neuroscientific study. To the extent, moreover, that the aim of psychoanalytic understanding is the enhancement of well-being, the strengthened capacity for a creative relation to the world, its connections with neuroscience bear implications for aesthetic pleasure that must also be profound. It is there that a distinctly new direction for what has traditionally been termed "applied psychoanalysis" comes into play.

I will argue in this book that, insofar as a number of dynamic, somatically based tensions are inherent in the creative process – that there is a discharge of bodily drive in representation – neurophysiological function is significant (in more than the obvious ways) for both the making and reception of art.

What I wish to show, more precisely, is that *the primary impulse of creativity is homeostatic in as much as creativity serves to augment self-awareness and it is on awareness of self that homeostasis depends*. Self-awareness is an amalgam of processes in which representation of the body in the mind is linked with cognition and affect. Its deep roots, as Damasio tells us, "are to be found in the ensemble of brain devices which continuously and *nonconsciously* maintain the body state within the narrow range and relative stability required for survival."[14] This is to say that homeostasis, which refers to the physiological mechanisms required to maintain the body's internal states, is necessarily implicated by the self however complex and multidimensional its constitution. And creative expression is homeostatic (conceived in the broad sense of the term) in that it passes through the filter of subjectivity, the nonconscious positing of the self as a performative agent.

How the biological matrix of subjectivity impacts the psychodynamic component of artistic process, then, is the subject of this book. Until recently, most studies considering the overlap of psychoanalysis and the literary or plastic arts have been what Freud termed pathographic; they have been concerned more with what the creative product tells us about the life of the creator than with the subjective experience of creativity itself. Owing largely to the neuroscientific efforts of Mark Solms, Jaak Panksepp, Allan Schore, and Damasio, among others, the work of a growing number of psychoanalysts displays a shift in focus. That of Drs. Arnold Cooper, Arnold Modell, Jerome Oremland, Morton Reiser, and Howard Shevrin may be cited in this regard. Extending beyond the "metabiographical" (the term is Oremland's), it seeks, literally and figuratively, to better balance the picture. Cooper, for example, has discussed changes in the psychoanalytic model of the mind imposed by findings in neuroscience. And Modell has considered structures of the imagination as the mind's metaphoric equivalents of unassimilated experience. For his part, Damasio has described creativity in terms of biological homeostasis and the impulse of every living cell to survive.[15] In fact, Damasio's notion of creativity as a regulation of the "life urge" will serve as a model for this work. To the extent that the mind, today, is understood in relation to functions performed by the brain, the neurobiological derivation of those tensions – between impulse and reason, say – at play within the creative process simply cannot be overlooked. My objective, therefore, is to explore such tensions as they are revealed within the aesthetic domain to see how they reflect, primarily in the work of a writer, a painter, and a dancer, the struggle for balance in the relation between soma and psyche, the struggle for the stability of a homeostatic state.

In Chapter 1 I consider what is meant by the subjectivity of aesthetic experience and why that subjectivity might be said to reflect the state of an individual's brain. What might constitute an enhancement of self-awareness in the creative acts of making and perceiving art and how might it be explained in neurobiological terms? More important, what remains of art's mystery when its biological foundations are revealed? Chapter 2 takes a new look at an old question; namely, whether art, and literature in particular, relates the specificity of sexual difference. My effort, though, is to reveal what "the decade of the brain" adds to the discussion of gender and art. The question underlying this chapter is whether or not the neurobiology of self-awareness supports the notion of a female (or feminine) expressive act. The work of Samuel Beckett is the focus of Chapter 3 where the direction I am proposing for applied psychoanalysis, one based on a new paradigm of creative purpose and process, is put to the test. All Beckett's characters (for lack of a better word) exhibit some kind of profound psychic disturbance; indeed, an impoverished body image and a distorted sense of identity are consistently latent within a markedly deficient emotional connectivity to the world. The defences of fragmentation, denial, and dedifferentiation have been widely considered with regard to Beckett's work since the 1960s. But a very different perspective on this writing may be derived from the paradigm of creativity as a somatopsychically efficacious act that I will put forth in Part II. The change in direction I am proposing for applied psychoanalysis is again put to the test in my discussion of the late work of Paul Klee. The vitality and rhythms of Klee's painting are well documented and Klee himself wrote prolifically about art. Little, though, has been said of the unique bodily distortions to which his deep sense of irony gave form. How was his belief in movement as the basis of point and line a manifestation of body sensation? More important, how did physical illness – more precisely, scleroderma, the rheumatological disease that only temporarily diminished his productivity but permanently altered the visceral perception of his self – reveal itself in his art? The link between self-awareness and the dramatic stylistic alterations characteristic of Klee's late work is the subject of Chapter 4.

In the 1920s Harvard psychologist W. B. Cannon defined homeostasis as the relative constancy of the body's "internal environment," the regulation of blood and tissue fluids determinative of circulatory, respiratory, and other biological mechanisms.[16] A concept widely used in the "hard sciences," its extension to psychoanalysis, where one may speak of psychic homeostasis, and even to the anthropological notion of cultural (or social) homeostasis is a fortunate outcome of the increase in interdisciplinary dialogues of late. Using the term in the broader sense of somatopsychic equilibration throughout this book leads me in the final chapter to the idea that both music and dance act upon this constancy in ways that literature and painting do not. To substantiate this view, and outline the specificity of dance's power to augment the self-awareness at the root of the homeostatic quest, I look at the work of Martha Graham. Both Graham's technique and choreography were built upon the most fundamental rhythm and motion of the body: the inhalation and exhalation that maintains its life. What I aim to show is that, through her aesthetic play on the kinesthetic experience of primary bodily function,

Graham accessed a deep sense of self and a degree of self consolidation she might otherwise not have known.

It is hoped that *A Curious Intimacy: Art and Neuro-psychoanalysis* will provoke further discussion of the relation between neuroscience and the creative imagination. Our understanding of artists' inhibitions, of connections between cognition and creation, of diverse effects of psychoanalytic treatment on artistic productivity, and of the compensatory-versus-innate-nature-of-creativity debate itself would surely be enhanced by continued examination of the interrelation of soma and psyche on the biological frontier.

Part I

Art and the brain

Introduction

Neuro-psychoanalysis is an effort to combine observations of subjectivity from two different perspectives. More precisely, it describes subjective experience and the relation of mental function to the brain by uniting the empirical data of neuroscientific research with the clinical evidence of psychodynamic study and treatment. The aesthetic or creative disposition of the mind/brain is one of several areas neuro-psychoanalysis may enter as, over time, it enlarges its terrain of investigation. This book, whose focus is how creativity is experienced, not what is created in a work of art, is a modest attempt to steer it in that direction.

Because creative states are inherently subjective, a sine qua non of creative thinking or activity, as I see it, is an impact on the creator. This is less obvious than it may seem. Indeed, the subjective component that drives creativity is sorely lacking in the literature. Howard Gardner, who has written prolifically and intelligently on the topic, speaks of the "new agenda" forged by creators, of the novelty and breakthroughs that relate the creator to his or her field. For Gardner, "all creative activity grows, first, out of the relationships between an individual and the objective world of work and, second, out of the ties between an individual and other human beings." But this "triangle of creativity"[1] stops short of what for me is the real evidence that creative work has taken place: some degree of change evoked within the self.

Similarly, Dean Keith Simonton discusses creativity from the perspective of the impact of the individual's thought on the work of the larger community, whether of scientists, artists, or others. Impact on the discipline is certainly a significant measure of the imaginative faculty but, as Simonton himself reminds us, the capacity for creative achievement is by no means synonymous with possessing the traits of a creative individual.[2] Simonton considers the roles of cognition and personality in the thoughts and behavior of the highly creative person and stresses the difficulty of disentangling the components of the richly associative network of thinking and imagining that constitutes the creative state. His insights are most valuable, in fact, for the empirical rigor of his investigations into the multiple determinants of creative praxis. To cite a brief example, he shows that one phase of the creative process, the incubation period, is vulnerable to a number of experiences that may affect the outcome of the creative endeavor. These include both external and internal events, events in the outside world of everyday life and mental events having to do, among other things, with unrelated creative projects that can "prime divergent associative pathways."[3] Though, like Gardner, Simonton does not go so far as to address the question of impact on the individual, he does distinguish between creativity's three essential components: "(a) the products that contain the creative ideas, (b) the persons who conceived those ideas, and (c) the processes those persons used to do so."[4] And this distinction is the first step in being able to speak of the interrelation of neuroscience and psychoanalysis in the context of creativity and aesthetics.

What Mark Solms, Howard Shevrin, and other practitioners of neuro-psychoanalysis endeavor to do is correlate neurobiological systems with psychoanalytic concepts that have been used to account for behavior, impulses, and thinking. A comprehensive review of the validation of an increasing number of psychoanalytic concepts (those of the unconscious and of drive not least among them) by recent discoveries in neuroscience is not possible here. But the point may nevertheless be made that the obvious incomparability of the quantitative data obtained in neurobiological studies with the cognitive-emotional data revealed in the clinical process of psychoanalysis in no way negates the value of considering their complementary bearing on creativity. For, indeed, there is a fundamental compatibility of the two kinds of information that emanates from their common subjective source. As psychoanalyst Morton Reiser explains it: "The mind principle of affective linkage [. . .] can be regarded as analogous to the brain principle of connection via limbic system linkage" precisely because "affect is a phenomenon that has both psychological *and* physiological manifestations."[5] In affect, then, we have the point of departure for a neuro-psychoanalytic understanding of creativity, the means, in fact, of exploring the psychological and physiological (or somatopsychic) aim of the creative endeavor. Affect is what separates the person from the product and the process. Having both psychological and physiological manifestations, however, it is also, as I will argue in the second part of this book, at the very center of creative purpose.

The implications of the premise of neuro-psychoanalysis – that there is an analogy to be made between the associative links in the neural memory systems of the mind and the limbic system links to cortical neural networks in the brain – are many and varied.[6] Reiser and others have demonstrated this in their investigations of, for example, the formation of imagery in dreaming and hallucinatory states, the role of traumatic memory in PTSD (post-traumatic stress disorder), and the transference relationship between analyst and analysand. In extending the neuro-psychoanalytic effort to the very different arena of aesthetic experience, we will see that many of the same issues dealt with by

Reiser and his colleagues – symbolization, mental representation, the meaning of meaning, the structural and dynamic relations between imaginative thinking and the perceptual operation of our sensory modalities, and intersubjectivity – come to the fore. It is therefore with these, and then with the question of the universality versus gender specificity of the creative process in view of what is now known of the brain, that I begin.

Chapter 1
Creativity and biology

As previously stated, this is a book about the relation between the biological matrix of the self and the psychodynamic dimension of art. What I wish to determine is this: As science increasingly accounts for the neurobiology of mentation and our inner representational world, for the neurobiology of emotion and of conscious and unconscious processes, does creativity assume a more positivistic significance than has heretofore been supposed? Do the neurobiological and neurophysiological substrates of mental experience have implications for the creation and reception of art that, previously, our views of imaginative expression and perception ignored?

To arrive at some semblance of a response, and perhaps at evidence of the power of art to resist reduction to the empirically validated roots in question, we must look at how aesthetic experience impacts implicit awareness of self. Only by considering how the awareness we call subjectivity reflects the brain's organicity, the province of neuroscience, will we advance our understanding of the "pleasure" of art. At the same time, however, only within the framework of neuroscience's dialogue with psychoanalysis will we facilitate an understanding of the dynamic constitution of the creative act.

In 1952 Ernst Kris put forth his oft-cited theory on the psychology of the artist. Briefly, Kris believed that creativity took place in a regressed state of mental function. This regression served the ego in giving it temporary access to the impulses or wishes of the unconscious without subjecting it to the risk of psychic illness. Working closely with Heinz Hartmann and Rudolph Loewenstein, Kris explored creative expression as a means of drawing energy from the id and converting it to energy of the ego. His view presupposed in the artist a kind of energic elasticity that allowed for the transformation of drive into acceptable form. Advancing her own thinking on the fluidity of the creative person's defense system, Edith Jacobson sought to validate Kris's id–ego perspective with the claim that the more flexible defense system of creative persons is what permits them to remain in closer touch than others with their unconscious.[7] Freud had already sought to demonstrate in his studies of Michelangelo, Leonardo da Vinci, and others the idea that artists benefit from the channeling of psychic energy in creative expression insofar as it spares them from repression. Kris took this notion a good deal further not only by equating the capacity for drive neutralization with psychic health but by expanding upon the nexus of neurological determinants that make of the creative act a reality-enhancing experience. Indeed, though insufficiently recognized, Kris's real contribution to our understanding of creativity resides in its appreciation of the relevance of the body – both its image in the mind and its fundamentally inseparable expressive and motor functions – for the making and perception of art.

In recent years, the noted psychoanalyst Charles Brenner has employed "modern conflict theory" to upset Kris's formulation of creative activity. Substituting for the ego–id–superego model of mind the paradigm of drive–unpleasure–defense, Brenner emphasizes those elements (such as drive, defense, anxiety, depression, superego prohibitions, and the like) that motivate imaginative expression.[8] In his paper "Creativity and Psychodynamics," however, Brenner arrives at the conclusion that "[C]reativity, like beauty, lies in the eyes and mind of the beholder, not in the psychodynamics of the individual who is called creative [. . .]." Brenner's point is that a distinct problem is posed by the notion that the creative person is unique in having access to childhood sexual wishes and the conflicts that derive from them. Over time, he observes, several solutions to this problem have surfaced: the idea, for instance, that one must be neurotic (or perhaps psychotic) to be truly creative. Or that creativity is the artist's alternative to what would, in the non-creative person, be a strained reconciliation of conflictual aims, a pathological compromise formation. Or even that the creative act is the equivalent of an altered ego state (Kris's "regression in the service of the ego"). Brenner explains that each of these solutions is associated with its own set of problems and the more accurate way to explain how it is that creative individuals have "special access to the wishes and conflicts of childhood origin" (i.e., to the unconscious) is by recognizing that they don't.[9] The psychodynamics of creativity are indistinguishable for Brenner from those of any other form of mental functioning insofar as every mental act, being a compromise formation, is inherently creative. Creativity is therefore neither uncommon nor in any way exceptional dynamically speaking.

But no exploration of creativity can be restricted to the psychodynamic arena alone. As Kris (and Freud before him) showed, one necessarily makes and reacts to art through the body. Whether or not one accepts the role assigned by Kris (as well as Hartmann and others) to the ego in the creative process, the body is implicated by the very construct we refer to as the self. And affect, an entity now known to have distinct neurophysiological components, is the primary source of the implication. Indeed, the subjective "I" is constituted precisely through the transmission of information from within the viscera of the body to the brain (a process that occurs by way of nerve impulses, cerebral spinal fluid, and the circulatory system controlled by the heart). What this information reveals is the *feeling* state or subjectivity of the individual. Current trends in neuroscientific research on aesthetic experience emphasize the significance of those areas of the brain controlling mood and motivation. The dorsolateral prefrontal cortex, for instance – the area of the brain under the forehead whose importance for mood is well documented – has been shown to be active during problem solving and creativity and magnetic stimulation to this region has shown an increase in creative function.[10] Additionally, the role in creativity of neurotransmitters – the molecules that mediate the transmission of chemicals in the brain – is now being considered. To cite but one example, critic Norman Holland has recently advanced a hypothesis on creative process based, in part, on the work of neuropsychologist Kenneth Heilman.[11] Holland's conjecture is that what creativity is about is a decrease in certain neurotransmitters (particularly norepinephrine) insofar as inspiration and creative insight appear to have much to do with the very states of mind for which such a decrease is responsible.

Distinguishing between two aspects of creativity, the "*inner process* of inspiration and illumination" favored by these states and the "*outwardly-directed process* of preparation and promotion" also necessary for creative achievement, Holland seems to navigate between Kris and Brenner. What results is a compromise negotiated between the idea that creativity resides in the regressed (or at least relaxed) ego-state of the creator and the notion that it is a value judgement of the reader or viewer. Holland calls it creativity's "transactive" constitution (employing a term he shares with John Dewey), by which he means that through the creation of the artist's personal identity (embedded in the forms, themes, and style of his work) readers or viewers re-create their own. Just how it is that a large number of people can use the same personal identity to re-create their own very different identities in a way satisfying to them all is, Holland ultimately determines, an unanswerable question. And therein, he claims, lies creativity's mystery.[12]

The biology of creativity, the study of the regional and chemical interactions affecting creative thinking and output, is relevant here to the extent that what it puts in high relief is the physiological foundation of self-awareness. What it attests to, in other words, is the potential of neuroscience to go beyond legitimizing one theory of mind over another. In providing information on the anatomical and physiological substrates of affect, motivation, memory, and representation, what neuroscience brings to the fore are the *perceptual* capacities of the mind/brain and the *nonconscious recognition of self implicit within them*. If Holland is right to stress identity and its re-creation as crucial to aesthetic experience, and if his argument justifies simultaneously, as I have claimed it does, both Kris and Brenner's positions, it is precisely because creativity extends brain function to enhance self-definition.

Among the most interesting writings on neuroscience and art that demonstrate how the aims of art extend the function of the brain and how knowing more about the brain tells us more about creativity are those by the neurobiologist Semir Zeki. In his work on visual art Zeki outlines a number of physiological laws of the part of the brain that processes vision, the primary visual cortex, and illustrates how aesthetic pleasure is dependent upon them. There is the law of opponency, for example, according to which "cells in the visual system that are excited by red are inhibited by green, those excited by yellow are inhibited by blue and those excited by white are inhibited by black and vice versa for each." There is the law of context effect that states that "cells in the brain concerned with colour can modify their responses profoundly by depending upon the background against which their preferred colour is presented." And so on. What such laws affirm, Zeki tells us, is that the visual brain seeks knowledge of the world by selecting, discarding, and comparing its selection of information to what it has previously stored, a task remarkably akin to that of the artist. If the brain's quest for knowledge is comparable to that of the visual artist, moreover, it is because each is fundamentally engaged in a search for essentials. And it is this that leads him to define "great art" in neurological terms: The most pleasing art is that which most closely approximates the many facets of reality, thereby satisfying the brain in its search for constants in an inconstant world.[13]

But why? What motivates the brain in this search and what motivates the artist in a comparable quest? No one would contest that, on the grand scale of evolution, survival of the species is served by the brain's seeking of knowledge through the senses. Nobel laureate Gerald Edelman's theory of "neural Darwinism," the idea that neural connections beneficial to life are strengthened while others become weaker from disuse and die, demonstrates the point. On the smaller scale of the individual the brain's objective, its targeting of knowledge, is homeostatic. Is this also what impels the artist? And how might the neurophysiologic motivation that is homeostasis be linked to the psychodynamic motivations associated with the creative urge?

Despite Freud's celebrated disavowal that "Before the problem of the creative artist analysis must, alas, lay down its arms,"[14] the psychoanalytically oriented have persisted in their attempts to uncover creativity's source. All too often, though, the effort has been diluted by the supposed connection between the practice of art and psychopathology. The assumption of mental disturbance, in other words, in framing investigations into creativity, has resulted in dislodging the actuality of making or otherwise experiencing art. It is often said that we cannot legitimately resurrect the inner life of an artist, any more than that of a dreamer, when we do not have before us a freely associating mind. With the more pluralistic approach afforded the psychoanalytic inquiry by neurobiology, however, what can be revealed is, on the one hand, how we process our selves and our relation to the world and, on the other, how we understand and communicate this processing through the varied forms of art. The value of understanding the role played by the biology of mind in the conception and transmission of innovative ideas and imaginative forms, therefore, resides in its potential for inhibiting the reification of the imagination that psychobiography effects.

It also, however (and this is more to the point), lies in the light shed on the generation of *meaning* in art. Maintenance of the body's internal environment (the homeostatic condition of life) depends upon the brain's capacity to absorb new sensory information, to evaluate its significance, and to integrate it into knowledge already stored. (The brainstem, hypothalamus, limbic system, and neocortex are perpetually engaged in this very purpose.)[15] Now the key to this homeostatic activity lies in the representational processes of the mind, and the neurophysiological systems upon which they rely, precisely because subliminal awareness is requisite to the mediation between inner needs and external environs. I refer here to not only the mental imaging that is representation, but the dynamic inner representational world, the self and object representations comprised of memories of experiences and the feeling states associated with them. Creative expression reorders these representations; it offers alternative perspectives on experience and does so through the *meaning* the creative communication of affect-laden representations suggests.

Prior to the newly emerging interest in the interface of neuroscience and psychoanalysis, the capacity for representation and even for the symbol formation from which creativity originates was a psychological conundrum. In 1957 Phyllis Greenacre noted: "The artist's persistent access to primary-process thinking and imagery means that he possesses a wider variety of symbols and related perceptions, which in turn make more choices of expression available to him than is true in the less gifted person."[16] To account for the quantitative difference, analysts tracked imaginative capacity along the developmental line that begins, as Linda C. Mayes and Donald J. Cohen have described it, with the "earliest symbiotic interactions between mother and infant, takes further shape as the child moves from dyadic to triadic relations, and culminates in a fully mature capacity to reflect upon in thought one's wishes and feelings vis-à-vis multiple others."[17] The developmental account implied that faults in the early subjective organization and internalization of the emotional environment could alone explain creative drive.

Melanie Klein and her followers, as I have already noted, sought the source of creativity in the need for reparation stemming from the depressive position, the infantile phase in which it is realized that the object of hate and destructive impulses and the object of love are one and the same. Restoration of the lost object, the re-creation or reparation of an inner world fragmented by aggressive impulses, was viewed as the basis of the sublimatory act. Hanna Segal went so far as to claim that an awareness of this need is present in the unconscious of every artist, that art is its symbolic expression, and that the ability to overcome the anxiety and guilt aroused by the aggressive urge, the ability to "work through" the depressive position, is essential for creative expression.

Others, certainly, viewed the role of child development in the determination of creative drive and capacity very differently. Anna Freud, as is well known, was hardly sympathetic to the Kleinian perspective. But if she situated the origin of creative inhibition in a fear of the "emotional surrender" that characterizes the dependency of childhood,[18] she nonetheless located the origin of creative capacity in the ability to sublimate acquired early in life:

> Sublimation is, thus, more than a mere mode of behavior which can be adopted at will in adult life when external circumstances, such as absence or other inaccessibility of the sexual partner, imprisonment, illness, etc. make the satisfaction of sexual or aggressive wishes difficult or impossible. It consists of an actual far-reaching modification of the instinctive processes themselves, as far as their fixation to particular aims is concerned. Where the ability to sublimate has developed in early childhood, the instinctive wishes become less inexorable in their claims, more ready to accept substitute gratifications and therefore more adaptable to the circumstances of life.[19]

Winnicott, as well, claimed the capacity for creativity in later life to be developmentally determined. Fantasy and play, the building blocks of adaptation to reality, lead to originality in the adult to the extent that that place between the child's mind and objective reality he called "transitional space" allows for a true exploration of self and world. Favorable conditions are required for this kind of play, for the free and imaginative use of internal representations that is based neither wholly in the psyche nor in the reality of the external world. Deprived of these conditions, the child has an impoverished capacity to play and will, eventually, make a limited, if any, contribution in the cultural domain.

It goes without saying that primary care can not be entirely separated from other environmental influences, such as the valorization of certain talents over others within a given society and the significance of creative activity relative to additional forms of socialization. But we now have sufficient evidence that the cultural or developmental considerations – the negotiation of the depressive position, the ability to sublimate, and a nurturing or "facilitating" childhood environment – cannot be construed independently of biological influences on creative need and success. The impact of biology on creativity becomes more evident every day: Factors such as prenatal development (the fetus's nutritional intake, for instance, which, affected by its position in the womb, influences the child's weight and related conditions at birth); genetics (the predisposition to both physical and emotional traits); and innate cognitive potential all play a role. Even certain features of personality, such as aggressiveness and the ability to tolerate frustration, are now known to be in some measure inborn, additionally complicating the nature versus nurture debate.

Furthermore, we now know that the formation of imagos (parental or other), considered by some requisite to the symbolization upon which creative thinking and expression depend, cannot be explained entirely as a function of environment and that more than a mere nod must be given to their biological roots. Memory, perception, affect, and a host of conscious and unconscious processes all interact with the mind's ability to represent. The means of verifying the structural design and functional processes whose complex interaction allows for the generation of internal representations are relatively new. The question of innate versus developmental representational faculties, however, is rapidly finding answers through the electrophysiological tracking of the chemical, sensory, and other biological systems from which mentation arises.

The principles of biology become all the more significant when one considers that creative achievement requires the ability to coordinate several elements of an art simultaneously and that various art forms require particular sensitivities. John Gedo has remarked, in this regard, that we have only to think of the poet who combines sound with imagery and semantic meaning or of the painter who must be especially sensitive to the aesthetics of color to appreciate the profound connection of neurobiological function to creative expression.[20] But how can we conceptualize the complexity of neurobiology's relation to the organization of the inner representational world? How, to put it somewhat differently, does creativity dynamically relate to the pre-cognitive awareness of self (to the experiential and affective memories and to the sensory inputs of the body schema) upon which artistic expression acts? To the extent that such questions can be answered, the problem of creativity's motivation will be resolved.

* * *

Neurobiologist Jaak Panksepp has neatly defined the mind as a tripartite phenomenon: brain, body, and environment. This is to say that the mind is a brain within a body that exists within a world. Panksepp's ontological view (reminiscent of early twentieth-century continental philosophy) is significant in that it simultaneously frames the singularity and universality of experience. As Mark Solms has stressed, we need to investigate what it is like to be a *particular* brain and it is precisely the *being* of a brain that interests the neuro-psychoanalyst.[21] Now a number of foci of research provide access into the subjectivity that Panksepp, Solms, and others are working to circumscribe. These include, as previously mentioned, perception, affect, and memory, but it is how they relate to the capacity for representation that is most critical to neuroscience as it seeks, through a rapprochement with psychoanalysis, to unveil the subjective experience of mind.

To be sure, the concept of representation has evolved since Freud first contemplated the infant's libidinal cathexis of primary objects and the contribution of the sexual instincts to the inner representational world is no longer thought to be determinative irrespective of early object relations. With the input of neuroscientists, some psychoanalysts, in fact, now consider representations to be continually encoded as templates in the brain whence they modify bodily states and act upon behavior as well. As Regina Pally explains: "When the brain is exposed to a new event, external (a face, a word) or internal (emotion, physiological state), a unique pattern of neurons is activated. In order to preserve this configuration, connections must be forged between the neurons, creating a new circuit that acts as a symbol, a representation of something in the outside or 'inside' world."[22] The greatest boon to the neuroscientific effort to unravel the mind–brain conundrum has been the growth of technology. Indeed, modern brain imaging techniques (position emission tomography or PET scanning and functional magnetic resonance imaging or fMRI) are said to survey more than the static structure of the brain (as revealed in computerized tomography or CT scans); they are described as providing access to the representational mind in "real time." But do they?

A starting point of Solms's work is the idea that consciousness, originating in bodily experience, projects both outwardly as our primary somatic sensations and inwardly as affect. For him, as for Freud, consciousness is precisely the perception of that activity. This is not to say consciousness *results* from brain processes, but that it is a *reflection* of mental acts. Now this is significant because, on the one hand, it attests to the mind's essentially unconscious nature and, on the other, it accounts for the view that the scanning of brain activity (the imaging of function in addition to anatomy), while not a direct access to the mind per se, entails its indirect inspection.

Some researchers, though, claim that what is revealed on functional scanning is the actuality of mentation (representation in the mind), not merely its neural signature. That there is a notable increase in neuronal activity in the frontal lobes during cognitive stimulation, which is proof of their "executive function," has led some, for example, to conclude that neuronal activation through visual, auditory, tactile, and motor stimuli yields a view of cognitive *process*.[23] Consider the work of Fred Levin who has underscored the relation of transference in psychoanalysis, a profoundly experiential phenomenon, to concrete neural activation and other biological mechanisms reflected in thinking. Levin first observed that certain primary cortical association areas are activated simultaneously, as opposed to serially, in people who are deeply involved in what they are attending to. Then he noted that the same simultaneous activation occurs in (or facilitates) the kind of insight known as the "aha" reaction, when the patient integrates (often by way of the analyst's use of an interpretive metaphor) different levels of experience. As Levin sees it, the complex connections between sensory modalities and judgments of similarity and difference that come into play in such moments are related to mechanisms of defense and control, self-regulation, and the plasticity of the brain itself. He draws from his data the conclusion that learning, which takes place in the mind and in the brain, is impacted by transference thereby substantiating the notion that experience has much to do with how neurons interrelate.[24] Does this mean imaging reveals mentation? Not, certainly, in the narrow sense of viewing the mind. But in a broader sense, it would seem so.

Similarly, Allan Schore's work on right brain development has shown the fundamental interrelation of brain structure and function with cognitive and affective experience. Insofar as they demonstrate that infant attachment to a primary caregiver influences the structural maturation of the brain, that the capacity for affect regulation is experience embedded, Schore's studies could be said to lend themselves to observation of the "psychobiological" mind/brain in actuality. So, too, Nancy Andreasen has shown the region at the base of the frontal lobe and structures connected to it, the orbitofrontal system, to be fundamental to preconscious awareness, episodic memory, and primary process mentation and she professes that in so doing she has localized, through PET scanning, freely associative thinking.[25]

Localization, however, is not actually observing the mind. Indeed, many vehemently argue against the notion that thought – or the processing of any affect with which it might be associated – is viewable on scanning. Robert Shulman and Douglas Rothman, for instance, have claimed that what functional imaging measures are merely neurophysiological responses to various sorts of stimuli. In other words, neuronal activity as indicated only by changes in the cerebral metabolization of glucose and oxygen and changes in blood flow in the brain.[26] More radically, Jonathan Brodie has asserted that functional imaging yields "vivid pictographic representations that can be manipulated to emphasize or distort anything."[27] In a sense, Mark Solms and Oliver Turnbull concur: people "want to elucidate the neural organization of particular mechanisms (e.g., 'repression'), or whole psychopathologies (e.g., 'hysteria'), or even whole functional systems (e.g., 'the Unconscious') by trying to visualize them in PET or fMRI scanners. In fact, it is not possible to do that with any degree of accuracy. *This is not because such things cannot be visualized (the neural correlates of literally any mental entity can be visualized), but because the mental entities in question cannot be artificially operationalized and manipulated in the laboratory conditions that such imaging techniques require.*"[28] Indeed, how do you ask subjects to repress? Furthermore, as Turnbull has noted, some law of nature seems always to produce in functional imaging, no matter how well designed the study, "at least five areas of activation, two of which will be in brain regions you have never heard of." It is not for nothing that the most hard-core cognitivists have had to retrain in neuroanatomy.[29]

But the real crux of the debate – and my reason for belaboring it – is not the potential of functional imaging, but the possibility of integrating two generic models of the relation between mind and brain: the clinically derived psychoanalytic model and the imaged neuroscientific model.[30] How the subjective, psychodynamic model of mentation is used to inform the objective model and vice versa is problematic precisely because it begs the question of the very meaning of "mind" – the question of how, not where, mental representation occurs. It even raises the question of whether visual representation is endemic to consciousness in the first place. It could be that some forms of thought consist in the production of meaning not circumscribed by visual imagery at all. Indeed, when psychoanalysts speak of the inner representational world, a good deal more than visual imaging is implied.

If the relation of consciousness to diverse brain–body systems remains the Holy Grail of scientists today, it is nonetheless assumed that the interplay of electrical signals within the brain is responsible for the levels of awareness that, when synchronized, allow for some sort of representation in the "inner eye." Antonio Damasio refines the question by making it two: He distinguishes inquiry into how the nerve-cell circuits make neural patterns that, in turn, become mental images from a related field of exploration, namely, *the brain's generation of a sense of self* as observer of this "movie-in-the-brain." His dual approach to the meaning of mind allows him to trace a trajectory of consciousness that begins with its neurobiological roots (the brainstem nuclei that receive bodily signals and interact with other regions of the brain) and progresses to the construction of a primitive and minimally attentive "proto-self." From this "proto-self" a self of extended capacity, an "autobiographical self" aware of what is occurring within it and able to orchestrate that knowledge in the service of creativity, is said to develop. A hierarchical view of brain anatomy and function, in other words, yields to the notion of a composite or "core" consciousness (what others consider the preconscious) equipped with memory, language, and intelligence, and interactive with a social environment.

For his part, Solms rejects any notion of cause and effect. Drafting an alternative view of mind, he maintains that the relationship between the brain and conscious experience is one of correlatives. Likening it to the relation of lightning and thunder – lightning does not cause thunder; rather, both lightning and thunder derive from something else – he claims human consciousness to consist in three things: the primary external and internal perceptions referred to earlier and those perceptions of previous experience associated with memory and cognition. Psychic representations are made of these perceptions, he maintains, and it is from these representational constructs that we develop our sense of self and world.[31]

As debate continues over the meaning of mind, the relation of mind to brain, and the significance of the various motor and sensory processes for the psychic structure that feels and thinks by way of representation,[32] two things are increasingly clear: First, that *physiological regulation, or biological homeostasis, is inseparable from the regulation of affect* and, second, that *consciousness is what joins the two*. Studies demonstrating the biology of consciousness are those that show the effects, for instance, of psychic representation on blood flow in the orbitofrontal regions of the brain (as seen in instances of episodic memory and in dreaming). They are what lead neuroscientists to conclude that, as Schore puts it, internalized representations operate as "biological regulators" and that the orbitofrontal region is "*uniquely involved in social and emotional behaviors, and in the homeostatic regulation of body and motivational states.*"[33]

Here, then, is where the deepest link between biology and creativity may be said to reside: *Homeostatic regulation is a phenomenon intrinsic to any living organism. It describes the effort of every biological system (in fact, of each individual cell) to maintain the bodily states that allow for life. In also accounting, however, for the modulation of affective states determined by the representation of self and object in the mind, homeostasis implicates meaning, the particular significance an individual assigns to internal and external events. Insofar as creative thinking acts on meaning, modifies one's appraisal (conscious or unconscious) of these events, creativity affects one's ability to thrive.*

This, certainly, is the primary assumption underlying both psychoanalysis and art: In seeking to uncover what is meaningful to a person and why, psychoanalysis focusses on the manifold origins of a particular view of the world so as to alter their significance and allow the individual to flourish. Similarly, the (re)construction of reality involved in making (and even viewing) art, insofar as it inaugurates something truly creative or "new," serves as a regulatory or adaptive process (whence the re-creation of personal identity Holland ascribes to art). My point, then, is this: Consciousness either results from (Damasio) or is perceptually correlative with (Solms) brain function but is irreducible to it. So, too, creativity is embedded in biology in the sense that meaning – conferred on consciousness through perceptual, recollective, and associative integration – aims to fulfill an essentially homeostatic goal.

The collaborative work of linguist George Lakoff and philosopher Mark Johnson on the "embodiment of mind" supports this thesis, as does psychoanalyst Arnold Modell's notion of the "biology of meaning." In *Philosophy in the Flesh*, Lakoff and Johnson discuss the grounding of thought in our perceptual and motor systems and describe how reason and concepts are formed through the body. The mind, indeed any subjective experience, relates to what they call "primary metaphors," the activation of neural connections automatically acquired by our sensorimotor functioning in the world. That the mind is thus embodied – that neural connections extend from sensorimotor function to subjective experience and the way we *feel* in relation to ourselves and the world – means that equilibration is unrestricted to the physical domain. Furthermore, the enormous number of universally acquired primary metaphors that allow for any but the most literal conceptualizations are not limited to ordinary language usage; they are manifested in art (as well as gesture and ritual) too.[34] The leap, therefore, from the homeostatic objective of the mind/body to its expressive modalities is really not a leap at all.

For his part, Modell explicitly claims that a coherent self consisting in psychic structures that not only organize perception and generate experience, but "contain *potential* for the creation of meaning,"[35] is a "homeostatic requirement of the psyche-soma." In suggesting that "to possess an open imagination is to be human,"[36] he points to creative capacity as the very means by which the self maintains such coherence and serves, thereby, the homeostatic goal. Citing Gerald Edelman's concept of value, defined "as evolutionary constraints favoring behavior that fulfills homeostatic requirements or increases fitness," Modell explains how current experience is valorized, or assigned meaning, by the "recategorization" of "perceptual events" in accordance with previous valorizations.[37] This is the basis of Edelman's "neural Darwinism," an evolutionary process that is both universal, owing to the anatomy of the human brain, and unique in its dependence upon the genetic makeup and subjective experience of the individual.

Modell explains the metaphoric transcription of bodily experience by differentiating between metaphors that generate new meaning through play with the juxtaposition of similarity and difference and those that he terms "foreclosed," those at work in transference, traumatic remembrance, repetition compulsions, and the like. The open or more supple metaphor stimulates the creative imagination by promoting the recontextualization of old affects, whereas the fixed form is a rendering of the present in terms of an unambiguous throwback to the past. Both, though, operate through "the perceptual and motor apparatus [that] serve memory by means of a scanning attempt to match current experience with old memory categories." These are thus stored as templates awaiting activation either through generalization/association or identification with a classification of affective experience to which "current perceptual inputs" metaphorically correspond.[38]

There is also another sense in which the metaphorical transcription of one sphere of meaning onto another may be said to be of somatic origin. Not only does the body interact with the external environment to produce affective memories that await reawakening over time but, as Modell confirms, "from infancy onward we also need to categorize experience arising from the internal world." What he calls "generic bodily metaphors" exhibit "a kind of synesthesia in that experiences derived from one sensory modality are transferred to another." The visual and auditory experience of bodily balance is an example. By virtue of its dynamic relation to affective memory, and to the synesthetic communication of such remembrance, then, metaphor – and thereby meaning – is both a physiological and psychological event.[39]

But how the neurobiological architecture, the organizing system of perceptual data, participates in the making of meaning is not the purpose of this book. Rather, I am interested in how art becomes psychodynamically meaningful through the artist's (or the spectator or reader's) *subjective experience* of that architecture and of the reflection of the somatosensory dimension in consciousness. Indeed, the neuro-psychoanalytic perspective on meaning distinguishes itself very clearly from the view of some neuroscientists who devalue subjectivity by reducing consciousness to the mechanics of neural activity alone. Believing that the correlation or binding of diverse, separately processed, neural firings in the brain (what Francis Crick and Christof Koch call "consciousness neurons") accounts for awareness, they essentially do away with whatever cannot be incorporated within that materialistic frame. Such a position, in other words, is antithetical to the efforts of those who seek to integrate the psychodynamic import of meaning with the neurophysiology that enables – though is not synonymous with – it at its core.

Among the most significant consequences of the union of the psychodynamic and neurophysiological orientations for our understanding of creativity is that it brings us closer to grasping the mechanisms by which the brain, and this is an extraordinary capacity, provides information where, perceptually, none (at least in reality) exists. Such, after all, is the meaning of imagination. And it is the imaginative capacity, the brain's ability to impose on sensory perception what it needs or wants for a picture to be made in the mind, which defines what happens in art. In *Phantoms in the Brain*, V. S. Ramachandran suggests the following:

> [W]hat we call perception is really the end result of a dynamic interplay between sensory signals and high-level stored information about visual images from the past. Each time anyone of us encounters an object, the visual system begins a constant questioning process. Fragmentary evidence comes in and the higher centers say, "Hmmmmm, maybe this is an animal." Our brains then pose a series of visual questions: as in a twenty questions game. Is it a mammal? A cat? What kind of cat? Tame? Wild? Big? Small? Black or white or tabby? The higher visual centers then project partial "best fit" answers back to lower visual areas including the primary visual cortex. In this manner, the impoverished image is progressively worked on and refined (with bits "filled in," when appropriate).[40]

In defining the perceptual process, the interplay between sensory input and the projective output (or filling in according to the needs of the brain) also defines how we make and look at art. The point is well made by the purposeful interference with the brain's inclination toward realistic imaging, toward completing the picture, by the intentional play, in other words, of some artists with the brain's proclivity to fill in the blanks. Both Rembrandt and Cézanne (particularly in their late work) did just that; they intentionally confused the viewer by leaving things out.[41] So, too, the Surrealists played on the mind of the spectator/reader by favoring incongruous images (like the mustache on the *Mona Lisa* in Duchamp's *L.H.O.O.Q*) in their paintings and freely associative texts. In provoking the viewer or reader's active participation by challenging his or her visual memory, "incomplete" art, with its irreconcilable images, is rendered a place of creative instantiation not only for the artist/writer but for the spectator/reader as well.

Indeed, the Surrealists' subversion of representation, their devaluation of mimesis or verisimilitude (and the violation of the laws of gravity, space, and time implicated therein), left much to the viewer or reader's own imaginative will. Exempt from all aesthetic and moral concern, as André Breton defined it in his *Second Manifesto*, Surrealism's "automatic" technique allowed for the generative power of images to dominate the mind. Thus with the dismissal of narrative or anecdotal forms and, above all, the privileging of chance, the iconoclastic themes of the Surrealist painters and poets of the 1920s and 1930s inspired fantastical associations that extended the work beyond the canvas or page. We have only to think of the titles of some of the paintings of Max Ernst, like *Saint Cecilia (the Invisible Piano)*, or of Joan Miró, such as *Stars in Snails' Sexes*, to appreciate the degree to which the artists exploited spontaneity to elicit innovation in the viewer too.

Later revolutionary challenges to the conventions of representation are comparable in their power to generate the "questioning process" that Ramachandran describes. The Pop Art of the 1960s (that of Robert Rauschenberg, Jasper Johns, and Roy Lichtenstein, to name but the best known) and the choreography of Merce Cunningham played with the viewer's visual memory. John Cage's exploitation of silence in music obliged the listener in some sense to fill in the blanks – or at least to question their relation to the sound surrounding them. Even the work of those associated with the Judson Dance Theater (Yvonne Rainer, Steve Paxton, Lucinda Childs, Trisha Brown, and others) played on the interaction of perceptual input with the stored record of the viewer's brain. Much of their movement was improvised and much of it was game-like or even banal everyday activity, with the result that the spectator was continually jarred by the imposition of originality on the familiar.

The literary movement known as the *nouveau roman* (or New Novel), a movement initiated by Alain Robbe-Grillet, Michel Butor, Nathalie Sarraute, Claude Simon, and others in mid-century France, is another good example. These writers actually investigated the novel genre within both the form and content of the so-called anti-novels they wrote. Uncertainty and contradiction pervade their work as they force the reader to determine the sequence and even the veracity (their conformity to the narrative) of the events described. Lacking the presumed omnipotence of their nineteenth-century predecessors, Robbe-Grillet and the others were intent on displaying both the changed reality of an increasingly chaotic world and, also, the indeterminate (as utterly subjective) constitution of the real.

Thus the artist, like the analysand who imposes past experience on the more or (increasingly) less blank screen that the "evenly suspended attention" of the analyst erects, makes deliberate use of this imaging capacity of the brain. As obvious as this may be, it obliges us to recognize something far less so, namely, that metaphor – the mode of discourse that allows us to comprehend – is a property of mind and not of language as the rhetorician would have us believe. Kenneth Burke was right to describe metaphor as that which "brings out the thisness of a that, or the thatness of a this."[42] Indeed, it is what permits us cognitively to "see." But this is not, as Modell and others have demonstrated, only because it is a particularly effective figure of speech. Or, rather, it is. But not in the sense that the metaphorical efficiency would be linguistic. Activating at once several loci in the brain, the use of metaphor reinforces right and left hemispheric integration. Indeed, constituted of sensory, imagistic, emotional, and verbal components, metaphors assimilate the various regions of the hemispheres[43] so that memory is accessed and insight achieved. The point is that art, like all forms of communication, organizes how we feel and what we experience in terms of something else. In the sense that it provides a means of apprehending a this through a that, its fundamentally metaphorical function cannot be denied. And as a primary structure of understanding, metaphors afford a sense of control: It may well be that conflict resolution or the "working through" of unconscious wishes, that the *re*-creation of lost objects for the purpose of mastering one's relations to them, is an objective of the creative endeavor. Most certainly, however, the metaphorical function of art serves the ego in its need to control predispositional sensitivities (what analyst Pinchas Noy refers to as the "constitutional factor") through an appropriate medium of expression.

The metaphoric construction of meaning is also significant for our present purposes in this respect: Neuro-psychoanalysis aims to shed light on the organization of our inner psychic worlds, worlds created from the coalescence of multiple layers of sensory-motor experience with instinctual need and unconscious desire. It aims to explain how individuals interact *as individuals* with the reality outside their corporeal selves, and it depends upon both neuroscientific data and clinical psychoanalytic observation to do so. This is to say that it holds to the basic tenets of psychoanalysis, with its emphasis on unconscious processes, and looks at how these processes render meaning meaningful.

Now artistic creativity is precisely the shaping of meaning; it resides in the giving of form to primary-process imagery and thought. The writer or painter shares a common discourse with all others, a common "currency of mind" (as Modell refers to it), namely, the metaphorical representation of unconscious processes. But the artist shapes it in accordance with a particular vision, a vision that projects a heightened awareness of self. If I belabor the point about metaphor it is because Modell's concept of the "biology of meaning," like Lakoff and Johnson's "embodiment of mind," reveals the usefulness of the neuro-psychoanalytic perspective for the understanding of creative process and the intersubjective constitution of art. Dream, fantasy, transference, the literary or visual work of art – all manifest the metaphorical interplay of ideation and internal representation (what Freud called *Vorstellung* or "presentation") with the bodily based ego. More important, they reveal homeostasis as motivating the imagination, as creativity's primary goal. In effect, what I am proposing is that *creativity* (the aesthetic experience of the artist or the spectator/reader) *is self-affirming and that it is so by virtue of the subjective constitution of meaning, the sine qua non of survival.*

We reach the same conclusion when we follow Damasio's reasoning on creativity. Briefly summarized, his argument, rooted in a "circle of influence," is this: Human existence is distinguished from any other form of being by consciousness. Consciousness reveals existence to us and allows us to better it by creative thinking and expression. Thus the circle of existence, consciousness, and creativity closes through the imaginative guidance being is afforded through knowing. Creativity, in other words, is dependent upon consciousness whose enlightenment continually informs us of existence. That perpetual revelation is what directs the creative process and makes it bear upon (and, hopefully, better) human life. Creativity's bearing upon existence is thereby regulatory; it allows consciousness to perform a fundamentally homeostatic role.[44]

* * *

In the second part of this book I will look at a literary depiction (by Beckett) of a deficit in self-consciousness, a visual depiction (by Klee) of an altered self-representation, and a choreographic depiction (by Graham) of a self-awareness sharpened through movement of the body in time and space. Prior to that I will consider a more preliminary question: namely, whether the experience of self as a gendered individual – that is, with desires and fears both conscious and unconscious relating to the biology of sexuality – might in some real way be determinative of creative expression. It remains for me here, however, to situate my thinking with respect to that of Gilbert Rose who, while certainly not the first to consider the biological underpinnings of creativity, has contributed to redirecting that discussion toward a psychoanalytic understanding of subjectivity.

Freud developed the idea of the body as the source of psychic representations or, more accurately, the external and internal perceptions from which they derive, in his 1923 work *The Ego and the Id*. There he claims that it is the projection of bodily sensations, particularly those arising from the body's surface, that constitutes the reasonable or commonsensical (as opposed to the passionate or moral) part of the mind. The "knowledge" that the psyche – specifically, the ego – obtains from the body is of interest to me primarily with regard to Freud's claim in that text that "the ego controls the approaches to motility – that is, to the discharge of excitations into the external world."[45] For it situates the point of convergence of soma and psyche within a distinctly mobile force. Already in "Beyond the Pleasure Principle," which appeared three years prior, Freud described as one of the primary functions of the mind the binding of instinctual impulses, the conversion of "freely mobile cathectic energy into a mainly quiescent (tonic) cathexis."[46] In this "economic" view of the mental processes, it was precisely the mobilization of a mechanism, whereby an unpleasurable tension is lowered and pleasure produced, which accounted for the union of body and mind.

Taking Freud's concept of resistance and discharge as a point of departure, Rose has made an invaluable contribution to our bio/psychological understanding of creative activity. Specifically, he has built upon the view put forth by Susanne Langer that aesthetic form resonates with the tension and release paradigm of our physical and mental life by giving it a Freudian twist. As he explains it, bodily tension and release are endemic to the making of art precisely because the ego is constructed on representations of the body. That is to say, the shaping of art (and its reception as well) externalizes the ego in its regulation of drive and externalizes its affective states as it reintegrates thought and feeling.

Let's look more closely at this model. In a trilogy that addresses the relation between form and perception, Rose argues that the energic interplay of tension and release is structurally embedded in aesthetic form because it reflects the control and ambiguity, thought and feeling, and separation and fusion[47] characteristic of the organizing function of mind. Emblematic of the relation between consciousness and the unconscious, the tension and release of aesthetic form reproduces the way in which we shape the world. "Creativity," he writes in *The Power of Form*, "is not just a vicissitude of id drives discharging themselves."[48] Rather, it is a "confluence of forces"[49]deriving from both primary and secondary processes. In other words, the libidinal (or unneutralized) energy of the primary process, seeking direct gratification in wish fulfillment, combines with the delayed energy of the secondary (neutralized) process, governed by the reality principle, in the making of art. As he has explained elsewhere: "Tension is associated with the flow from primary process immediate discharge to secondary process delayed discharge; release of tension with the flow in the opposite direction."[50] Aesthetic experience (whether the creation of art or its reception) replicates, in sum, the dynamic tension and release characteristic of the coexistence of primary and secondary process mentation.

Speaking more directly to the question of the emotional expressivity of art, Rose has expanded upon this thesis that artistic form reveals the form of primary and secondary process interaction to include the generation of affect. "[N]ot merely an epiphenomenal accompaniment" to thought and perception,[51] affect in art originates, he claims, not from the projection of emotion itself, but from the energy system defining that interaction. In highlighting aspects of everyday life, art elaborates visually or in sound the rhythms of tension and release inscribed by the two modes of psychic processing. In so doing, it intensifies their relation to pleasure and unpleasure stimulating the "personal associations and individual emotions" of aesthetic experience.[52]

The lowering of tension in primary process imagination and the increase of tension endemic to secondary process logical thinking is responsible, then, for the dialectical constitution of art. In *Trauma and Mastery in Life and Art* (1987), Rose reiterates this argument and convincingly demonstrates that artistic form magnifies the organizing structure of mind. But he goes further: Extending the idea introduced in *The Power of Form* that this congruence of art and psyche renders the former capable of strengthening the latter, he contends that mental function is *enhanced* by the power of art and therein lies the biological significance of his thesis. In providing "the ego with problems on which it can test and perfect its capacities,"[53] in helping "to sharpen the coordinates of orientation as to time, place, and person, aesthetic form is said to "*facilitate* mastery," to expedite "the interaction of primary process imagination and secondary process knowledge of reality that underlies all perception and thought."[54] In the more recent *Between Couch and Piano* (2004), he explains the reception of art in similar terms: The "responsive resonance" on the part of an audience issues from the validation and reinforcement of its "own sense of wholeness," from its recognition of an "implicit motion and structural concordance between the external wholeness of aesthetic form and one's original internal wholeness of thought and feeling."[55]

Rose's idea of the impact of art on the mind is valid and profound. In view of the most recent achievements of neuroscience, however, particularly those related to the neural mechanisms of emotional learning and memory, I believe the argument for the biological function of aesthetic experience runs considerably deeper. *Art is a powerful mediator of affective experience because it acts on the neural circuitry underlying mood.* Particular brain regions are crucial to self–other differentiation, to the shared representations of intersubjectivity, and to the sense of agency. In as much as creativity shapes implicit self-awareness and the construct that is the body schema, it impacts these areas of the brain and hence the stability of somatopsychic linkage. I would suggest, therefore, that the tension–release model is not only reflective but *derivative* of the homeostatic battle fought on the most rudimentary level of human existence.

On what is this argument based? First, it derives from the neurobiological origins of the affective constitution of self. We know that the limbic system controls the drives, that neurotransmitters modulate the rate at which neurons fire and thereby have much to do with mood, that affects are evidence of subjectivity, and that they reveal our subjective experience of the body's neural circuits. (Of the neurobiological foundation of human emotion, Jaak Panksepp and Joeseph LeDoux, among others, have offered elegant proof.) Second, it results from the exquisite sensitivity of the brain and of the self-consciousness embedded within its functions to affective experience. Attachments (or the lack thereof) to primary caregivers in infancy are known to alter the future emotional growth of the individual by affecting the maturation of the brain itself. (There is evidence that the imprinting of traumatic attachments within the limbic and autonomic nervous systems of the developing right brain results in insufficient mechanisms for coping with stress and predisposes the individual to stress-related disorders later in life.)[56] Biological changes are also known to occur as a result of psychotherapy.

Cognitive behavioral therapy (CBT), for instance, produces changes in the orbitol frontal cortex of patients with obsessive-compulsive and anxiety disorders like those produced by medications (specifically, the SSRIs or selective serotonin reuptake inhibitors). Similarly, changes in affect regulation and behavior, such as may be achieved in analytic treatment through interpretation of the transference and other forms of insight, have been linked to the establishment of new functional patterns within the brain. (As we saw in the studies cited by Levin above, insights achieved through the synthesis of recollection with the present – "aha" reactions – correspond to the neurophysiological activation of relevant parts of the brain.[57] The freely associating patient, moreover, is not only arousing the multiple brain systems involved in the retrieval of past experience. Reconstruction also entails the modification of what is remembered by the brain's consolidation and encoding of features of the treatment situation itself.)

For decades, psychoanalytic theoreticians have addressed the connections between emotional states and creative functioning, from the aims of sublimation to its impediments, and sought links between the affective psyche and art. If the time has come for those in the social sciences, and the humanities as well, to look to neuroscience for a deeper understanding of creativity's relation to the link between psychic and somatic processes, it is because research has shown the effects of the physico-chemical systems on "cognitive flexibility," as neuropsychologists call creativity.[58] Demonstrating that it is, in fact, a two-way street, recent studies provide concrete evidence that creative expression has measurable effects on mood, that positive emotions are intensified and negative ones diminished by creative activity, as artists themselves have often claimed. Given the considerable knowledge of the neurobiological foundation of affect gained over the past 15 or so years, knowledge that has resulted in our no longer conceiving of the emotional processing of the environment as independent of an influence on the brain, can the equilibrating effects of creativity be ignored? As the impact of creative expression on somatopsychic function becomes empirically measurable over time, a number of interesting questions about the disposition of the human being to creativity will be raised. Among them is the role of adaptation in our passion for, say, literature, music, or dance. I will have more to say about this later for it constitutes an important direction for future research. Now, however, I turn to one register of the subjectivity of creative experience, the specificity of gender, to see what can be said in this post-feminist era of its relation to the making of visual and verbal art.

Chapter 2

Re-dressing the question

Neuroscience and the "feminine" in art

Applied psychoanalysis has a tradition of subversion. In seeking to explain a literary or visual work of art, it extends the aesthetic situation to the psychoanalytic, puts the artist on the couch, and offers a diagnosis. While not without interest, criticism that traces art to psychic illness (or any sort of psychic limitation) runs the risk of neglecting the virtuosity and aesthetic intelligence of a text or painting. (It also neglects, by necessity, the reasons why other artists having the same or similar diagnoses have not produced the same or similar works of art.)[1]

Feminist criticism has an analogous history: All too often, it has subverted the primary objective of critical interpretation – analyzing a given work and accounting for its specificity – by attempting to define a distinctly female aesthetic. Though initially the feminist effort was to signal female stereotypes in art and repudiate their political charge, somewhere along the line it shifted to defining female identity and to viewing how women write and read, paint and look at painting, as a collaborative endeavor. The shift was unsurprising insofar as the cry for equality implicated sameness as well as difference, but the point is that at its zenith feminist criticism submerged art and literature in social and cultural theory. As is well known, a number of feminist critics turned to contemporary psychoanalysis to bolster their views of the creative experience. Re-reading Freud non-proscriptively, they sought a means to withstand a biological determinism that devalued the feminine. Their effort, of course, was to resituate it outside the patriarchal order.

The situation, however, was not quite so simple. Within their ranks one discerns the so-called "gender" feminists (for whom gender is undeniably a social construct), the "difference" feminists (who maintain the opposition to biology, but stress other natural differences between the sexes), and the "equity" feminists (who advocate for equal treatment on the basis of moral rights). Despite the divergence, feminist criticism has remained subservient to identity theory for, as one feminist critic put it, it "provides us with a sophisticated and multivariant theoretical apparatus with which to explain differences between writing by women and by men in matters of both form and content."[2] And what contextualizes that theory is the female body, more precisely, the *feeling* a woman derives from her physical and emotional capacities as a woman.

The subjective experience of female corporality is what inspired Anaïs Nin, an avant-garde writer best known for her diaries, to call for women's creation to "be exactly like her creation of children." It must, she declared, "come out of her own blood, englobed by her womb, nourished by her own milk."[3] As though in response to this appeal, painter Judy Chicago sought in the early 1980s to shape images that would "resonate" to the essence of women's reproductive capacity, to the "glory and horror of the birth experience itself."[4] Chicago made a great many drawings and paintings that were sewn by hundreds of women into the needlepoint *Birth Project*. Conceived (pun intended) for the purpose of rendering metaphorically the creation of the universe as a profoundly feminine act, the images do not depict the process of labor so much as transcribe the pain and joy of the laboring woman into an equivalent visual expression. From the deep satisfaction of giving and nurturing life, Chicago made forms that are visually comparable to what is felt within the very tissues of the procreative body (Figure 2.1). From the cries and screams of a laboring woman, for example, she created, as she called it herself, "a visual wail."[5]

I cite Chicago's work here for three reasons: First, insofar as *The Birth Project* is composed of images that "visually radiate outward into a series of rhythmic forms reminiscent of the rhythm of labor,"[6] it wonderfully illustrates the view of creativity as play with psychic patterns of tension and release that allow both artist and viewer to (re)create their emotional sense of self. Experiencing art, whether by making or seeing it, is a means of reorienting oneself, as Rose describes it, to "inner and outer, subjective and objective reality."[7] And Chicago's raw images in this project metaphorically confirm that thinking.

Creativity, moreover, also serves, as I have said, the equilibration of mind and body that impacts homeostasis and Chicago's forms, insofar as they achieve her goal of being "recognizable at a cellular level," reflect that function of aesthetic experience. The "ovum of life,"[8] in fact, was the very vision she sought to render and her exploration of the congruity of configurations within nature (the patterns of a river, for instance) or the larger cosmos (like supernova) with those of the human body (such as the nerve cells) tell the homeostatic story.

Third, what interests me in Chicago's project is the way in which she visually expresses the subjectivity of female experience non-representationally. Though fascinated by the similarity between biological and cosmic forms, by the likeness of shapes having to do with the reproductive and solar systems, she does not use one to stand for the other symbolically. Rather, she looks to the movement of the image and to its illusory quality to access analogically the essence of womanhood and express her reverence for the psychobiological qualities that make a woman a woman. In the *Crowning*, a series of works

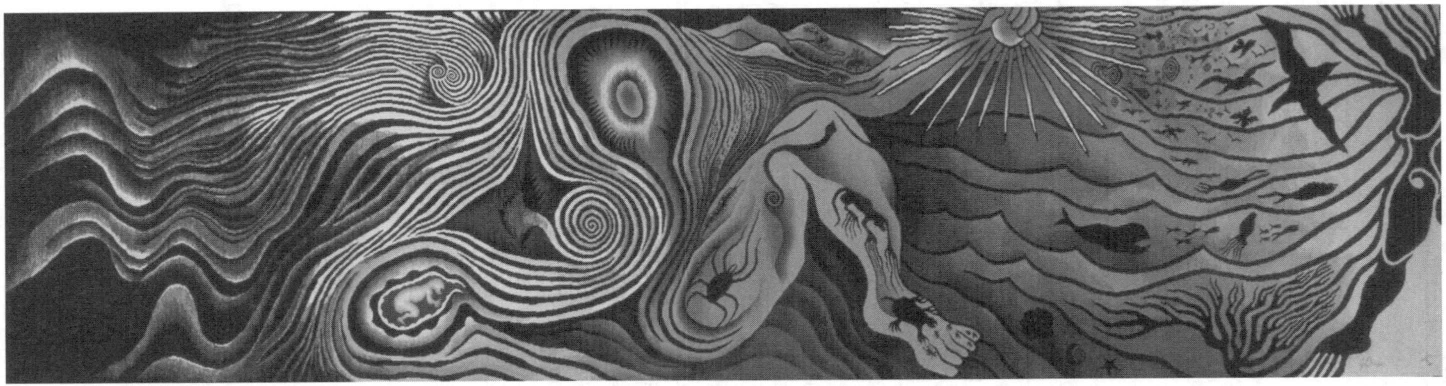

Figure 2.1 *Creation of the Universe*, © Judy Chicago 1980–4, tapestry (woven by Audrey Cowan), 42 inches × 14 feet

in which the vagina is majestically revealed as the point of origin of life, for instance, several kinds of needlepoint stitches and intricate design patterns complement each other in such a way that one is drawn into the luxuriously threaded and exceedingly rhythmic images much as one is enveloped within the undulating movement of waves.

In *Birth Figures #1* to *#4*, to cite one other example, Chicago projects various feelings women may have toward their pregnant bodies. As the artist describes the figures: "One is staring at her bulging stomach in dismay; the next gazes at the milk pouring from her breasts; the third sees a monster growing from her womb; and the last figure ponders with horror the miscarriage that is carrying away the child she wants to bear."[9] Remarkably, the faces of all four are featureless and thereby lack any expressiveness one would associate with these descriptions. This is to say that the lived experience is not rendered by a signaling of emotion that would be shown on a face but experienced within the viscera of the body. Through the images' transparency, texture, and color, the pregnant bodies themselves provide access to the emotional responses elicited by the women's conscious positing of their pregnant bellies.

I return to Nin's appeal and to a related question – in fact, the defining question posed by feminist writers and artists throughout the 1970s and 1980s – namely, whether a form of expression particular to women can truly be envisaged outside our habitual phallocentric frames of reference. Poet Adrienne Rich articulated it as follows: "I am really asking whether women cannot begin, at last, to *think through the body*, to connect what has been so cruelly disorganized."[10] Can Chicago and other feminist visual artists (Alice Neel, say, or Lynda Benglis) be said to have achieved this? And what about writers? Critic Domna Stanton wondered if a mode of writing that would subvert "the syntax, the semantics, and even the Cartesian logic of the Logos" could exist in a locus "from which woman might speak her difference."[11] Without succumbing to what has been called "the pathetic reverence commonly given Gallic obscurantism by American academics,"[12] I want now to look at what the best-known French feminist theorists had to say in response to this question. My purpose in doing so is not to renew the politically charged debate over sameness and difference, over gender as a social construct versus biological determinant. Rather, I wish simply to return to the principal site of cohabitation of feminism and psychoanalysis to better appreciate how neuroscientific findings that postdate the discussion clarify and refocus it and help us to understand the reciprocity between biology and art.

* * *

Some years ago the critic Susan Suleiman noted that if you "ask any fashionable Parisian intellectual these days about feminism or feminist theory – let alone, heaven help you, the 'new French feminisms,'" you will be met with "a pitying stare." She clarified this unusual observation by adding: "Nothing is more embarrassing, to a fashionable Parisian intellectual, than to be caught quoting last season's watchwords. Feminism, like Marxism, structuralism, poststructuralism (or like the narrow striped tie?), is definitely *passé*." With a verbal shrug of the shoulders – "Ah, well, so much for *la mode*" – Suleiman then proceeded to introduce the work of French feminist Hélène Cixous who, like Hokusai "drawing his two hundred nineteenth lion," Rembrandt "painting his hundredth self-portrait," and Monet "his twenty-sixth cathedral or *n*th water lily," returns indefatigably to, among other things, the relations between writing and gender.[13]

Cixous, with Julia Kristeva and Luce Irigaray, completes the triumvirate of French women theorists who first celebrated the connection between writing and the body and contextualized the link psychoanalytically. A prolific writer (her work includes 50 novels, plays, and texts of literary criticism, plus innumerable articles), she persists, as do they, in formulating the ways in which women relate to their expressive voice. At the center of their shared concerns – which include otherness, exile, loss, love, and maternity – is biology, more precisely, the manifestation of bodily excitation in the use of words. However tied to the now dated "new" French feminist milieu, this is a preoccupation that knows no temporal limits and, indeed, it is one that assumes new meaning when we consider the implications of neuroscience for our understanding of literary and visual art.

The focus of French feminism on the relation of the body to verbal expression presupposed a question that Phyllis Greenacre voiced as early as 1960. Citing data indicating that creativity, whether in the arts or sciences, is significantly less frequent in women than in men, she asked: "[A]re there differences between the sexes in constitutional equipment and functioning which have bearing in this special sphere?"[14] Greenacre saw creativity as determined by a number of biological (inborn, though not necessarily inherited) potentials. These consist, in particular, of "an especial range and intensity of sensory responsiveness present from the first months onward, including marked kinesthetic as well as other sensory responsiveness to rhythm and an innate capacity or tendency to feel sensory responses in gestalt or patterned ways but with great flexibility and variability."[15]

Greenacre was careful to distinguish, however, between inherent creative potential and productivity, between creative capacity and its realization, and while she concluded that sexual difference has bearing on the latter, she claimed we cannot determine whether it impacts the former. Specifically, she tells us, it is body build and one's relationship to one's own genitals that determine those character traits, different in men and women, which account for the quantitative difference in artistic achievement. In a word, their anatomy predisposes men to a greater concern with the externalization of the creative impulse.

Additionally, Greenacre found, artistic achievement may have a greater risk of interference or inhibition in the female insofar as disturbances arising at the anal level of development (anal function being prototypical of productivity itself) can evolve from the little girl's inclination to associate the anus with the vagina. So, too, the vicissitudes of the Oedipal period, and its conflictual nature, are borne differently by the male and female and may influence the degree of interference or blocking in the adult's creative output.[16] But productivity is not ability and the biological determinism to which Greenacre subscribed is not the Freudian determinism that would spark the ire of feminist critics on both sides of the Atlantic a decade or two later.

It was Freud's much berated "anatomy is destiny" and its aftermath that provoked the question of a form of expression that might defeat the Freudian fatalism, the notion that "anatomy is textuality," as it was paraphrased by Elaine Showalter.[17] While painters like Judy Chicago were engaged in finding forms that would challenge the prevailing (male-centered) modes of visual expression, writers (particularly in France) were preoccupied with the two- versus one-sex model of language. In the 1975 article for which she first became known, "The Laugh of the Medusa," Cixous described how women, through their writing, would remake culture irrespective of its phallocentric past: By articulating the body's integrity, writing a body intact (not one defined by a lack), the woman writer would repossess, from the margins to which they had been relegated, her identity, her feminine unconscious, her generative power, in a word, her self. Cixous implored woman to return to the wholeness of her body, that body from which she had been alienated by man: "Write! Writing is for you; you are for you; your body is yours, take it." What woman would find in writing the body are her maternity ("There is always within her at least a little of that good mother's milk. She writes in white ink.") and desire. In writing her libido, in fact, woman would "produce far more radical effects of political and social change than some might like to think."[18]

If, in this and her subsequent writings, Cixous repudiated Freud's theory of sexuality, in which the penile organ is the referential context of both female psychic development and female anatomy, she did so because it masks the true nature of difference. She believed then and continues to believe now that the binary opposition of gender conceals woman's experience of her sexuality and precludes the inscription of her body in her expressive voice. "Feminine" and "masculine," in other words, in rendering sexual difference oppositional, veils distance itself as the real issue at hand. In much of her work, Cixous rejects the words "femininity" and "feminine writing" for their throwback to the masculine. When she does use them, it is only for lack of better terms. In her teaching, she finds it preferable to speak of a "libidinal femininity"[19] which marks the difference/distance outside of the discord and defensiveness the other expressions evoke. Also, "libidinal femininity" indicates that female desire from which not only male domination is absent, but also the dehumanizing force of our postmodern world. For this is a desire that emanates from the deepest connection of the human being to its body where the subject is in a loving, which is to say harmonious and not technologically driven, relation to the world.

The language that Cixous continues to propose, then, is one in which women will write their sexual difference and in so doing reveal the pleasure, or *jouissance*, that is uniquely theirs. Cultural transformation depends on the expression of that pleasure in which the female imaginary and the anatomical are conjoined. Habitually, woman's pleasure has been defined in accordance with male fantasy that is restrictive in focus (genital) and inhibitory of woman as a creative (inspirational) source. But "libidinal femininity," true feminine pleasure, can be reclaimed through the act of giving voice to the body integrity of which women have been deprived.[20] In fact, for Cixous, the very act of recovery – the regaining of one's own body, of one's childhood, and one's being-in-the-world – is in itself a "feminine gesture," as Verena Conley has called it; it is a means by which the "she" carried within the self is reclaimed by the "I" as its own. While postdating the separation of subject and object, of writing and living, that the postmodern era supports, the language that Cixous beseeches women to script simultaneously precedes those schisms in its expression of, above all else, immediacy and pleasure.[21]

Like Cixous, Luce Irigaray has long proclaimed the ethical necessity of establishing a female-specific discourse that will define woman's identity and make known the particularity of her sexual economy. For the revolution to take place that will reposition women on the socio-cultural horizon, her entire relation to the world and to the language that articulates it must be reassessed. Women differ from men, Irigaray tells us, in "their relationships to fluids and solids, to matter and form, to the sense of touch through skin and mucous membrane, to symmetry, to repetition, and so on." Moreover, "woman's temporality is complex hormonally, and this has an effect on the body's organization and general equilibrium." A woman's puberty, loss of virginity, pregnancy, and menopause "mark a much more continuous temporality than do the ruptures of male sexuality or its continuum without irreversible momentum." As a consequence, the cyclical temporality of women is inextricably linked to the rhythms of the cosmos and women must find a way to distance themselves from the imposition of laws restrictive of this compatibility. The creation of "a discourse neither seductive nor reductive" is the means to that end.[22]

En route we need to remember, Irigaray forewarns, that no language is neutral, that the rules of language impact female identity and the way women interact not only with men, but with each other. In *Thinking the Difference*, she takes the example of French – with its masculine, feminine, and neuter nouns; the congruence of the neuter with the masculine form (where, most often, the sexual difference has been obliterated); the masculine plural when the two genders are named together; and so on – to demonstrate the consequences of the rules of language for each sex. Discourse that truly reveals the female identity, that allows women to speak as women, will clearly distinguish itself from the controlling and objectivity-oriented syntax of men. As she explains in her best-known work, *This Sex Which Is Not One* (where woman's specificity is marked by alienation, by her exclusion from the symbolic order of patriarchal law):

> [W]hat a feminine syntax might be is not simple nor easy to state, because in that syntax there would no longer be either subject or object, "oneness" would no longer be privileged, there would no longer be proper meanings, proper names, "proper" attributes. . . . Instead, that "syntax" would involve nearness, proximity, but in such an extreme form that it would preclude any distinction of identities, any establishment of ownership, thus any form of appropriation.[23]

Nathalie Sarraute, a novelist and playwright associated with the French New Novel (or *nouveau roman*), may be thought of as having, in some sense, written in this way. Though she denied the feminist appellation for herself, trademark ellipses running throughout her work speak to a rhetorical question posed by Xavière Gauthier in the French journal *Tel Quel*: If " 'replete' words (*mots pleins*) belong to men, how can women speak 'otherwise,' unless, perhaps, we can *make audible* that which agitates within us, suffers silently in the *holes of discourse*, in the unsaid, or the non-sense."[24]

However conspicuous they may be, though, the points of suspension were not Sarraute's primary means of manifesting the inner agitation of those who populate her novels and plays. What drive her texts are the preverbal movements, both instinctive and irrepressible, that she called "tropisms." These paradigmatic sensations are "generally provoked, like those of plants, by an exterior excitement, by the presence of someone or some object" as she explained. And they propel not only the content but the textual language itself: Holding on to each, she "develops" them, "ripens" them, "so that they [. . .] make the language spring, give it its rhythm, its images."[25] By no means the sole province of women, however, Sarraute's tropisms skirt the issue of sexual difference. They attest to a heterogeneity that appears to disassociate her from those favoring *l'écriture féminine*. Her writing neither cultivates nor even recognizes difference as a motivating or psychological force. A speaking subject is inscribed, nothing more. Or so it seems. It has been noted that Marguerite Duras, a writer on the periphery of the *nouveau roman* (and one better known than Sarraute in the United States), also uses silence, non-speech, to display what she calls in her 1964 novel *The Ravishing of Lol V. Stein* "a word-absence, a word hole." Again, there is something not to be spoken, but made to "resound."[26] What occupies, or at least indicates, the place of the unspoken in Duras and Sarraute? Is it a sublimation of women's negative self-image, of her castrated body (of which her decapitated mind is but a derivative)? Is it, rather, the "dynamic force" of a uniquely female desire whose potential, once named or defined,[27] is precipitously brought to an end by the linguistic imprinting of patriarchal constraints? Or is it, after all, something more sensuous and somatically derived?

In her many texts on literature and art, Julia Kristeva has focussed on the creative expression of desire and the erogenic body. In *Polylogue*, *New Maladies of the Soul*, *Time and Sense*, and elsewhere, she described how libidinal impulses are discharged in the signifying process. A semiotician and (like Irigaray) a psychoanalyst, she has long been concerned with the constraining and reductive forces of our socio-cultural environment on the construction of linguistic meaning. In fact, she first became known for juxtaposing to them the pleasure of mastering signification in the articulation of libidinal desire: *Jouissance*, about which she has written so prolifically, is, it will be remembered, *j'ouis sens*, or I heard meaning.[28]

Distinguishing between two dispositions inherent in the signifying process, the "semiotic" and the "symbolic," Kristeva aimed from the start to demystify the articulation of subjective experience by returning language to its earliest bodily origins. The distinction between the "semiotic" – which may summarily be described as the effect on language of the body's instinctual drives – and the "symbolic" – which refers to language's structural constitution, the referential dimension by which the subject identifies itself as distinct from its objects – substitutes a dual determination of meaning for the rationalism imposed by male-referential thinking on meaning's biological base.

Kristeva does not emphasize difference, which is not to say that it plays no role in her thinking. On the contrary. The difference in question, though, is not gender determined: Insofar as one's sense of self develops from the differentiation from mother and, ultimately, from all others, female or male, femininity is thought by Kristeva to "take as many forms as there are women." She therefore denies the existence of a feminine writing for the essentialism it implies:

> If we confine ourselves to the *radical* nature of what is today called "writing", that is, if we submit meaning and the speaking subject in language to a radical examination and then reconstitute them in a more polyvalent than fragile manner, there is nothing in either past or recent publications by women that permits us to claim that a specifically female writing exists.[29]

How can there be a truly feminine writing if femininity – or even woman – cannot be defined? Not only is the idea that one *is* a woman absurd to Kristeva in the extreme, but a woman cannot be said to "be": "In 'woman' I see something that cannot be represented, something that is not said, something above and beyond nomenclatures and ideologies."[30] Yet, precisely because she views the feminine as a subjectivity whose sexuality is thereby unique, does Kristeva not beg the question of a female libidnous expression after all?

There are writers who, to Kristeva's way of thinking, have moved in the direction of expressing libidinal drive in a renewal of signification, an "infinitizing" of meaning, in accordance with the rhythm of a text. But is this renewal of meaning expressive of the "libidinal femininity," the distinctly female desire, to which Cixous and others subscribe? Can we even conceive of libido as being of a specifically feminine order?

Freud was, to some degree, inconsistent in his response to the question of the nature of libido. Or, at least, he was sufficiently puzzled by it to provoke considerable disagreement over what he said even today. A forerunner of the concept of libido appeared in his 1894 paper "The Neuro-Psychoses of Defence" where he described "a sum of excitation – which possesses all the characteristics of a quantity (though we have no means of measuring it), which is capable of increase, diminution, displacement and discharge, and which is spread over the memory-traces of ideas somewhat as an electric charge is spread over the surface of a body."[31] In the *Three Essays on Sexuality* (1905), however, he refined his notion of what by then he called "libido" to claim that, as sexual energy, it had three component parts: an object (the mother, father, lover, and so on); an aim (to be nurtured, penetrated, etc.); and a mode of gratification (sucking or intercourse, for example). And it was in this context that he developed his hypothesis of the sexual instinct in terms of two polarities, *activity and passivity* and *masculinity and femininity*. Though the former was said to relate more to instinctual aim and the latter to the post-Oedipal choice of object, this is where the dissension in contemporary readers begins.

It is unarguable that Freud increasingly came to view activity and passivity not only as the province of instinctual aims in both the male and female pre-Oedipal child, but as part and parcel of the masculine–feminine dichotomy generally. Already in 1905 he wrote:

> [I]f we were able to give a more definite connotation to the concepts of "masculine" and "feminine", it would even be possible to maintain that libido is invariably and necessarily of a masculine nature, whether it occurs in men or in women and irrespectively of whether its object is a man or a woman.

In a footnote added to that text some ten years later, he is even more definitive:

> "Masculine" and "feminine" are used sometimes in the sense of activity and passivity, sometimes in a biological, and sometimes, again, in a sociological sense. The first of these three meanings is the essential one and the most serviceable in psycho-analysis. When, for instance, libido was described in the text above as being "masculine", the word was being used in this sense, for an instinct is always active even when it has a passive aim in view.[32]

Clearly it is on a masculine-centered model of sexual energy that Freud constructed his theory. But there are moments in his subsequent writings where he appears less convinced by his own penchant for calling libido masculine. For example, in one of his last statements on the matter, the paper on femininity in the *New Introductory Lectures* of 1933, he briefly equivocates with regard to "the motive force of sexual life":

> It would not be surprising if it were to turn out that each sexuality had its own special libido appropriated to it, so that one sort of libido would pursue the aims of a masculine sexual life and another sort those of a feminine one.

Yet he does not end his reflection there. He retracts the possibility of a dual-gendered libido and he does so with force: "But nothing of the kind is true. There is only one libido, which serves both the masculine and the feminine sexual functions." Moreover, he withdraws the sexual identification entirely: "To [the libido] itself we cannot assign any sex," only to reverse himself once again by returning with even greater insistence to the masculine-centered view: "[I]f, following the conventional equation of activity and masculinity, *we are inclined to describe [the libido] as masculine*, we must not forget that it also covers trends with a passive aim."[33]

Countering "the juxtaposition" of a "feminine libido," which he claims to be "without any justification,"[34] Freud conceptualizes libido, then, as qualitatively masculine in nature. He does so because instinctual drive is necessarily active in as much as it is a search for gratification and for Freud active and masculine are mostly synonymous. At the same time, though, he stresses that the male may possess passive aims just as the female's aims may be active which brings me to an important point. Despite his declared opposition to the notion of a "feminine libido," Freud does incorporate in his theory what some see as a defeat of the active-is-masculine equation. It is this, I believe, that legitimizes the call for a feminine discourse that concerns us here. Psychoanalyst Peter Dunn has articulated it as "the libidinal *pleasure* associated with the *gratification* of passive aims."[35] Interestingly, Kristeva gives form to this concept of female libido when she writes of those avant-garde texts where clarity of meaning is lost to the very rhythm of a story or sentence. Ruptures, ellipses, and blank spaces provoke ambiguity as linguistic holes are introduced in narrative or verse. What's more, all the writers she cites as expressing this sort of feminine libido are men.[36]

According to some, what Freud really seems to have in mind is a bisexuality that goes unnamed. That he speaks of passive aims (which is not to speak of passivity) whose achievement may well require significant activity appears to support the idea. Elisabeth Young-Bruehl has observed that recognizing libido as bisexual, or at least organized for bisexuality, would have been more consistent with Freud's understanding of libidinal drive. He never did identify it as such because, according to her, he was unable to connect the concept of bisexuality (with regard to aims and objects) to his theory of instinctual motivation.[37] Rosemary Balsam agrees. In a recent paper she notes that the equation of "active" with male and "passive" with female is a "forced dichotomy" seemingly "imposed almost for theoretical neatness."[38]

We must not lose sight, however, of the fact that Freud's libido theory was primarily a way of thinking quantitatively about the *energy* of the sexual instincts, that what it addressed was the very dynamism of the drive itself. Thus the analyst David Milrod, for one, can "strongly agree with those who object to giving the libidinal drive a sexual identity," either masculine or feminine. It is Milrod's claim that making a clear distinction between the libidinal drive energy and the objects, interests, and activities that are invested (cathected) with that energy would go a long way toward demonstrating that the libidinal drive is singluar and the same in the male and female. It is the objects, interests, and activities (the targets of libidinal drive investment) that are characteristically different for males and females.[39] Yet, it is precisely this economic perspective that provokes others to proffer that because libido (whose etymology, we recall, is "desire") is biological – it emanates within a body that is structurally (anatomically) and chemically (hormonally) constituted – it is qualitatively masculine or feminine. That is, because it is *of a particular body* and not merely a byproduct in the mind, it is determinative of a creative sublimation rooted in sexual difference. Perhaps, though, this is to confuse the female's libido with the abstract concept of a feminine libido, even if it might be argued that they are synonymous.[40] This much is clear: On the order of metapsychology alone, the matter of the feminine libidinal impulse to which Cixous, like so many other verbal and visual artists, beseeches women to become attuned remains unresolved. Hence the need to reframe the discussion neuro-scientifically as I will endeavor to do below.

Both Cixous and Irigaray have situated the feminine voice in that bodily delimited space (as initially defined by the symbiotic connection of infant to mother) which precedes the acquisition of language and acceptance of the Law of the Father. Kristeva also turned to the pre-Oedipal emotional environment to establish the origin of *jouissance* in its link to the imaginary. In fact, she went so far as to connect the discourse of fantasy in free association with the Kleinian concept of "protophantasy," the idea that drives and desires aimed at the object (the breast, the mother) are articulated by babies in a "quasi-narration."[41] All three, then, however diverse their positions, looked beyond Freud for affirmation of their thinking and appropriated the developmental model of Jacques Lacan wherein ordinary language usage obfuscates the direct relation of the body to pleasure in imposing a symbolic inbetween.[42] They took from the French psychoanalyst the idea that the phallus, more than an organ, linguistically enacts in symbolic representation the authority of Father over the familial triad. And they located in the pre-symbolic not only the bodily source of writing, but also incompletion and loss – from which desire, as creative pursuit, unfolds.[43]

But neither Lacan's thinking nor the French feminists' appropriation of it is new. Why return to them now? Why here? In "Coming to Writing" Cixous claimed that "[A]ll women feel, in the dark or the light, what no man can experience in their place, the incisions, the births, the explosions in libido, the ruptures, the losses, the pleasures in our rhythms." What she was at a loss to explain, though, is *how* what affects her, *how* what she feels as a woman, could "[come] into language, [come] out fully worded" as the "writing springs forth." She described it as "a fusion, a flowing into fusion" that would be incited by woman within herself: " 'Let yourself go, let the writing flow, let yourself steep; bathe, relax, become the river, let everything go, open up, unwind, open the floodgates, let yourself roll . . .'." Yet the mystery of creativity surpassed her as she wondered *how*, "in the movement of her instinctual economy," women would risk the dangers of submersion to live "in direct contact with writing" and gain "instant access" to words.[44] In what follows I will redirect the question to neuroscience in an effort to glimpse how what Cixous envisaged as women's " 'coming' to language" is clarified by recent research on the brain. In its collaboration with psychoanalysis, as we shall see, neuroscience sheds significant light on the relation of the female body to verbal and visual expression with the result that much of what was previously intuited by the French feminist triumverate is now scientifically confirmed.

* * *

The question at hand is essentially this: While a number of feminists have called upon women to create through their bodies, is there any reason to suppose they ever did anything else? Does expression mediated as literary and visual art by a female brain, in other words, necessarily (and therefore already) differ from that mediated by the brain of a man? To answer we must begin by noting that what is at issue is the existence of a female consciousness and by resituating the discussion on the order of the biology of subjectivity. Sex-based biology is slowly beginning to revolutionize research and the medical treatment of women. How women experience pain and metabolize medication, the rate at which they pump blood through their hearts and how their immune system functions, the size of neurons in their brains and how they synthesize neurotransmitters – these are the basis for changing views of sexual difference. What must keep pace with this change is our perspective on its socio-cultural manifestations. The idea that women are concerned with "psychological events, rather than with abstract philosophical assertions or with external, dramatic happenings" (as one critic put it), and that some sort of "interior monologue" is therefore the stylistic province of the female has been characteristic of a kind of simplistic thinking that may be traced back to early modernist reactions against nineteenth-century realism. (It was modernism's rejection of the authoritative and analytic mode of writing characteristic of that male-dominated literary tradition that impelled this shallow taxonomy.)[45] Seeking the biological foundation of a female aesthetic outside such archaic formulations means looking beyond stylistic affinities, beyond shared verbal and visual structures and the commonality of certain kinds of images in texts and paintings by women. In truth, the repeated recurrence of such structures and images does not reveal much about their origin, whether they reflect something within or without, something inherently female or something responsive to what being female may socio-culturally represent. With the proviso in mind that it is always a matter of an individual's creativity, even when the overall focus of the discussion is the creativity of women qua women, we need rather to consider what might be meant by *female awareness* in art and what constitutes its origin.

The 1970s and 1980s saw an upsurge in the subversion by feminist artists of male images of women; they worked to reclaim them and make them their own. The turn in feminist criticism (particularly in France) to post-Freudian (particularly Lacanian) psychoanalysis was in support of that effort for an alteration occurred in psychoanalytic thinking around 1970 (as Rosemary Balsam has demonstrated) that made gender less of a competitive issue and fostered recognition of the female psychic experience as a phenomenon to be reckoned with in and of itself. There was a "shift of emphasis to the centrality of the female habitus," Balsam tells us, with the result that clinical treatment and theory became more attuned to "the blend that becomes a person's gender portrait" than to the anachronistic notion "that maleness must be 'overcome' to 'create' female development."[46] Psychoanalysis alone, however, has proved insufficient in accounting for the "feminine subjectivity"[47] underlying the idea of a female aesthetic. Greater attention to the biological substrates of that subjectivity is required precisely because it is neural systems that determine our consciousness of ourselves and the feelings dependent upon it. To that end we might consider the primary structural and functional differences that have been noted between the female and male brains. Interestingly, we run into a problem right from the start, for the human body has a default system, a physiological blueprint that is female and this includes the brain.

It is generally accepted by biologists that, despite genetic differences between the sexes (the last of the 23 pairs of chromosomes being XX in the female and XY in the male), structurally there is no differentiation in the embryo. Rather, sexual organs develop from "ducts" as hormones are secreted (in the first six or so weeks after conception). Insofar as we all start out as females, should the maturational process go astray and the hormonal mechanism whereby some brains are masculinized be inhibited, a male body could contain a female brain. This is to say that the biochemical maturation of the fetal brain is not directly linked with that of the rest of the body; their symmetry, in other words, is not to be assumed.[48] The condition in which a female infant's genitals appear male, congenital adrenal hyperplasia, and other intersex conditions where anomalous genitalia are present prove the point.

Now the dissimilarity in brain chemistry has profound functional implications. These derive mainly from the fact that the body's primary gland, the pituitary, whose hormonal secretions affect most of the other major endocrine glands of the body, is directly connected with and is also instructed by the hypothalamus (a part of the brain so determinative that it is sometimes referred to as the brain's own brain) and that in the hypothalamus there are significant gender differences. Also, certain hormones (oxytocin and vasopressin – those largely responsible for the sexual behavior of women and men respectively) may act as molecular messengers (or neurotransmitters) and relate thereby to the greater activation of certain regions of the brain in one or the other sex. This would account for the fact, for example, that the anterior cingulate gyrus (a region in the medial frontal lobes intimately connected to ancient subcortical emotion systems) is more active in females while the same is true of the amygdala (an area of the anterior temporal lobe) of males. The former, in fact, appears, as Solms and Turnbull tell us, "linked with the expression of *nurturant* behaviors and concern for *social* connections" and the latter "probably relates to the finding that boys are typically more *aggressive* and *active* than girls."[49]

While there is no structural differentiation in the embryonic brain, there are structural differences between the mature female and male brains worthy of note. These include the size of the nucleus of certain cells (those in what are called the preoptic area and the ventromedial hypothalamus), synaptic and dendrite organization, and the volume of particular cell groups.[50] More important in the present context, however, is the difference commonly thought to exist in the network of fibers, known as the corpus callosum, which connects the two hemispheres of the human brain. There is considerable evidence that in the female brain this network is larger than in the male. In the great majority of the population (some 90 percent), language is primarily a function of the left hemisphere where such tasks as the relating of word symbol to meaning are achieved. The right hemisphere, though, also plays an important role: Instrumental in producing emotion, it allows for the prosodic embellishment of language, for the variations in usage that extend beyond literal meaning. Because there is considerable evidence that the corpus callosum (in particular, the posterior segment called the splenium) is larger in the female brain, women are commonly said to enjoy better connectedness between the left and right hemispheres with the result that they have language abilities considered superior to those of men. In fact, there is additional evidence that the two areas that process language (the Broca and Wernicke areas situated in the frontal and temporal lobes) are also larger in women and that both sides of the frontal brain are active as the female processes language while only the left side is activated when the male does. (It goes without saying that none of this has to do with intelligence. Moreover, while women have, on the average, verbal and other abilities exceeding those of men, the male brain affords its own superior capacities: Topographical spatial abilities, for example, are typically greater in men than in women.)[51]

Other structural differences have been indicated in the cerebral cortex where larger and fewer neuronal units have been found in the female brain upon autopsy and in data obtained by magnetic resonance imagining. Again, gender-specific abilities, most notably the language advantage in women, are supported by these findings.[52] Can we conclude from these studies that women think and feel differently from men? Certainly they process language in another way and this alone has cognitive (again, having nothing whatsoever to do with intelligence), affective, and social implications. But are there real implications for the consideration of a "feminine" art?

Since the publication in 1962 of a seminal work by the Russian neurologist Aleksandr Romanovich Luria, *Higher Cortical Functions in Man*, we have come to understand that mental functions are dynamically determined. Just as bodily functions (like digestion and respiration) result from a number of interactions between various organic systems, mental functions are situated between and not within particular parts of the brain.[53] What this means for our understanding of language is that it, too, is to be "dynamically" as well as structurally situated. Specific regions of specialization – the area for the production of language identified in 1861 by the French anatomist Paul Broca, for instance, or that recognized some 12 years later by the German psychiatrist Carl Wernicke as the site of its comprehension – are now considered within the context of their profound, if complex, interactivity. And the processing of primary speech sounds (of which there are about 110) is viewed in terms of its integration of sensory and motor functions, an amalgamation that calls both the perception and memory of auditory and visual patterns into play.

The dynamic view of language, moreover, begs the question of the relation between language and consciousness. As previously noted, consciousness exists for the purpose of regulating the human organism. Without consciousness, as we are reminded by Solms and Turnbull, we would not know how we feel: "It tells us whether something is 'good' or 'bad'; and it does that by making things *feel* good or bad (or somewhere in between). That is what consciousness, feeling, is *for*."[54] Insofar as the striving to maintain a condition of constancy (homeostasis) originates in the neuroanatomy and neurochemistry of the automatic nervous system, then, consciousness is inherently biological at its core.

This is highly significant, for monitoring of the organism by consciousness could not be accomplished were *meaning* not implicated in the process. It is what feeling *means* to us that delimits homeostasis and determines its success. Our very survival depends upon our ability to evaluate what is happening within and outside us, and it is the brain (specifically, the posterior cortex) that perceives and evaluates data so that consciousness may represent and assign meaning to our inner states. Consciousness modifies the brain's intake of information, in other words, and thereby preserves the status quo. It monitors the state of our various bodily systems and "report[s] whether they (i.e., you) are 'contented' or not."[55]

In short, when we remember that consciousness exists to give meaning to feeling, we can appreciate the importance of structural and chemical (hemispheric and hypothalamic) differences in the female and male brain: They are precisely what determine how "feminine" or "masculine" one *feels*. Also, language, thought, and the meaning ascribed to feelings are so intimately connected that language bears on our understanding of reality, of our perception of time and space, and of ourselves within it. To the extent that the female brain differs from that of the male in ways that impact verbal expression, it follows that woman's identity – her sense of self whence her creative voice emerges – *psychodynamically* reflects the physiology that is uniquely hers.

A caveat, however, is in order: When Elaine Showalter wrote in 1981 that "Organic or biological criticism is the most extreme statement of gender difference, of a text indelibly marked by the body,"[56] the fall-out from Sandra Gilbert and Susan Gubar's monumental *The Madwoman in the Attic* (1979) was still strong. Gilbert and Gubar had proclaimed the pen a "metaphorical penis" and the writing of women deeply inscribed with the anxiety of sexual difference. Showalter was protesting that analogy and the biological perspective in general, not because the idea of anatomical inferiority (bequeathed by Freud) was any less objectionable to her than to those writers, but because its backlash in "biocriticism" was just as offensive. In looking now to neuroscience for clarification of the feminist discussion, in no way do I seek to diminish the significance of myriad ways in which socio-cultural forces act upon language. Nor do I wish to overlook scientific research that counters the argument that the female instinctual economy has, or can have, an expressive voice (verbal or visual) unto itself.

Indeed, it cannot be left unsaid that the observation of infants has led some cognitivists (and some psychoanalysts as well) to believe that basic narrative or preverbal structures intrinsic within the brain render the notion of the gender specificity of creativity untenable. Pointing, rather, to the universality of image formation and expression, such "pre-narrative envelopes" (as Kristeva calls them) are said to be at the root of drive regulation and affect control. Activating early drive interactions with primary objects, they would stimulate object relations and the fantasies to which they give rise. An extension of Noam Chomsky's notion (developed in the late 1950s) of the brain's genetic encoding or hard-wiring for language, the idea of narration as an elementary object relational structure finds support in Melanie Klein's belief in the neonate's inborn awarenesses – the preconception, for instance, of the breast (and other "part objects") – and in the existence of unconscious fantasy from birth. It is also supported by Damasio's concept of the endless interweaving of data (the preverbal narrative to which I referred earlier) in the higher reaches of consciousness. To the extent that such storytelling, in which what happens is registered in the brain, is a prerequisite of language, a condition for language learning, it may not render the idea of gendered expression more credible, but the reverse.

Similarly, some biological principles of image making are known to be universal. Research has demonstrated that pictures drawn by children (of the human figure and the house, for instance) are astonishingly uniform and that several factors underlie the uniformity. To begin with there is a muscular factor, in which gratification is obtained from making certain arm and hand movements over others that are more difficult and less pleasing to make. There is also an optical factor, the preference for visual arrangements more acceptable than others to the eye.[57] And, of course, there is the psychological component, the desire to be like others that is more powerful at certain times in a child's development than at others.

The complexity of the matter becomes even more evident when one considers the discharge of tension achieved through the creative act. To call for artistic expression to be congruent with or flow from within the rhythms of the female body is to affirm a process already inherent in the making of art. Such is the basis of the aesthetic paradigm developed by Rose, the late music theorist David Epstein, and others, the model founded on the belief that all art has a distinctly biological function executed through the building of tension and its ultimate release:

> Painting is a visual model of how the brain works, dealing with the separateness and unity of perception; music is an acoustic model, working with variations of sameness to reconcile time's change with its constancy; poetry mediates between physical feeling-impulses and discursive thought. All build tension, sustain and resolve it, in order to rebuild it – which is what the mind does.[58]

Still, there are two important points I wish to stress: First, the structural and chemical differences between the male and female brains referred to above are no less significant for the universality of organic function. For even if the infant is born with the apparatus for, say, language acquisition, the actual inscription of language in the brain is experiential. It depends upon human interaction and the affective associations, mental representations, and hierarchy of meanings it yields. This, of course, is where the supporters of the socio-cultural side of the debate have long gathered their evidence. At the same time, however, the point lends credence to the other side of the argument: Insofar as the brain continues to develop for many years after birth, the structural maturation of its language and other centers is subject to the hormonal differences between male and female all during the time such conditioning is taking place. Nothing, moreover, can be said to be more experiential than bodily sensation. Thus the notion of a primary femininity or a primordial sense of femaleness from which women create is immediately implicated by the feeling, the "knowledge," and the meaning sensation in the body imparts.

Second, there is the remarkable plasticity of the brain. As we saw in Chapter 1, experience provokes change in the brain's neurobiology. (Howard Shevrin, in addition to those mentioned earlier, has impressively documented the brain's reactivity to experience citing research on modifications both in the synaptic organizational patterns of the brain and in neurotransmitter activity produced experientially.)[59] Differences in brain structure account for differences in perception and in the processing of what is perceived; but these, in turn, affect the structure of the body's primary organ of life. This point, too, has been used to support the nurturists' argument over that of the naturists: It is socio-cultural conditioning, the reasoning goes, which explains the male/female distinctions and accounts for the differences between the male and female brains. Yet, the belief in an innate male–female dimorphism, what the eminent psychoanalyst Peter Blos referred to some years ago as a "core gender identity," is validated by both not-so-new observational data showing sexually linked differences in neonates[60] and very new and compelling neuroscientific evidence of the connection between psychic representation, the sense of self, and bodily experience. To the extent that the brain's plasticity, its responsiveness to what is perceived through the senses, contributes to the psychic evolution of the self through mental representation (and I will have more to say on this in Chapter 5), it can be said that the feeling of femaleness is a psychophysiological phenomenon (as is the feeling of being male).

In short, then, the implications of the question of gender identity for art are rich precisely because it is in *subjectivity* that gender awareness resides. And it is in the concrete evidence of the *biology of subjectivity*, in the neuroscientific substantiation of the self's psychophysiological constitution, that the notion of a feminine presence in art is legitimized. To be precise, it is the discovery of the neurobiological substrates of affect, memory, representation, and all the constituents of self-awareness that explains the subjective nature of consciousness and it is this that is responsible for a woman's "sense of primary femaleness," as it is now sometimes called.

The notion, though, that subtending the question of a female creative voice is the biology of subjectivity is rendered exceedingly complex by the implication of neurological referents of that indistinct phenomenon we call the "self." In fact, among those questions preoccupying neuroscientists at this time are these: How does the mental circumscription of bodily boundaries relate to the neural mechanisms essential not only to early attachment but to the differentiation of self from non-self? How does the sense of self relate to the neural substrates of affect and emotion? Where are internal representations (of self and object) encoded? And a real consensus on the answers has yet to be reached.

Neuroscientists generally agree that psychic functions involve a range of brain structures and that the real work lies in coming up with the full list and function of each. Some of the more cognitively oriented, however, argue that the representational system, at once spatial, conceptual, and linguistic, resides primarily in the cortical regions and that a self/non-self distinguishing mechanism is pre-wired within the brain. Others see representation in terms of something else. Joseph LeDoux, for instance, considers the representation of subjective phenomena as determined by emotional mechanisms that in turn are determined by consciousness which is really all about memory. In a word, he redefines "the problem of emotional feelings as the problem of how emotional information comes to be represented in working memory."[61] Still others, on the basis of clinical observations, view differently the continuum of mnemic traces on which self (and object) representations are erected. (These extend from the higher cortical regions, where the more elaborated and more "cognitive" aspects of the self are registered, to deep within the subcortical regions where the more primitive aspects of the core self are encoded.) Solms and Turnbull, for example, distinguish a "simple awareness" from the "reflexive awareness" that is more intimately connected with "inner speech." The one is directly linked with the visual generating part of the right cerebral hemisphere while the other, the ability to reflect on what is represented within the mind, has to do with the working of the left cerebral hemisphere where words are generally produced.[62]

Damasio and Panksepp would concur that basic awareness emanates from core structures while the more elaborated forms of awareness are linked to the higher cortical areas. Panksepp, in fact, accounts for the neural basis of self and object awareness in an elegant theory he refers to as Simple Ego-type Life Form, or SELF. For him, representations develop from the coherent, if exceedingly intricate, organization of a motor process located in the midbrain. Essentially subcortical, they extend to the brain's higher regions through a variety of neurological and psychological maturational processes, but of particular significance to us here is that Panksepp goes so far as to claim a distinct neural referent for the pronoun "I." This is an archaic or "primary template" of the SELF system found deep within the layers of the colliculi (or little swellings) on the dorsal (which is to say upper) surface of the midbrain and in the primary circuits of the gray matter of the brainstem, the periaqueductal gray (PAG).

Some recent research indicates that self-awareness depends not only on a network of interconnections, but on the overlapping perceptions and representations of both self and others. For example, Jean Decety and Jessica Sommerville have reported that the right inferior parietal cortex (a central region towards the back of the brain), along with the prefrontal cortex in the right hemisphere, is critical to self–other differentiation. And they have claimed that self-awareness relies on an identification with others, on shared representations, as much as on the apperception of the self as unique.[63]

Whatever the neural activation, though, it is through its interaction with our most fundamental emotional circuits that the regulatory input of memory, association, and body schema are, as Arnold Modell reminds us, "the record of the experience of an *individual*."[64] This is to say that despite the universal structure and function of the central nervous system, there are sufficient genetic and experiential variables to generate an incalculable diversification of subjective meaning. This is what obliges us to rethink the matter of gender with regard to the arts in terms of neurobiology. It is the biology of subjectivity that gives credence to the notion that the female artist writes or paints from within her womanhood. It is the biology of subjectivity that legitimizes the claim of some feminists that she must recognize the bodily source of her work in the same way she experiences her self as distinctly female. Rather than "anatomy is destiny," this means she has her own *body memory* to celebrate, her own visceral sensations and *body-knowledge* to honor for harboring feelings unique both to her gender and to her self. And it means that it is from there that she makes art.

In his 1915 paper "Instincts and their Vicissitudes," Freud described the motor factor of instinct or drive (*Trieb*) as pressure (*Drang*), that is, "the amount of force or the measure of the demand for work it represents."[65] More recently, neuroscientists have realized, as Pankepp tell us, "that such a broad abstract *intervening variable* cannot be credibly linked to unitary brain processes" and thus the notion of "bodily *need state*" is preferable to the concept of drive.[66] However the motor arousal that increases in response to regulatory disparities or insufficiencies is described, researchers are now coming to understand what fuels it – motivation – and how motivation is anchored in the very experience of one's self as an actor, as an agent initiating action. Neuroscience, in other words, is yielding the secrets of the self's *experiential* constitution and its determination of the *motor factor* at the heart of drive theory (in Freudian terminology) or of energy balance regulation (as Panksepp would have it). Howard Shevrin articulates it thus: "From a neurophysiological and neuroanatomical standpoint agency appears to be instantiated in a particular brain circuitry characterized by a particular transmitter. But the behavioral and experiential observations accompanying the activation of this system are actions of the entire individual as agent." The word *motive* itself, he reminds us, comes from the Latin *movere*, to move or to be in motion and it is as "active agents" that we "adaptively learn and prosper."[67] If the implications, evolutionary and homeostatic, of the neuroscientific understanding of the self as agent validate the energic model of the mind, they also illustrate the biology of subjectivity and, thereby, the primacy of gender, the sense of one's body not as the same as or different from another's (gender identity is not established before the second or even third year of life), but simply as one's own. I do not mean to imply here that any real sense of self is present from birth, though interesting studies of late suggest that the degree of psychic symbiosis in the infant and mother dyad is perhaps not as extensive as classical psychoanalysis has presumed. (On the other hand, the refutation of any distinct phase of undifferentiation between self and other, such as Melanie Klein advanced, is far from being confirmed.) The point, rather, is that the concept of agent as fundamental to motivation implicates a however discreet bodily sense from which a fuller self-awareness grows.

By virtue of neuroscience's uncovering of the links between motor processes and neural referents of self-awareness, its detection of the brain circuitries responsible for the agency motivating drive, and the physicochemical and anatomical explanations of mental representation itself, the notion of gender identity has taken on a very new meaning in recent years. Indeed, psychoanalysis for the most part now acknowledges that the development of the female is psychosexual and determined by her relation to her body,[68] a notion supported by the evidence that psychobiological differences exist because of differences in mechanisms within the female and male brain. Increasingly, the sense of femaleness is seen not as derivative of learning or as the consequence of a psychological-coming-to-terms with not being male. Learning and cultural bias, of course, do play a role – and a significant one – in the fine tuning of female identity, but there is overwhelming empirical evidence of intrinsic biological substrates of gender which subvert the parameters of phallocentrism that have long defined female subjectivity in terms of the male. Though the gender portrait constructed by the self harbors varying degrees of ambiguity (dependent in part on parental internalizations), within the neurophysiology of motor arousal and the biology of subjectivity subtending it, we have a distinct psychophysiological basis for the primacy of feeling female.

Interestingly, it was the socio-cultural extension of the energic model of the mind that Irigaray and other radical feminists condemned for a phallocentric bias. As Irigaray explains: "The energy involving tension, release and return to homeostasis [. . .] seeks to become more and more intense, faster and faster. It must 'pulsate', it must 'explode', etc., and at any cost, otherwise it goes limp, it falls apart." It is this "escalation towards human and technological entropy [that] makes us forget our condition as living beings." Put somewhat differently, it is this "pathos of increasing energy, of economic growth, both individual and collective, out of harmony with natural rhythms, [that] sacrifices us little by little."[69] But if Irigaray's remarks affirm what neurobiologist Lesley Rogers has eloquently demonstrated, namely, that no biological concept is entirely "value free,"[70] it is nonetheless in the play between pleasure and unpleasure (tension and release) and its implication of an awareness of self, that the idea of a primary feminine element is validated. I say this, fully aware of the irony, precisely because the somatic determination of psychic energy – the mind's derivation from neuronal activity and the interactive functionality of the subcortical structures that motivate our behavior to ensure homeostasis – is now empirically verifiable.[71]

The sculptor Louise Bourgeois once told an interviewer "I'm a woman, so I don't need to be a feminist."[72] What she meant was that her art is based not on a feminist perspective, on a conscious effort to correct a male-centered image of women or of the female body, but on her female experience; and the subjective apprehension of her womanhood is evident everywhere in her art. Consider the series of drawings from the 1940s known as the *Femmes-Maisons* ("House-Women") in which houses appear as heads and torsos of naked female bodies. Like so much of her work, these emotionally charged drawings resurrect the well-known trauma of her childhood, her father's ten-year-long relationship, within the confines of the family home, with the English governess hired to care for his children. Bourgeois has often referred to her father's disloyalty as the target of her anger and, indeed, these house-like amputations are aggressive attempts at reparation by revenge. But what comes though these images is less her anger at the paternal object than the sense of betrayal she felt as the daughter of this man. It is from within this rejection of her self as a feminine self that the aesthetic tension of the work arises and if the *Femmes-Maisons* have been called "anthropomorphic," it is because they appear as formal extensions of the vital functions of her own female body.[73]

So, too, in *Cells*, a series of sculptures dating to the late 1980s and early 1990s, one perceives an affinity between body and sculpted matter that addresses the trauma on the level of its somatopsychic juncture. "The Cells represent different types of pain: the physical, the emotional and the psychological, and the mental and intellectual," Bourgeois has said. "When does the emotional become the physical? When does the physical become emotional? It's a circle going round and round. Pain can begin at any point and turn in either direction." It is undeniable that in certain of her works tension emanates from the interplay of her womanhood with distinctly male imagery. In the pink marble *Femme Couteau* of 1969, for instance, we see her identification with the phallus as a means of defending herself against the aggressor.[74] But it is also the case that Bourgeois expresses in her work an equivalency between her body and her sculpture, a fact to which she has openly attested: "For me, sculpture is the body. My body is my sculpture."[75]

Louise Bourgeois conceives of art as inherently organic. This is how she describes the congruence of body function and the content of the artistic endeavor:

> Content is a concern with the human body, its aspect, its changes, transformations, what it needs, wants and feels – its functions.
>
> What it perceives and undergoes passively, what it performs.
>
> What it feels and what protects it – its habitat.
>
> All these states of being, perceiving, and doing are expressed by processes that are familiar to us and that have to do with the treatment of materials, pouring, flowing, dripping, oozing out, setting, hardening,

> coagulating, thawing, expanding, contracting, and the voluntary aspects such as slipping away, advancing, collecting, letting go –

Judy Chicago defines as her aesthetic objective a specifically female iconography meant to replace the passive and seductive images of women created by men. In fact, she has described her artistic exploration of what it has meant to her to be a woman and articulated her desire to configure "an active female" identity within an "energetic shape."[76] Thus the utterly dissimilar work of these two artists displays a common feature: a preoccupation with the subjective apprehension of their feminine constitution. In so doing it draws attention to the gratification obtained from the apperception of an equivalency between external aesthetic form and internal psychophysiological milieu.

In effect, what I am arguing is that their art achieves more than the mastery of sensitivity to prior experience. Bourgeois reshapes her self in shaping her sculpture; she regulates her affective response to the trauma of her father's betrayal by reworking her feelings through the perceptual and cognitive processes at play in her making of art. But the biological function served by her creative state is more profound than a facilitated interaction between primary-process imagination and secondary-process knowledge of reality. Chicago's "desperate" need (as she calls it) for affirming rather than denigrating images of women finds similar satisfaction in the restorative achievement of the creative act. (The incongruence of the representations of the female she observed in her youth with what she felt herself to be was a powerful determinant of the direction her art would take.) But here, too, the creative experience is in the service of a deeper biological objective: the renewal of self-definition that the mediation of affect (through the neural circuits subtending it) and somatopsychic (re)integration affords.

Freud made explicit the body's role in stimulating activity of the mind. When he wrote of instinct as the "psychical representative" of endosomatic forces, he was describing the intimate connections constituting the very substance of neuro-psychoanalytic research. The critical component of analysis is the transference because psychic change depends upon the reconsolidation of affective experience that depends, in turn, upon the operation of neural circuits. *Creativity effects change in a comparable way: Memory traces and affects set progressively over time within an initial framework of (pleasurable and unpleasurable) bodily states are edited by the making or viewing of art.*

That creativity occurs via a body whose mental representations constitute, in part, the subjective definition of self is precisely what allows us to speak of a female aesthetic and to understand what Cixous intuited as she contemplated the creativity of woman within "the movement of her instinctual economy." Further supporting the significance of the biology of subjectivity for the validation of a female aesthetic is the body's responsiveness as the work of art is visually or aurally experienced. This has been the subject of a considerable number of studies, among the most interesting of which is one by Panksepp and Günther Bernatzky where it was discovered, among other things, that females and males score differently in their physiological reaction to music. Some of the data from this study suggest, for example, that "pro-social, nurturant dynamics of individual emotional patterns" account for the higher incidence of the "automatic 'rush' " or "chill response" – encountered in females listening to music. It was also found that music serves females more than males in the regulation of mood.[77] As noted above, functional differences in the hemispheric processing of language have been documented in relation to structural asymmetries between the female and male brains. While the implications for the viewing of plays and the reading of texts have not, to my knowledge, been evaluated as yet, hypotheses may be formulated based on such functional corroborations of anatomical difference. In fact, additional distinctions in gender responsiveness to music may be forthcoming insofar as some data already indicate the greater reliance of males on left lateralized hemispheric processing for certain musical functions (like pitch tasks).[78]

Jaak Panksepp claims the understanding of subjectivity to be "an especially important key to the deep neural nature of many homeostatic functions." And he attributes the majority of our feelings of sensory pleasure to "the various stimuli that signal the return of bodily imbalances toward an optimal level of functioning."[79] Aesthetic experience is one source of such pleasure and, in exploring the French feminist concern with "*l'écriture féminine*" – and the idea of a female aesthetic generally – in terms of the subjective apprehension of feeling, I have aimed to show the connection between art and gender to be profoundly biologically motivated, however much it is mediated by social (object relational) goals. The belief that the physical and chemical components of the brain's interaction with mentation are the province of neuroscience while its dynamic function (and its byproduct: behavior) is the domain of psychoanalysis has long kept these disciplines apart. We need now to arrive at greater acceptance of the fact that the two are intimately conjoined. It is not merely a question of nature versus nurture: Gender identity – previously dichotomized in the neuroscientific focus on the genetic determination of sex and the psychoanalytic focus on the pre-Oedipal phases of early childhood – is increasingly viewed as a matter of subjectivity and how equilibrated one feels becomes ever more defining as neuropsychoanalysis corrects this and other such schisms.

Part II

A new direction for interdisciplinary psychoanalysis

Introduction

Psychoanalysis has so infiltrated our thinking that it is difficult these days to speak about its application to a discipline outside it. Nonetheless, when we return to the premise upon which psychoanalysis was founded – namely, that the mind is of a biological nature – we are obliged to rethink our understanding of the relation of psychoanalysis to the areas it has infiltrated. All parts of the body, from its skin surface to its internal organs, transmit sensory information via the upper spinal cord to the brain stem, midbrain, and cortex. Thinking, feeling, and even self-awareness depend upon the structural pathways that allow for this transmission and the chemistry that regulates it. Yet the idea that the totality of being we call the "self" is a perception of the ego, that mental structure whose origin Freud located within bodily sensation, has been sorely neglected by the tradition of applied psychoanalysis now thrown into question by neuroscience. The practice of psychohistory aims to resurrect a past that, in truth, can only be resurrected through inference. What neuroscience is now imposing is a change of paradigm that necessarily follows from the reconnection of creativity with biology and it is this that will be the focus of the next three chapters. In a word, this paradigm is not the past as origin of the psychic need for reparative fantasy in art, but *the present as evidence of creativity's somatopsychic efficacy, its profoundly integrative or self-consolidating function.*

While everyone knows that art is the domain of subjectivity, a neuropsychoanalytically inspired aesthetics recognizes the significance of the fact that subjectivity is rooted in what is objectively verifiable. Semir Zeki and his colleagues have been striving to outline the common organization of the neural circuits upon which the variability of visual and emotional responsiveness depends. Mark Solms and others using the clinico-anatomical method of relating objectively to subjectively derived data aim to understand the meaning symptoms have for the individual. Taking his inspiration from Zeki, Solms, and other neuropsychologists and neuroscientists, Norman Holland has recently posed a number of important theoretical questions relevant to thinking about literature neuropsychoanalytically: "Where is a text?" "Why do we do literature?" "What do we enjoy about literature?"[1] Taking my inspiration from many of the same sources, I will follow in the next three chapters a divergent path. I will test the hypothesis that somatopsychic stability is served by the self-consolidation that defines creativity's primary purpose.

To do so, I will look, first, at the work of a novelist and playwright whose characters (more accurately termed "voices") reveal their creator's preoccupation with mental illness. Instead of seeking in the disturbance in psychic boundaries that characterizes each of them a deficit in the psychological biography of the writer, I will aim to disclose how the obsession with illness functioned in Beckett's art as a stabilizing force. Of course, such an effort implies some biographical reassessment, but the difference is more than one of emphasis. This discussion of a play in which a woman's incapacity to articulate the pronoun "I" is the narrative focus will show that what the playwright was after was an iconic re-enactment of human mental function, a function whose health is measured according to the proportion of seeing and not seeing, of insight and repression. And in supporting the astute observation of cultural historian Peggy Phelan that what Beckett dramatized in his work was the very "rhythm of looking" – a rhythm that "oscillates between seeing and blindness, between figuration and abstraction, between the void at the center of sight and the contour of the slender ridge that brooks it"[2] – it will illustrate precisely how art mirrors the mind. But the play also depicts an exceedingly poignant failure, that of this distilled female consciousness to perceive the autonomy of her bodily self. Beckett's rendering of ego diffusion, of the dedifferentiation associated in its severest form with psychosis, was an ongoing effort to comprehend the suffering that may plague the self having a limited capacity for boundary delineation. In all his work, in fact, there is a problematizing of psychic attunement with the body and a sharply curtailed tolerance for de-fusion, for the emotional acceptance of the separation between self and non-self supported by the universal biological blueprint for human consciousness. How this might account for Beckett's enigmatic belief that all art is necessarily doomed to expressive failure is not without interest, for the insufficient self-consolidation would also account for his concurrent sense of the artist as one obliged, nonetheless, to pursue his creative mission.

I will then turn to the work of a painter who, himself, suffered from a severe illness, this time a degenerative physical affliction. Traces of undifferentiation took the form – both aesthetic and conceptual – of a cosmic merger, the union of self and universe, in Paul Klee's creative activity. We will see that the phenomenon significantly intensified precisely at a time when he was out of sync with his body, when he was at a complete loss for control over the reality of its ill health, and that the need to create was reinforced by the need to lessen the distinction between his private experience and a world on which he lacked a hold. Thus the biology of subjectivity will once again frame the investigation of an artistic output revealing the largely kinesthetic basis of the self and its emanation from sensations within the body. Indeed, in his last years Klee's bodily sensations were drastically altered by his illness and the result was that his work became not only far more abstract (objectless) but extraordinarily abundant. The point will be made that Klee's late creativity resided in the furnishing of a newly *felt* equilibrium.

Illness certainly need not frame the neuro-psychoanalytic study of creative experience. Equilibration is the primary objective of everything living and would appear to be determinative of all art, whatever the medium, as we will see in the final chapter on music and dance. Nowhere is the kinesthetic role in the maintenance of the integrity of self more obvious than in the dancer in whom the apperception of the self as the embodiment of internal states is achieved through movement. Martha Graham was convinced of the integrative power of the body's control of physical energy in dance and, as we will observe, her creative impulse sprang precisely from the enhancement of self-awareness afforded by the spatial and temporal sensations associated with moving.

In essence, then, what I am suggesting is that the vision of the artist – whatever the gender and whether healthy or ill – is informed by the integrity of the self. Insofar as we know this integrity to be dependent upon the apperception of feeling in the body, self-awareness – whose brain patterns or neural circuits are increasingly traceable – necessitates a change in applied psychoanalysis. If the conventional measure of creativity is the innovative impact on a field at large, the argument I wish to develop is that art is more accurately deemed creative by virtue of its impact on – *its meaning for* – the creator (and re-creator) at hand. Once again, the basis for this thesis is the immeasurable, but no less real, subjective feeling generated by the brain as it seeks harmony and pleasure in art.

Chapter 3

Psychic boundaries in the work of Samuel Beckett

In an article that appeared in the fall 1987 issue of *The Paris Review*, journalist Lawrence Shainberg describes Beckett's fervent interest in a book he had written on the medical community: "Whenever I saw him," Shainberg tells us, "he questioned me about neurosurgery, asking, for example, exactly how close I had stood to the brain while observing surgery, or how much pain a craniotomy entailed, or, one day during lunch at rehearsals: 'How is the skull removed?' and 'Where do they put the skull bone while they're working inside?' "[3] Beckett's interest in the human brain was a variation on his philosophical interest in the mind–brain relation and the psychology of the mind more generally. Indeed, his readings in philosophy and his literary efforts to come to terms with the Cartesian duality are well documented. Less well known, however, is that he read voraciously, in the 1920s and 1930s, on psychology and even psychoanalysis. Though both his figurations of psychic states and numerous references to Freudian, Jungian, Gestaltist, and other psychologies in his fiction and plays have been the focus of critical studies,[4] these appeared prior to 2001 when the author's copious notes on his readings first became available for consultation by scholars.[5] What the notes attest to, above all, is the extent of the writer's interest in and study of the psychology of the mind and its vicissitudes.

Some of Beckett's interest in the mind–brain may have derived from members of his family: Two uncles on his father's side were doctors, one cousin was a psychiatrist, and another a nurse. A sure source of his learning, though, was his close childhood friend, Geoffrey Thompson, a Dublin physician and, later, a psychiatrist in London who was instrumental in persuading Beckett to seek his own psychotherapy. Beckett visited Thompson at the Bethlem Royal Hospital, a mental asylum in Beckenham, on several occasions. He recounts in a letter to another close friend, Thomas MacGreevy, his experience visiting the wards there where he "saw everything, from mild depression to profound dementia."[6] From his lengthy correspondence with MacGreevy we know that Beckett was inspired by his treatment with Wilfred Bion (from 1933 to 1935) to learn more about mental illness, particularly its manifestation in the ills of the body.[7] There was also a lecture by Jung in 1935 (to which he was taken by

Bion) that had a profound effect on him. (His 1956 radio play *All That Fall* contains direct references to it.) But Beckett's detailed notes bear witness to the fact that most of what he knew came from his readings in the history and development of psychoanalysis.[8]

The significance of this is that he did not populate his prose and drama with the mentally ill willy-nilly, but that he knew very well whereof he spoke. At least as early as his 1938 novel *Murphy*, the fictive voices of his texts were afflicted with neuropsychological ailments uncanny in their clinical accuracy. In that text, for example, he refers to the severe memory disorder known as Korsakoff's syndrome and does so with more than a passing knowledge of the illness: "A hypomanic teaching slosh to a Korsakow's syndrome"[9] is a play on the chronic alcoholism that most commonly produces the condition. Other characteristics of Korsakoff's are consistently woven throughout Beckett's works, but none so conspicuously as the "misremembering" typical of his incessantly confabulating voices. The false memories of the Unnamable (he calls them "hypotheses"!) that constitute the entirety of the 1953 narrative of the same name are perhaps the best example.

The resemblance of Beckett's late play *Footfalls* (1976) to a case study of psychologist Pierre Janet is also telling. The many analogues between the psychopathology of the patient known as Irène, who suffered from terrifying somnabulism and hallucinations, and Beckett's haunting portrayal of May, the primary character in that play, have been enumerated already and it is not necessary to restate them here.[10] Suffice it to say that Janet's patient's tortured story seems clearly to inform Beckett's own. The exploration of other such cases (of schizophrenia and aphasia, in particular) known to the author would further exemplify his interest in neuropsychology and his familiarity with the distorted sense of self in which neuropsychological disorders may result.

Indeed, the matter of self is Beckett's primary concern in all his plays and novels. As Bennett Simon has noted: "Any reader of Beckett's works, or viewer or auditor of his plays, quickly concludes that there is something amiss with the 'selfhood' of his characters."[11] If they are more aptly called "voices," it is that they are never clearly situated in time or place; that they do not interact with others on any but the most primitive of levels; and that their incessant storytelling is little more than a desperate attempt to fill the space left uninhabited by the normally integrated agent we call "I." Each such "voice" is a profusion of selves, fragmented and in search of coherence. In *Molloy* (1951) and *Malone Dies* (1951) we follow an extraordinary metamorphosis of one voice into another as the self wanders in search of its truer or more meaningful incarnation. So lacking in autonomy are Beckett's characterizations that they relate to inanimate objects as though they were extensions of themselves. Crutches and bicycles, bowler hats and tattered garments, are inseparable from their owner rendering the self a something muddling somewhere along the indistinct animate/inanimate boundary:

Lucky, in *Waiting for Godot* (1952) can think only while wearing his hat. The narrator of *How It Is* (1961) holds steadfastly to his sack as he makes his way, belly down, in the mud because it is equated with his life. More radically, Molloy conceives of himself only in relation to the infinite parameters of the universe with which he is fused.

Doubling (such as we have in *Godot*, the novel *Mercier and Camier* [1970], and the 1981 play *Ohio Impromptu*) lends an additional fragility to the self of Beckett's speaking subjects. The replication of their voices on tape (*Krapp's Last Tape* [1958], *Rockaby* [1981]), like their intense craving to be recognized, or at least so much as seen (*Murphy*, *Endgame* [1957], *Play* [1963], *Happy Days* [1961]), complements the coupling of identities that harbors a profound terror of extinction. Beckett's penultimate work, *Stirrings Still* (1988) – where the lone image is of one who sees himself seeing his previous comings and goings – illustrates the hypervigilance employed by Beckett's characterizations to thwart the disintegration. In focussing the character's (mental) eyes on himself and, specifically, on a self whose only real activity is mentation, the narrative depicts extreme self-awareness as a primary means of triumphing over the persistent threat of dissolution:

> One night as he sat at his table head on hands he saw himself rise and go. One night or day. For when his own light went out he was not left in the dark.[12]

"Ghosting"[13] serves a similar purpose and takes a variety of forms in Beckett's oeuvre (Figure 3.1). To cite but a few examples, there are the ghostly presences (such as are found in *Quad* [first televised in 1982] or the short prose piece *Imagination Dead Imagine* of 1965); the ghostly absences (*First Love* [1946], *Waiting for Godot* [1952]); and the ghostly recurrence of names (or the letters that substitute for them), all of which play on the instability of me/not me boundaries. Indeed, the phantom projection of self onto the exterior world is the very basis of Beckett's only film, aptly titled *Film* (1963), in which the principle character is obsessed with obliterating any objectivation of self, as in a photograph or mirror, with eradicating, in fact, his own self-representation or self-image.

The opposite side of the same coin is found in the 1981 play *Rockaby*, a powerful monologue driven by a woman's search for completion in the self of another. Seated throughout the play in a rocking chair, the unnamed woman verbally creates the visual image of the other so as to become its self. Interestingly, consultation of *Rockaby*'s original manuscript reveals an important variant with respect to the final version: a periodic slippage from the first to the third person. References to "I" are amended to "she" by the recorded voice of the lone subject thereby establishing a distinct connection between this play's initial version and another, at which we will look more closely below, the 1972 play *Not I*.[14] In both plays, in fact, it is in the conflation of self

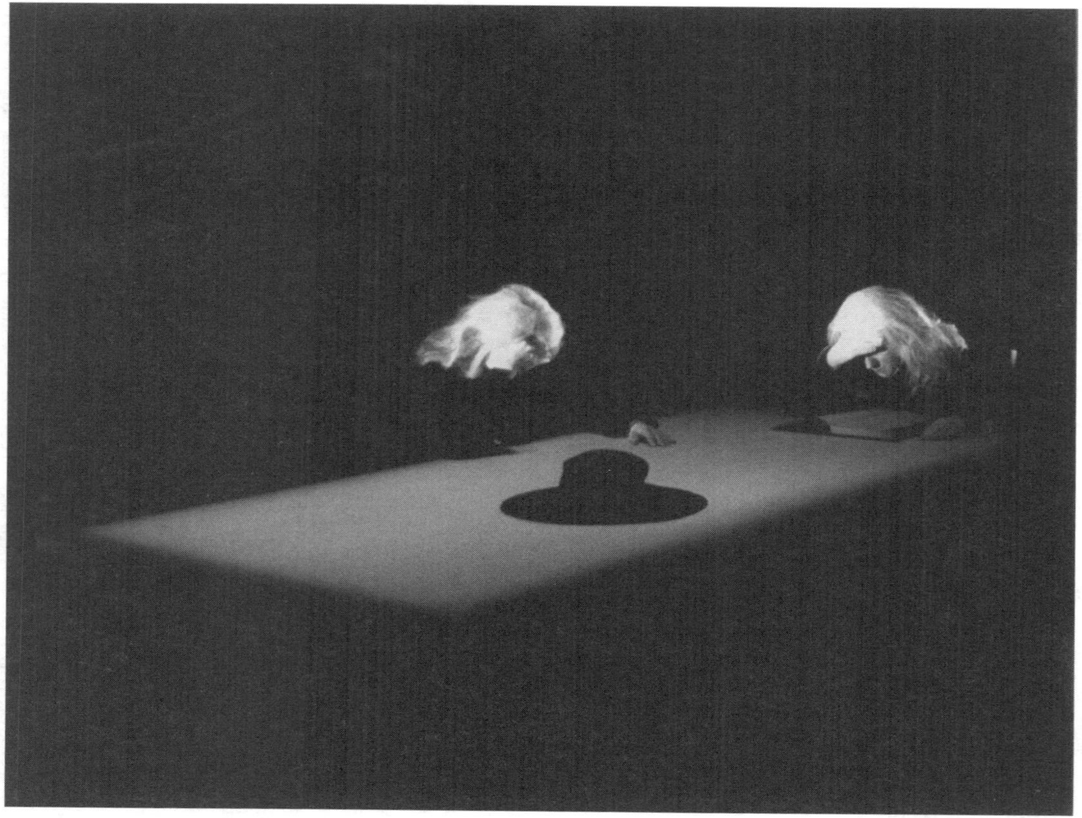

Figure 3.1 Sam McCready (Reader) and Walter Bilderback (Listener) in *Ohio Impromptu* by Samuel Beckett. The Maryland Stage Company, Baltimore 1990, Strasbourg 1996, Berlin 2000. Director Xerxes Mehta. Photographer Robert Dold

and other, in the autoscopic hallucination of self as other, that the primary disturbance of the me/not me boundary is manifested.

The preoccupation with material objects that runs throughout Beckett's narratives and plays is yet another attempt to define the purity of "I" (while not closing in on the specificity of identification) in the ego-distant world this writer privileges throughout his work. In one of the best known passages of Beckett's fiction, Molloy explains how he shifts 16 small smooth stones from his pockets to his mouth and from his mouth back to his pockets so as to suck each of them equally. Similarly, objects of all kinds (from lipstick to a revolver) are lovingly withdrawn from Winnie's handbag in *Happy Days* in a painstaking effort to define where the "me" ends and the "not me" begins. In its most extreme form the fetish-like obsession with things points not only to a fault in the constitution of self, but to the complete annihilation of autonomy, and to the sense of oneness with the world that Freud described in the context of infancy as "oceanic". It is in this spirit that the Unnamable can utter: "Nothing to do but stretch out comfortably on the rack, in the blissful knowledge you are nobody for all eternity."

Generally speaking, then, Beckett's narrative and dramatic fictions have in common a profound preoccupation with differentiation and dedifferentiation, with identity and self-representation as contrasted with ego-world fusion and boundary loss. This is the principle focus of the trilogy, *Molloy*, *Malone Dies*, and *The Unnamable*, where, in the last of these novels, it is succintly expressed as follows: "For to go on means going from here, means finding me, losing me, vanishing and beginning again, a stranger first, then little by little the same as always, in another place [. . .]."[15] It is also the crux of Beckett's earlier narratives, like *Murphy* and the short stories of *More Pricks Than Kicks* (1934), and all his dramatic works too. In *Rockaby* the woman seated in a rocking chair seeks to become her self through the image created by her own voice on a recording. That is, she seeks to solidify her self-image through the sensory modality of hearing. As critic Enoch Brater puts it, she is "literally nothing until she is united with her own image."[16] The narrative voice of *Stirrings Still* strives similarly to distinguish his self, in this case by vigilantly watching himself come and go.

Examples of the effort to establish me/not me boundaries, of obsessively differentiating and dedifferentiating egos, abound in Beckett's writings. What unifies these fictions, however, is not just the fluidity or diffusion of self and the quest for identity that make up the proto-fantasy of Beckett's work. What the texts are *about* is superseded by a mode of expression strategically shaped to appear shapeless so metaphorical is the correlation of language with perception. But I will return to this in a moment, for it is precisely in the form of his writing that the work acts upon the creator (and re-creator) as evidence of the inventive force of Beckett's art. First, however, I wish to explore its raison d'être, the origin of the creative fantasy and the purpose it served.

Psychoanalytic considerations of Beckett's work have, for the most part, emphasized its depressive, nihilistic even, nature, the meaninglessness of a world inhabited by physically degenerate or disembodied voices who do little more than observe themselves moving ever closer, but not rapidly enough, to death. So defining of his art is this world-weary affect that Beckett enthusiasts have long been disposed to seeking the psychohistorical origins of the sense of loss and despair that permeates this work. From the complex and, at times, anguished relationship he had all his life with his mother, his critics like to unpack the torturous pull of the maternal imago in many of his texts. Beckett's biographers recount that May Beckett was of uncertain temper and that she suffered from powerful changes in mood. Profuse clinical data on children's experience of maternal depression (whose silence may pass for rejection or even hostility) that alternates with phases of acceptance and warmth attest to the kind and degree of pain that can ensue. Reared in an atmosphere of emotional uncertainty and unreliability, children may respond, for example, with profound ambivalence, anxiety, and depressive disorders. Both separation from his mother and closeness to her posed a threat for Beckett throughout his life. Even in his last months his feelings for her were turbulent. James Knowlson, Beckett's official biographer, says they struck him in conversations with Beckett then as "still intense, almost volcanic."[17] Certainly this troubled relationship caused a degree of suffering that his writing allowed him in some measure to work through. Works such as *Footfalls*, *Rockaby*, *Company* (1980), and *Ill Seen Ill Said* (1981) have been interpreted by critics from this perspective. But the reparative function of Beckett's writing, the extent to which it served as a corrective measure, as a means of re-forming the relationship with his primary objects (and with his mother most of all), can only be inferred. Did Beckett seek in his work to assimilate the loss of the object and in some sense restore what had been previously experienced as deprivation? Did Beckett need to satisfy aggressive wishes toward his mother or expiate the guilt they provoked? These are the questions of psychobiography and they can only be answered speculatively. What I would rather ask is this: Did something more fundamental impel Beckett to write? Did writing, and writing primarily about disturbances in selfhood, affect his feelings about himself and the world? How might we understand on a more rudimentary level the gratification he derived from creative work? These are questions I believe we can answer by looking at his novels and plays.

So constant and so desperate is the anxiety of dissolution underlying all his texts that Beckett's gratification in creativity must be qualified as of a particular kind, that which derives from the projection of a fear onto the outside world. In projecting his own fear of disintegration onto the characters he creates, the author is able to situate the sense of impending debilitation and loss outside himself and gain thereby control of it. This in itself is a source of satisfaction, or at least of relief, and I would contend that it also had much to do with his distinctive brand of humor. Indeed, externalizing his anxiety and subjecting it to the finite limits of the book or stage rendered it malleable, as Beckett's famously precise stage directions affirm. And it fostered an atmosphere of existential absurdity in which his Chaplinesque wit would thrive. Listen to Sander Gilman whose views on the projection of the fear of dissolution I echo here: "The fixed structures of art provide us with a sort of carnival during which we fantasize about our potential loss of control, perhaps even revel in the fear it generates within us, but we always believe that this fear exists separate from us. This sense of the carnivalesque provides us with exactly the missing fixity for our understanding of the world," an understanding the dread of loss of control denies.[18]

The fear of loss of control, of the disunity of self, with which all Beckett's voices struggle and whose projection, I submit, was a source of the primitive gratification Beckett took in writing, is generally considered evidence of the failure of some sort of defense system. In his paper "Fear of Breakdown," Winnicott offered a number of examples of defenses and the "primitive agonies" (a term he preferred to the weaker "anxieties") against which they protected. Their relevance to Beckett's characters is nothing if not uncanny. Consider these three: Disintegration as a defense against the "return to an unintegrated state"; depersonalization as a defense against the "loss of psycho-somatic collusion" (or the "failure of indwelling"); the autistic state or "relating only to self-phenomena" as a defense against the "loss of capacity to relate to objects."[19] The list of those characters not only displaying, but incarnating one or more of these defenses would be far too long to enumerate. But what is more astonishing than the consistency with which these defenses appear throughout the oeuvre is the psychological correctness of Beckett's depictions.

I will return to the extraordinary accuracy of the writer's dramatizations of defense below. What I wish to emphasize here, though, is that the creative subversion of the obsession with psychic boundaries – more precisely, the fictive depiction of extreme ego weakness and identity diffusion – afforded Beckett a means of delving deeply into the unit of self. And I believe this to have been very much in the interest of consolidating his own selfhood. Writing was not for him a mode of recovery, a modification of past experience, so much as the way of constructing or affirming an integrated self-representation. This integration, the achievement of the focus on mental illness, moreover, is evidence of the work's creative function. To the extent that any form of therapy is ultimately biological, which is to say that it works precisely by altering the brain's neurochemistry and neuroanatomy, over and above its aesthetically innovative value, Beckett's writing was creative in being therapeutic.

This is not to say that writing always came easily to Beckett; on the contrary. He went through many periods of creative stagnation when he was devoid of motivation. "At such times of impasse," Knowlson tells us, "he was irritable and fractious, sometimes even insufferable."[20] Beckett was also prone to prolonged bouts of depression (for which he sometimes took lithium) and he suffered from a deep sense of alienation. But the connection between the writing inhibition and the depression is not nearly as obvious as some would have it. Neurologist Alice Flaherty, for one, has recently demonstrated the complexities between what we commonly refer to as writer's block and depression: The former is not necessarily the result of symptoms of the latter (though loss of enjoyment, energy, and concentration may contribute to diminished productivity). Flaherty makes a strong case for viewing depression not only as a cause of language inhibition, but as a different manifestation of the same frontal lobe malfunctioning that may otherwise be responsible for it.[21] Similarly, Mark Solms's research has shown that those brain regions involved in motivation are also implicated in the workings of the imagination (whether the subject is asleep and dreaming or awake). The point is that depression reflects not only a state of the mind, but of the brain and we need not seek a direct cause-and-effect relation between Beckett's periods of creative stagnation and his depression to appreciate the benefit he derived from writing. If we do not, however, need confirmation that the termination of a play or novel regularly alleviated some form of anguish (it didn't), what we do need are concrete indications that his longstanding interest in abnormal psychology was not gratuitous. That his interest in mental illness was more emotional than intellectual – in fact, he modeled several of his characters after patients he knew or heard about attesting to the extent of his emotional engagement – provides such evidence. May in *Footfalls* is but one example. The patients at Beckenham, those at the hospital in France where he had visited Lucia Joyce (the schizophrenic daughter of James), the young patient described by Jung in the lecture he had heard by the analyst in 1935, and possibly others provided real-life associations for his characterizations.[22] Beckett was deliberate, in other words, in the assimilation of his sources and the extension of this deliberateness into a pervasive focus on the inner world of the psyche points to the need to externalize his own preoccupations and discomfort. In persistently dramatizing shifting or insecure self–other boundaries, Beckett was effectively countering the disintegrating force of his own anxieties.

There is little information on the alteration of brain activity following any type of therapy, least of all what might be considered therapeutic about creative expression, though this is rapidly changing. (New studies are increasingly able to register the neural correlates of the mental events involved in creative activity.) Nonetheless, from systematic animal studies we know a great deal about limbic control of emotion. And from victims of stroke, aphasiacs, and others who have suffered damage to the brain we have come to understand how the areas determinative of language usage interact directly with this system. In this way, neuroscience has been able to establish that the brain functions differently as a result of the "talking cure," that the functional alteration occurs in the prefrontal lobes, and that *language* is itself an exceedingly powerful and precise mode of effecting therapeutic change.

While no such biological confirmation of the therapeutic efficacy of Beckett's writing is possible, it is significant that writing not only afforded him an escape from the emotional distress of a variety of physical ailments – including headaches, boils, and insomnia – but a means of investigating and coping with their psychic sources. From his correspondence with MacGreevy we know to what extent he was self-absorbed and disturbed by his physical symptoms. From his notes on psychoanalysis referred to above, we know how eager he was to explain their psychogenesis. (The physical manifestations of his anxiety attacks, with heart palpitations at the head of the list, concerned him most of all.) Lines in red ink, for instance, and, next to Freud's descriptions of anxiety neurosis and hysteria, the words "mine own" appear in the margins. And certain phrases taken from his readings – those, for instance, having to do with wishes as the source of such symptoms – are underlined. Through writing Beckett was able to temper his obsession with the relation between mind and body and even strengthen the sense of control lost to what appears, from his novels and plays, to be his own poorly delineated inner representational world. The therapeutic benefit of his writing is further confirmed by Knowlson who writes: "By externalizing some of the impulses of the psyche in his work [. . .] he would find it easier to counter the self-absorption that had seemed morbid and destructive in his personal life. Writing thus became essential to his later mental and physical well-being."[23]

So it is that the preoccupation with self, to which he himself attributed his physical ills, and the fundamental disturbance in selfhood that is the sine qua non of his work are never isolated there from the corporeal arena. Yet, while the deep relation between psyche and soma is continually scrutinized by the author, it has been virtually overlooked (other than within the Cartesian philosophical context) in the critical writings on his work. In fact, the similarity of his characters to patients presenting with the somatization of psychic disturbance or to those with real somatic dysfunction endowed with psychic pathology (such as in a number of acute neurological disorders) is most extraordinary. A close look at one of Beckett's late plays should be helpful in putting the somatopsychic relation – both the source and real focus, I would argue, of the writer's narrative and theatrical preoccupation with self – in high relief. This, in turn, should allow us to see his entire creative endeavor as a projection of Beckett's own subjective experience, the projection of an awareness, however unconscious, of feeling fragmented and of a self rendered more autonomous and stable through writing.

Not I is certainly one of the most innovative plays of the twentieth century. First, it takes place almost entirely in the dark. Only a disembodied mouth (appearing suspended stage left) and a silent figure, an "Auditor" (of undetermined gender, clad in a "loose black djellaba, with hood," and standing stage right), are illuminated. Second, the play consists in an extraordinarily rapid outpouring of words: Beginning unintelligibly behind the curtain and ending, some 16 minutes later, in the same incomprehensible way, Mouth (as Beckett calls this female voice) spews forth at breakneck speed the sad tale of her life. All that accompanies the voice is Auditor's four-time repetition of a single brief movement, a "simple sideways raising of arms from sides and their falling back, in a gesture of helpless compassion."[24] Mouth's own intermittent screams provide the sole interruptions of her speech. Third, for all her logorrhea, Mouth is unable to appropriate the first-person singular pronoun though she speaks only of herself. Holding steadfastly to the third person, she throws into question the experience of self by her incapacity to linguistically objectify it (Figure 3.2).

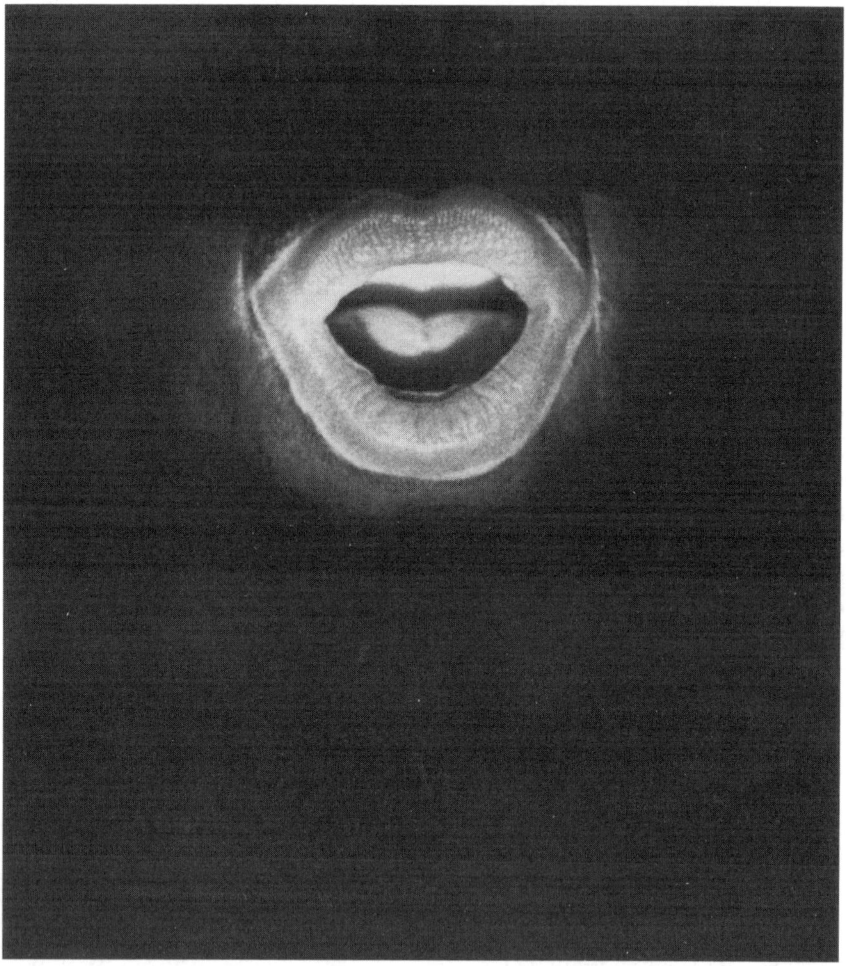

Figure 3.2 *Not I* by Samuel Beckett. Teatro Franco Parenti. Director Anna Nogara, with Anna Nogara (Mouth)

A powerful and exceedingly difficult piece to execute, *Not I* has been succinctly described by actress Billie Whitelaw (whose agonizing performance is legendary) as " 'something akin to verbal vomit' " and "Beckett's inner scream."[25] The central image of very red lips (suggestive of vaginal labia) from which words and more words endlessly gush remains forcefully imprinted in the mind's eye. Indeed, the visual image is more enduring than the words. Yet the play does tell a story. There is the narrative recounting of the traumas of birth:

> . . . . out . . . into this world . . . this world . . . tiny little thing . . . before its time . . . in a godfor- . . . what? . . . girl? . . . yes . . . tiny little girl . . . into this . . . out into this . . . before her time . . . godforsaken hole called . . . called . . . no matter . . .

abandonment:

> parents unknown . . . unheard of . . . he having vanished . . . thin air . . . no sooner buttoned up his breeches . . . she similarly . . . eight months later . . . almost to the tick . . . so no love . . . spared that . . . no love such as normally vented on the . . . speechless infant . . . in the home . . . no . . . nor indeed for that matter any of any kind . . . no love of any kind

and loss:

> . . . wandering in a field . . . looking aimlessly for cowslips . . . to make a ball . . . a few steps then stop . . . stare into space . . . then on . . . a few more . . . stop and stare again . . . so on . . . drifting around . . . when suddenly . . . gradually . . . all went out . . .[26]

And it is the congruence of that fiction with the forceful visual image that renders the preoccupation with psychic boundaries and the vicissitudes of selfhood compelling.

Antonio Damasio suggests that the self originates in the brain's representation of the body (which, as for Freud, means, primarily, the sensations of its surface) and that it depends precisely upon those brain mechanisms that maintain the body in a state of survival. This is to say that the coherence or integration of the self requires a process of constant, moment to moment even, reconstruction. On the most primitive order of organic function, then, it is subject to the vulnerabilities of the body's neurological and chemical systems and their interrelation, to the liabilities of the body's cells and tissues. It is subject, as he puts it, to "the entire biological edifice," a structure that is "held alive by the constant execution of construction plans, always on the brink of partial or complete collapse should the process of rebuilding and renewal break down. The construction plans are all woven around the need to stay away from the brink."[27]

What Damasio is describing is the connection between the sense of self and homeostasis. Psychoanalysts, too, view selfhood as fundamentally dependent upon the extraordinary biological network that, in the developing infant, allows for the representation of one's own bodily constitution as distinguished from that of the parental other. From the earliest creative experience of the individual – the formation and use of the maternal imago – through the various stages of individuation, the self seeks consolidation and coherence. And the quest does not end with the individuating process of early childhood, or even with its reworking in the various identity-seeking phases of adolescence. Rather, it is endemic to all that is imposed on the individual for a lifetime by human biology, genetic disposition, and personality. Throughout life the self remains fundamentally elusive in nature and vulnerable to the disorganization and fragmentation that result from disruption of any of the forces operative within the intricate circuitry of the living organism.

But how do we get from here to the assertion that creativity is impelled by a somatopsychic search for equilibration? (How is the homeostatic urge transferred from its most elementary level of biological function to the higher order of creativity?) And where do we see this in Beckett? Broadly speaking, the answer to the first question lies in the particular form of thinking displayed in any work of the imagination. It was the notion of unconscious mental activity that allowed Freud to fathom the nature of dreaming. Dreams, he reasoned, serve a purpose; they exist to give new form to our unconscious instinctual impulses and disguise their wishful essence. Freud insisted in many of his papers that dreams are merely a form of thinking and he extended this idea to include waking dreams and the fantasies of art. Like the dreamer, the literary or visual artist shapes his wishful thoughts into a representation of fantasy, one that evades the repressive forces of the ego. This liberation from inhibition, from ego censorship, is a source of pleasure to the dreamer/artist precisely to the extent that the fantasy is represented as fulfilled.

Not unlike dreaming, in other words, creating or viewing art involves what Norman Holland (after Coleridge) calls the "willing suspension of disbelief."[28] Knowing that we are attending to an enactment on the stage, for example, and not to reality, we shut down those brain processes that, were we faced with real events, would cause us to act. This is just as in dreaming when only particular regions of the brain are activated and others cease to operate as they do in the wakeful state. More precisely, we know from neuroradiology that it is those parts of the brain engaged in arousal, emotion, memory, and motivation (the frontal and limbic parts) and those involved in abstract thinking and visual perception (whose parts are situated at the back of the brain) are active when we dream. We know as well that the outer, most anterior regions of the frontal lobe (the dorsolateral frontal convexity), known to be exceedingly active in wakeful mentation, are rendered inactive by the dreaming brain. What happens, then, is that dreaming involves a switch from the motor to the perceptual areas; the motor system is blocked though the dreamer, rendered inactive, believes what is perceived is real. What happens with the artwork is much the same: The creator or re-creator is taken in, however briefly, by what is occurring in the work of art, but it is known not to be "real."

Now, over and above the diversion of libidinal energy that Freud identified as the origin of imaginative thinking, whether in the dream or in the fantasy of art, the creative act is stabilizing in emanating from an evolutionary drive to communicate need. Alice Flaherty argues that the desire to write is often homeostatic in the sense that suffering triggers limbic system and temporal lobe activity which triggers communication that can recruit the aid of others to ease the suffering. This accounts for the finding in several studies that writing has measurable positive effects on mood. Like the child who first uses language to create a mental image of mother to soothe him in her absence,[29] the creative writer employs language to bring relief from what Freud termed "unpleasure." If we consider that the continual play with psychic boundaries and the relation of psychic to somatic function in Beckett's work constitutes a proto-fantasy that takes a variety of forms in his prose, dramas, and poetry, we see that the pleasure–unpleasure principle defined by Freud is enacted by Beckett over and over. In any work of art, the gratification of wish and the avoidance of pain are accomplished by an imposition of form that provides access to the unconscious. In Beckett we see the degree to which creative drive may function in the distinctly therapeutic service of stabilizing the writer's own somatic and psychic function.

In fact, Beckett's texts have much in common with psychoanalytic therapy and this is where we come to the answer to the second question. As I have demonstrated in greater detail elsewhere,[30] free association is everywhere in Beckett's narrative and theatrical monologues where the interplay of words and silence recalls the therapeutic environment. In the radio play *Cascando* (1963) automatism is the modus operandi of one who recounts the descent of "gentle slopes" of mind to uncover "what's in his head"; "I associate" are the less than subtle opening words of the short prose work "First Love" (1970); and the disembodied voice of *Not I* associates endlessly as the Auditor's almost imperceptible efforts to make sense of it all are stifled by the verbal onslaught. Beckett's dramatization of the analytic session is replete with resistance: "All that goes before forget. Too much at a time is too much" ("Enough" [1963]); with recurring sysmptoms: "[His] old terror of night laid hold on him again" (*Ohio Impromptu*, 1981); and compliance: "Myself I cannot save. He sat down on the couch, still tossed from the last patient. After a while he lay down on it" ("A Case in a Thousand" [1943]). And by its very structure, the logorrheic narration recalls the therapeutic alliance of the patient who speaks and is sometimes silent and the analyst who is silent and sometimes speaks.[31]

But to return to *Not I*, Mouth's characterization is dramatic precisely because it reflects the playwright's painstaking effort to write an integrated self into existence. What Beckett so forcefully and eloquently articulates (both visually and verbally) in this play is what might be called a "somatopsychic anesthesia," an extraordinary device not unlike the deconstruction of narrative coherence that occurs in each of his dramas and fictions. Critic Porter Abbott refers to the unwriting of narrative emblematic of Beckett's texts a "narratricide," a means of disjoining each episode from what came before. And he goes so far as to equate it with the theme of the "horror of fatherhood" so evident in Beckett's work. "Children, babies," the narrator of the 1958 short story "The Expelled" tells us, "I personally would lynch them with the utmost pleasure"; Molloy forgets if he ever had a son; and in *Endgame*, Hamm not only "bottles" his "accursed progenitor" but, as Abbott puts it, "orders the death of a flea for fear that humanity might start from there all over again." Abbott's argument is that this narrative theme is linked to the killing of narrative and that "unwriting the father" is precisely what allows the son to be.[32] (Not surprisingly, Beckett himself chose not to have children.) But what is the connection to what I call the "somatopsychic anesthesia" of *Not I*? While it is through Mouth's disembodiment and through her incapacity to articulate the first-person pronoun that Beckett projects the feeling of identity dissolution, it is also through them that he arrives at the unity of psyche and soma, the unified sense of self that defines his creative need.

In her monologue Mouth takes us through the experience of losing her sense of a bodily self. Noting that nothing worthy of mention occurred in her first seven decades of life (beyond a premature birth into a loveless, parentless world), she relates the story of that April morning when "suddenly . . . gradually . . . all went out. . . ." Beside a buzzing in the ears and an intermittently perceptible ray of light, all that remained was a dullness of feeling. At the same time, though, there is the potential for the recurrence of feeling in the body Mouth refers to as a machine. Long after the event in question feeling is thought to return ("starting at the top . . . then working down"), but it is rapidly recognized as just that: a *thought of feeling* (however "awful"), *a feeling existing in the mind/brain*. Persistent allusions to the physical organ of consciousness, to a brain said to "[flicker] away on its own," serve to make the point. First there is protest – ". . . but the brain. . ." – and then a plea – "the whole brain begging . . . something begging in the brain. . . ." But the whole body is dulled and "like gone."

A number of psychoanalytic concepts may be useful in interpreting Mouth's disembodiment or loss of her bodily self-image. We might speak of regression and, specifically, of the reversion to the most primitive phase of ego-feeling that Freud termed "oceanic". That earliest mode of mentalization when the "me" is not yet differentiated from the "not me" would certainly provide a valid interpretive context in which to regard Mouth's desensitation or feelinglessness. Indeed, the loss of bodily boundaries in severe regression is linked to the orality of the infant who does not differentiate its body from the breast. I need not stress the appropriateness of this to a play about a mouth.

Alternatively, there is the radical decathexis or affective blankness that the French psychoanalyst André Green calls the "zero state." The bizarre split from her body that Mouth describes is certainly evidence of the kind of depersonalization of which Green has prolifically written. The loss of feeling, in this sense, renders the body machine-like (and Mouth herself describes it as such) in a defense against its sexuality. Psychoanalyst Roy Schafer has noted the etiology of the expression "to lose face," the connections between shame and de-facing, between that and effacing, and an argument could certainly be made for Mouth's renunciation of self with regard to the affects of shame and of guilt as well.[33] For the lack of suffering and, indeed, the desire experienced by Mouth on that April morning elicits the "notion of punishment . . . for some sin or other . . . or for the lot." Ego fragmentation or collapse, finally, has long served critics of Beckett's work (myself included) in their efforts to come to terms with the insentience of his narrative theatrical "voices."

Clinical cases exemplifying severe boundary loss bear an uncanny resemblance, in fact, to Beckett's portrayal of Mouth. In a 1949 letter addressed by Winnicott to a colleague, for instance, the psychoanalyst writes of an extraordinarily difficult female analytic patient described as without access to the shared reality of the external world. What is startling in Winnicott's letter is the way in she is not only chacterized as dwelling entirely in her head, but living in a place unrelated to her body as an entity perceptible to herself or to others. She is, in short, divested of any corporeal existence.[34] Other cases illustrative of the diffusion of selfhood that characterizes Mouth – and, indeed, of all Beckett's "voices" – are easily found in a review of the literature on borderline personality disorder. In short, a variety of manifestations of the deficits in identification and internalization, deficits that may be experienced on the level of the self as agent or the self as object (to borrow Roy Schafer's useful distinction between kinds of subjective apperception), are reminiscent of the very kind of pathology so forcefully displayed by Mouth.

But clinical cases similar to Beckett's imaginative fantasy of disembodiment and the dissolution of self are not of interest merely for their comparability. They are worthy of our consideration for what the somatic origins of the psychic dysfunction may lend our interpretation of the play. And, more relevant to our present purposes, they are of interest for what they tell us of the creative need satisfied by Beckett's preoccupation with mental illness in his work. To make the point I will briefly look at how *Not I* may be viewed in terms of two clinical syndromes, one where patients present with the somatization of psychic disturbance and one where real somatic dysfunction is endowed with psychic pathology, though the body may be said to be the origin of each.[35]

The first is hysteria. Much has been written of Mouth's disembodiment, but only in the broad thematic context of the bodily disintegration significant in all Beckett's work. To my knowledge it has yet to be regarded in the more narrowly focussed symbolic context suggested verbally and visually by the play itself, namely, conversion hysteria, one of the two kinds of hysterical neurosis distinguished by Freud at the start of his career. Initially, Freud viewed hysteria as the result of an event that produces unacceptable feelings in an individual. When attempts to repress these feelings fail, they are symbolically represented in the form of a conversion symtom. More precisely, Freud qualified hysteria as an illness of representation, a term not to be understood as re-presentation, but in the sense of the body's having an emissary or representative in the mind.[36] His idea was that early trauma may produce an unbearable image, understood as a psychic trace, one that is overburdened with affect against which the ego must defend itself by means of a repressive force. The result is a conflict between an excessively charged representation needing to rid itself of its surplus energy and a repression that prevents it from doing so.[37] What may ensue is the conversion of that energy into the overinvestment of a bodily region, the discharge of sexual excitation through bodily zones or processes not normally sexualized. The symptomatology of hysteria, however, also includes the conversion of conflict into dissociation, the loss of awareness and control on the part of the ego of certain basic functions. In Beckett's extraordinary visual image both forms of defense are evident: On the one hand, there is the conflation of the orifices of speech and female genitalia that in itself recalls the etiology of the word "hysteria" (however prejudicial that may be). And, on the other, there is the sensory impairment, the hysterical anesthesia, that Beckett totalizes in the complete dismemberment of Mouth. Indeed, confronted for some 16 minutes by the sole image of a red mouth isolated in blackness, the audience visually perceives as corporeal numbness the profound dissociative emptiness to which Mouth's monologue attests.

That there is an association to be made between *Not I* and hysteria is defensible not only visually but textually, for Mouth's monologue centers around the very events of that April morning from which the hysterical anesthesia, Mouth's bodiless image, may be said to derive. Events that remain unarticulated throughout the monologue, they are nonetheless narratively implicated as the source of the conflict and the repressive defense. Furthermore, with respect to its form, the play simultaneously projects an extreme tension – the *physical* strain of uttering comprehensible sounds at such great speed – and a discharge of that tension – the *psychic* release the verbalization affords – evocative of the kind of conflation of psyche and soma that occurs in the conversion process. That is to say that Mouth's monologue conforms to the "anomaly of the nervous system," the "different distribution of excitations, probably accompanied by a surplus of stimuli in the organ of the mind," by which Freud defined the disorder. Both in the form of her monologue, the spewing forth of words interrupted only by her own agonizing screams and periodic pauses, and in its content, with its memories of trauma, flashes of thought, and insistence on the insurmountable brain, Mouth puts in high relief precisely what Freud described as "*changes in the normal distribution over the nervous system of the stable amounts of excitation.*"[38]

We know, however, that Freud ultimately modified his thinking on the pathogenesis of hysteria by saying that hysterical symptoms emanate from unconscious fantasy, not from the psychic trace of an actual traumatic occurrence. Abandoning the idea of childhood seduction as the morbid source of the disturbance, he demonstrated how desire itself (specifically, incestuous Oedipal wishes) may stimulate anxiety sufficently intense to result in a symbolic transformation designed to defend against the pleasure that threatens. Reading Beckett's play along the lines of hysteria is by no means contradicted by this modification in theory for, as is his way, the playwright equivocates: We are faced simultaneously with the account of a trauma (presumably a rape) and with the scenario of a fiction within a fiction, an uncertain story (presumably a wishful fantasy) that appears to serve the distinctly protective purpose of defending her against the danger of limitless pleasure. This is apparent in the inconsistency of her anguish, the repeated references to the realization that "she was not suffering . . . imagine! . . . not suffering! . . . indeed could not remember . . . off-hand . . . when she had suffered less. . . ." The disclosure that it was "just all part of the same wish" is equally telling.[39]

Turning to the second symptom complex, *Not I* may similarly be viewed as a fictional case of asomatognosia, as a metaphorical depiction not of hysterical anesthesia, but of the neurological condition in which there is a partial or total lack of body recognition. Whereas hysteria involves the body in a process of psychic conversion, asomatognosia engages the body in a process of psychic rejection.

A related disturbance, anosognosia – the incapacity to recognize a physical impairment or illness in one's body – is even more revealing of the psychic component. The currently accepted model of this form of bodily rejection is a deficit-based disturbance, a neurological disorder reflecting a deficiency of the brain in its capacity for body imaging. Recent research, however, supports a competing model in which there is an implicit awareness of the body or bodily region whose explicit recognition has been rejected. This dynamic explanation of anosognosia is that it is a motivated defense, that there is an affective benefit to be had from the refusal to acknowledge the body's disability. Rather than viewing the absence of body recognition in terms of, say, a real loss of so-called "negative emotions" (a physical inability to experience the anger or sadness that would normally result from the awareness of impaired bodily function), some (V. S. Ramachandran, Mark Solms, and Oliver Turnbull among them) emphasize the notion, and there has been convincing evidence of it, that the patient is psychologically defending against the affective consequences of the recognition in question.[40]

But to return to the more generalized form of impaired body awareness,

Damasio has described an asomatognosic patient who, as a result of seizures produced by vascular lesions caused by a stroke, had no awareness of her body, though she knew she was thinking. In other words, she didn't lose her sense of being; she continued to have a sense of her core consciousness, as visceral and vestibular signaling was not interrupted despite the loss of any integrated representation of the musculoskeletal structure of her body. While the cause of her condition was clearly neurological, the transient inactivation of a significant part of the somatosensory cortical complex within the right hemisphere, what was compromised was her mind.

Despite hysterical anesthesia's distinctly psychodynamic objective (the function it serves is clearly defensive), asomatognosia has in common with it the impairment of what Damasio refers to as the extended consciousness. A biological phenomenon, the extended consciousness is the highest level of self-integration which, evolving over time, depends on memory and is enhanced by language. It is unlike the core consciousness – also biologically rooted, but stable throughout the life of the organism and independent of memory and language – in that it does not remain intact in somatopsychic disturbances like hysteria, asomatognosia, and anosognosia. But what does this tell us of Mouth?

First, it tells us that Beckett's fictive characterization is remarkable for its biological accuracy. Mouth retains her awarenesss of herself as a thinking core consciousness: The "whole brain begging," the brain's "begging the mouth to stop," and, more important, its effort to piece together and make sense of the "stream of words" she utters are surprisingly analogous to the implicit self-awareness observed by clinicians. The likeness between Mouth's inability to translate the self into an appropriate pronoun and the linguistic impairment of certain patients with neurological damage is also impressive. Damasio recounts the story of one, for example, a stroke victim whose severe aphasia, though significantly improved over time, left her able to correctly make use of a number of different words though she was unable "to find consistently the correct pronoun to denote herself."[41] That is, her thought processes remained rich and sophisticated and her core self, a nonverbal phenomenon, was unaltered; as is all too often the case, however, that awareness simply could not extend to a translation of her self into "I."

Second, it tells us that Beckett's fiction is just as remarkable for its psychological accuracy. As in the clinical syndromes described above, what is especially poignant is the psychodynamic significance of Mouth's failed representation of her autonomy. Affectively speaking, were she to experience the fulfillment of her desire, she would further imperil an already fragile sense of self; she would further jeopardize her exceedingly frail me/not me boundaries. Hence the hysterical anesthesia, the suspension of sensory reflexes, she so clearly describes: ". . . no part of her moving . . . that she could feel . . . just the eyelids . . . presumably . . . on and off . . . shut out the light . . . reflex they call it . . . no feeling of any kind." At the same time, though, were Mouth to accept ownership of her (abused?) body, were she able to process the word "I," she would endanger a self whose only remaining integrity lies in its objectivation in the third-person pronoun. Hence the asomatognosic-like rejection, the denial of her body as her own: ". . . what? . . . who? . . no! . . she! . . ." If Beckett's fictive depiction of Mouth is comparable to such patients, it is that, in ways similar to theirs, she has withdrawn her sense of relatedness to her extended sense of self.

Beckett grappled in his work with the mind–body problem cognitively and emotionally. We see this not only in the narrative content, but in the way he used language. This is to say that the syntactic and syntagmatic shaping of language referred to earlier may also be said to reflect the preoccupation with identity, with psychic boundaries, and with self and object representation in which the psycho-biologically accurate narrative content originates. It was not for nothing, for instance, that Beckett wrote an auditory perceiver into so many of his plays: Krapp in *Krapp's Last Tape*, Willie in *Happy Days*, the spotlight in *Play*, Joe in *Eh Joe*, Auditor in *Not I*, Listener in *That Time* and *Ohio Impromptu*, May in *Footfalls*, F in *Ghost Trio*, M in *. . . but the clouds . . .*, the Dreamer in *Nacht und Träume*.[42] But he also posited the immediacy of perception in his characters' use of words. Consider, for example, that, like his other fictive voices for whom speaking is equated with being, Mouth never articulates what she feels. She has registered the events of her life as if they lacked any emotional significance, though the projection of her monologue belies her impassivity before the events she describes. How are we to view the compulsive gushing of words devoid of any reflection on what or how Mouth feels?

In one sense, her inability to verbalize emotion is very much in keeping with the overall constrictive or withholding nature of Beckett's writing. Much has been said of his effort to reduce textuality to a minimum. It accounts for the absence of names (characters are often identified by an initial or simply by their gender: Woman in *Rockaby*; W1, W2, and M in *Play*; and so on); the stripping of action to inaction (nothing "happens" in *Waiting for Godot*); the diminished length of his productions (the 1969 play *Breath* is performed in a matter of seconds); and the total absence of words in many of his writings (*Film*, for instance, or the 1956 mimes *Act Without Words I* and *II*, and the 1982 television play *Quad*). But this aesthetic of constraint – often seen as a sign of anality, an all too facile point of departure for conflating artistry and artist – is more than willful reduction; it is the sign of a recurring tension between representation and abstraction.[43]

What happens when the images of a text are emptied of what Sidney Feshbach calls "the structure of feelings based on actual experience"? We are left with a kind of conceptual art in which what the reader or viewer apprehends is raw perception.[44] None of Beckett's characters is capable of differentiating between feelings perceived. None is able to distinguish between real emotion and sensations produced in the body as a result of emotional arousal. For the most part, they are merely preoccupied with the concrete minutiae of the external environment – and with being.[45] I would even submit that many meet the criteria for yet another disorder of the interrelation of psyche and soma, alexithymia, a condition in which individuals cannot fully experience and communicate emotions. Why? When we consider that Beckett uses language to display perceptuality, that the primary unifying force of his literary and dramatic oeuvre is a metaphoric transcription of subjectivity, we see that his alexithymic-like characters ultimately advance, aesthetically, the very same project of self-consolidation: In focussing on what, from the time of Brentano and Husserl, has been called the intentionality of mind, he reveals not the object of perception, such as an emotion, but the perceptualizing process itself. And this, after all, renders him the ultimate perceiver, the autonomous subjectivity holding the various selves together.

In an oft-cited letter of 1937 to an acquaintance, Axel Kaun, Beckett asked:

> Is there any reason why that terrible materiality of the word surface should not be capable of being dissolved, like for example the sound surface, torn by enormous pauses, of Beethoven's seventh Symphony, so that through whole pages we can perceive nothing but a path of sounds suspended in giddy heights, linking unfathomable abysses of silence?

What he envisioned was an "unwording" of literature to be achieved through silence, absence, lacunae of whatever kind:

> To bore one hole after another in [language], until what lurks behind it – be it something or nothing – begins to seep through; I cannot imagine a higher goal for a writer today.[46]

Beckett is calling to our attention the essence of consciousness where internal and external indices are not synthesized or are nonexistent, where timelessness is substituted for any objective sense of past, present, and future, which is precisely how Freud described primary process ideation.[47] In his every text, Beckett struggled to move closer to attaining this ideal.

In *Not I* three forms of elision serve this aesthetic goal. The first, of course, is the unarticulated pronoun itself. Not despite, but on account of its unuttered status, what is so vehemently renounced by Mouth is rendered in virtual high relief. To put it otherwise, Mouth's refusal to speak the word that would say her is ironically what reveals her awareness of her core self. Second, Mouth's disassociation from her physical self similarly confers on the body the value of a virtual image, one as metaphorically significant as the unarticulated self. Not only is the disembodiment "seen" on the stage, but it "appears" in the monologue where words like "disconnected," "numbed," and so on are used to convey her detachment from the corporeal entity she calls "the machine." Again, the mental representation of self is made all the more dynamic by virtue of absence.[48] A third form of elision similarly depicts the tension between representation and abstraction: the persistent use of ellipsis throughout this and several of Beckett's other texts. Ellipsis has so powerful an impact on the narrative construction that it appeals to what Porter Abbott calls the "schematizing imagination" of Beckett's voices who, like Mouth, do little more than tell tales to fill the "egregious gaps."[49] What the sudden breaking off of words in *Not I*, like the other forms of elision, metaphorically reveals is the mind *in extensa*, intentionally projected toward the object of perception. What Beckett seeks in the "unwording" of literature, then, in all the "egregious gaps," is to divest language of its surface materiality in order for its perceptual charge to ring through. For, once again, in depicting consciousness at a distance from the self, in depicting a speaking subject unable to circumscribe its boundaries and utter, as an agent of self, "I feel this or that," he locates his own unified selfhood within his role as creator.

Remarkably, then, the linguistic form of Beckett's work, the expressive strategy that projects the tension between representation and abstraction, may be said to emanate from the same problematic from which the narrative arises. It is also to be found on the level of the playwright's vision of performance. When Billie Whitelaw played the role of Mouth in London, Beckett insisted not only that she not project, but that, in a sense, she not even act. Whitelaw has described the *non-acting* required of her as agonizing: Beckett "didn't want anything *presented*," she wrote in her autobiography. "He wanted to get to some unconscious centre"[50] and his means of doing so was to remove the body, as much as possible, from the stage. Dressed in black, seated in a similarly camouflaged chair, with only a single ray of light restricted to her mouth, Whitelaw was required to articulate at great speed under conditions that felt like "a form of torture" and left her feeling totally disoriented:

> Usually, when you are acting a part, you are given some physical movement to use the accumulated energy. Here there was nowhere for the energy to go. [. . .]
>
> What now happened in performances was that my head started to shake; all the energy was going into the back of my head and neck. When I was building up speed, that was the only place the tension could go. As my head started to shake violently. my mouth was juddering in and out of Jack Raby's very precise lighting, so I was given two big lamps placed at either side of my head, while I was strapped to the chair. In effect, my head was now held in a vice, clamped at either side of my temples.[51]

If Beckett wanted Whitelaw to act, as he often said, "without color," it was that his plays, like his prose texts, are not meant to tell stories. Rather, words are clearly in the service of the visual image, sound in the service of the eye. If

Endgame was preferred by Beckett to *Godot* – "I suppose," he is reported to have said in 1978, "the one I dislike least is Endgame" – it was precisely because it was "better visualised."[52] In both plays, though, the image outweighs the word: The two tramps of *Godot* and the heads peering from within trash cans in *Endgame* have a force more enduring than the scripted text. A remark made by the playwright about *Footfalls* – "the walking up and down is the central image . . . the text, the words, are only built up around this picture"[53] – has relevance for all his work. (The title of the 1981 short prose work, *Ill Seen Ill Said*, succintly makes the point.) Beckett's texts are thus, to borrow a term from the late BBC producer Martin Esslin, "concretized metaphors." As Esslin says, "they are not about an experience, they *are* the experience"[54]; they are rich metaphorical images that resonate with others that are the perceiver's own.

Arnold Modell is right to call metaphor a "currency of mind," to consider it a cognitive tool as opposed to a mere rhetorical device. "As a mode of cognition," he writes, "metaphor is doubly embodied, first, as an unconscious neural process and, second, in that metaphors are generated from bodily feelings, so that it is possible to speak of a corporeal imagination."[55] It is this concept of a "corporeal imagination" that enables us, obliges us even, to consider Beckett's narrative focus on psychic boundaries and his use of language itself as a metaphor for the intentionality of mind in the context of somatopsychic regulation. Indeed, invoking the paradigm of dynamic change as a criterion of creativity should not evoke a reductive reflection on symptomatology (be it depressive, anal, or any other) as identifiable with Beckett's art. Rather, it should stimulate thinking on the neural underpinnings of the creative mind/brain itself. Beckett's novels and plays are alike in consisting in monologues of multiple voices: In *That Time* (1976), Beckett stipulates that speakers A, B, and C are "moments of one and the same voice." In the trilogy, as previously mentioned, voices morph from one to another. In *Not I* Mouth hears another's voice in her head. In focussing on the boundaries between the me and the not me – Is it I who is speaking or someone else? Is it I whom I visualize or the parental imago I resemble? – Beckett dramatizes what Esslin calls "dialogues between parts of the self," fantasies in which "the self debates with the self."[56] So consistent a preoccupation makes one wonder about the writer's own inner representational world, about the contribution of his psychic development to this deep fascination with the mind. But it also provokes curiosity about the universal self-signaling and nonself-signaling areas of the brain upon which it depends. And it elicits reflection on how these may be altered as the creator, and even the re-creator, engages in the creative act.

Beckett told Jessica Tandy, who played Mouth in New York in 1972, that he hoped the play would work not on the intellect of the audience, but on its nerves.[57] To Whitelaw it seemed that "Mouth was not going *out* to an audience," that "the audience had to be sucked into this rioting, rambling hole."[58] Beckett had his way and Whitelaw wasn't far from the truth: Through the schemas we have formed from our own prior experience neural networks combine to constitute our aesthetic response. And through our psychological needs and resultant fantasies, our cognitive strategies and expectancies, the viewer/reader gives meaning to the visual image and verbal text.

The idea that our perceptions are necessarily mediated by the schemata of prior experience was introduced in philosophy by Immanuel Kant who held that the mind actively organizes experience into patterns. It was ultimately developed in neuroscience, however, by Henry Head and G. M. Holmes and later in psychology by Jean Piaget.[59] Briefly, Piaget's idea of intellectual development was that structural units, or schemata, make up a skeletal cognitive system whose form is continually modified by sensory input. The assimilation of such input allows the system to alter itself in a process of accommodation. The impetus for Piaget's theory, and the principle that remained embedded within his thinking, was equilibration, the perpetual seeking by the schematic structures to counteractively balance the imperfections or inconsistencies revealed as the system assimilates and accommodates to the stimuli in question.

Piaget's contribution to schema theory, then, stressed the processes by which the individual, precisely through cognitive strategies and psychological expectancies, actively shapes his experiential world. Psychologist and psychoanalyst Paul Wachtel summarizes the Piagetian position as follows: "Neither as children nor as adults do we respond directly to stimuli per se. We are always constructing reality every bit as much as we are perceiving it." Both neuroscience and psychoanalysis are rooted in the belief that, as Wachtel puts it, "man is not stimulus-bound, that he does not just reflexively respond to external stimuli, but rather selectively organizes and makes sense of new input in terms of the experiences and structures which define who he is."

In a paper on transference Wachtel has illustrated how Piaget's perspective on schema theory functions in the psychoanalytic setting where the patient's perception of the analyst is determined by his or her needs and fantasies.[60] Similarly, Janet Baird, describing the usefulness of schema theory for constructing a unified theory of mind, has argued that the concept of schema, originally conceived as a cognitive structure, may easily be transposed into psychological constructs. She offers convincing evidence of this by illustrating how any number of psychoanalytic concepts – from conscious and unconscious fantasies and screen memories to compromise formations and self and object representations – can be reframed in accordance with this theory. I will not reproduce her reasoning here, but simply observe that she succeeds in moving schema beyond the formalism of cognitive neuroscience to the psychodynamic (conflict/compromise) model of the mind. And, in so doing, she reveals the plasticity of connections within the neural networks of the brain as schemata negotiate on a functional level the cognitive and affective responses to perceptual input of whatever kind.

In arguing that emotion and feeling are expressions of biological regulation,

Antonio Damasio takes our understanding of response to perceptual stimuli to yet another level. He hypothesizes the existence of "somatic markers," instances of a particular kind of feeling, a visceral or nonvisceral sensation in the body, that is also a positive or negative image. An incentive or a deterrent of a given choice of action, the "somatic marker" originates in the innate regulatory predispositions of the brain and is developed over the course of socialization to result in an individual's making automatic connections between "specific classes of stimuli" and "specific classes of somatic state."[61] "Somatic markers," which are aimed at reducing unpleasant states and strive for equilibration or homeostasis, account for the assimilation of perceptual stimuli to representations of the past. Like Piaget's schemata, then, they are an effective conceptual tool for framing the creative functioning of the mind.

In view of the broadened notion of schema theory and the biological underpinnings described by Damasio, it may be said that art implicates the mind/brain of the reader/spectator as the co-creator of the work at hand. Insofar as components of our neural networks combine in the constitution of schemata to compete in the constitution of aesthetic response, the mind of the reader/spectator assimilates and accommodates the perceptual input of the brain to give meaning to art. As Steven Pinker has recently noted: "Oil paint, moving limbs, and printed words cannot penetrate the brain directly. They trigger a cascade of neural events that begin with the sense organs and culminate in thoughts, emotions, and memories."[62] Wachtel concurs: "Rather than dichotomizing between perceptions that are accurate and those that are 'distorted,'" he writes, "the schema notion helps us to see that all perception is a selective construction"; it is, in short, an act of creation.[63]

Reminiscent of the *Rezeptionsästhetik* of Hans-Robert Jauss, Wolfgang Iser, and others, wherein it was the reader who was said to be the maker of textual meaning, schema theory appears to offer a solid basis for rethinking the viewing of dramatic or plastic art. I would illustrate the point by returning to the predominant me/not me struggle of *Not I* to which spectators respond with the reanimation of their own self-schematic states. As in the analytic situation, where a given schema is called into play because something corresponding to stimuli that previously nourished that schema is activated, the spectator projects schematic fantasies onto the work that will, in large part, constitute its meaning.[64] When there is a fundamental withdrawal of self-relatedness, as in this play, the projections and subsequent generation of meaning through the arousal of self-schemata is particularly compelling.

Modell posits "two characteristic pathologies of the self that can disrupt its homeostasis: splitting and decentering."[65] Both are pervasive throughout Beckett's work. While it goes without saying that the generation of meaning is infinitely variable, I would suggest that the somatopsychically determined impulse to reinforce self-centering would engender the however disparate associations to and ultimate valuations of the play. The inseparability of meaning from biology is itself supported by the idea that the sense of self, its affective and somatic centering, is what allows experience, aesthetic or other, to assume meaning. When the experience in question focusses on decentering, on the discontinuity of self even, as it does in Beckett's work, what will be activated, in a sense defensively, are templates of self-centering schemata that the homeostatic brain holds in reserve. As Modell explains:

> The continuity of the self is preserved by means of the self's linkage with the homeostatic brain systems. [. . .] Perceptions occurring in real time are recategorized through a "matching" with the value-laden memories of former states. A sense of the continuity of the self amid the flux of perception is assured, because the self acts as a dominant template imposing order and coherence on current perception.[66]

That such templates, or pre-existing object-schema, are activated in exposure to novel perceptual experiences (whether actual or in fantasy) has also been suggested by Baird who claims that their mobilization provides for the "interaction with the new object and/or the formation of a schema specific for that object."[67] Historian Lynn Hunt elegantly demonstrates the point: In a recent paper she goes so far as to claim that the credibility of human rights developed from the new sense of self afforded by the reading of novels in the eighteenth century: "[R]eading epistolary novels," she tells us, "ha[d] somatic effects that translate[d] into brain changes and [came] back out as new concepts about the organization of social and political life." What she is suggesting is "that reading novels create[d] new individual experiences (empathy) which in turn [made] possible new social and political concepts (human rights)." More explicitly, she says:

> Individual men and women read epistolary novels and through their identification [. . .] they learned to empathize with ordinary people they did not know personally. This learning process was activated by the bodily sensations they got through reading; they learned that society was constructed through social roles; that individual identity was not entirely determined by social roles [. . .]; that selfhood depended on qualities of interiority; that all selves had interiority, and consequently that all selves were in some sense equal because alike in their possession of interiority.[68]

Consideration of the kinds of fantasies elicited and of the aesthetic conditions that allow for the activation of various schemata, then, summons the interrelation of neuroscience and psychoanalysis to the interpretive arena. Insofar as the somatosensory cortex, limbic system, and cortical regions form the basis of a neural network fundamental to body awareness, to one's corporeal representation,[69] the thematic and imagistic projection by Beckett of unstable me/not me boundaries acts on the somatopsychic stability of both creator and re-creator. I would therefore amend Gilbert Rose's observation that art is "a working model of how the brain works"[70] to include dynamic homeostasis.

It is true that tension mounts in *Not I* as Mouth accelerates her refusal to employ the first-person pronoun. It intensifies within the philosophical conundrum the play poses; namely, are the self apprehended as subject and the self apprehended as object two sides of the same perceptual coin (as psychologist William James maintained) or is there some degree of autonomy to each? Tension builds further from the peculiarity of the character's disembodiment. It is also true that, at the same time, there is discharge in both Mouth's intermittent screams and the defensive anesthetization of feeling metaphorically expressed in her existence as a non-corporeal entity. From the interplay of tension and release – most conspicuous in the conflation of the orifice of speech with the image of genitalia that is at once taboo (on the level of secondary-process thought) and titillating (on the level of primary-process mentation) – there is a deepening of bodily and psychic integration.[71] But there is an even more salient interpretation of the preoccupation with ego weakness and psychic boundaries underlying all Beckett's work.

The very pronunciation of words had an existential significance for this writer: As long as there was language, as long as there was a voice to go on saying, there was being. Thus each of his narrative and theatrical depictions is demonstrative of the inherently dramatic human condition, a condition defined by the capacity for adaptation. Mouth's dissociative functioning, like that of all Beckett's characterizations, reveals a kind of perverse adaptational competence. If she spews forth words at a speed rendering them almost incomprehensible, it is precisely to compensate for an excessive libidinality with an excessively antilibidinal renunciation of self. Only in hysterical intensity, in other words, can she find a measure of stability. There is, however, also this: In a letter dated October 16, 1972, to his American director Alan Schneider, Beckett explained that Mouth screams "in illustration of what she might have done if able," had she not been "numbed" in the experience she relates in her tale.[72] From the actuality of this scream an equilibrium emerges – in the character and in the spectator. I believe that what impelled Beckett's writing – and, specifically, the compulsive rendering of disintegrated self-states – was of a similarly equilibrating (and thereby therapeutic and adaptive) nature. In a sense, the creative act served him as abreaction serves the analytic patient. Beckett was well aware of the immediacy of art's impact: He said so when he wrote, or words to this effect, "The text as is, the words as is, that's all I know. The rest is Ibsen."[73]

Chapter 4

Paul Klee's late style

In 1903 Paul Klee, aged 23, created a small (5 × 9.6 inches) etching entitled *Two Men Meet, Each Presuming the Other to be of Higher Rank*. Like much of his early work, it combines satire with an uncommon sense of the grotesque and displays the artist's superior analytical skills. Anecdotally, the work is rich: With two caricature-like human forms, one bowing deeply before the other, it makes a humorous statement about the hypocrisy of the human species. Fine lines playfully delineate the contours of the elongated bodies and their surroundings in nature while bristly hair and similarly depicted bristly grass, each interspersed with patches of smoothness, unify the composition. Fast-forwarding some three and a half decades, we come to a 1939 drawing in colored crayon entitled *A Super Sycophant*. Remarkably unlike the etching (which preceded by three years the first exhibit of some of Klee's earliest work), this late tableau nonetheless confers a distinct symmetry on the artist's career: The positioning of the single human form on the paper reflects that of the two bodies seen in the etching. The horizontal flow of energy is comparable in that the lone body, which appears to be walking, is bent forward from the waist at an angle of 90 degrees to resemble the bowed torsos of the early work. And there is the notably primitive quality in the drawing that one associates not only with the etching, but with much of Klee's work of the intervening years. It is the differences, however, that are most interesting and they are obvious: The somewhat larger 1939 drawing contains none of the detail of the 1903 etching. In fact, it is exceedingly simple both in conception and execution. A few geometric shapes make up the entire picture rendering it one of the artist's most minimalist drawings. Broad strokes replace the early fine lines, the use of a single color (orange) projects a now exaggerated uniformity, and the composition assumes a new and powerful force, a surety of expression characteristic of the art made by Klee near the end of his life.

That Klee's late work reveals profound changes, as this brief comparison is meant to show, is indisputable. A number of Klee's interpreters have sought the origin of the bolder, more abstract forms characteristic of the late work in the psychological impact of the illness, scleroderma (systemic sclerosis), that lay waste to Klee in the last five years of his life. Very few attribute the stylistic changes to the crippling effects or other physical symptoms of the disease. And some, curiously, do not make any allusion to the illness at all. Even Klee's biographers make little or nothing of the debilitation which, except at the beginning, not only did not diminish the artist's productivity, but may even have produced the opposite result. Indeed, the artist's own catalogue of his work reveals an extraordinary productivity in this period. Other than in 1935, when he produced only 148 works (down from 219 in the preceding year), and in 1936, when his output slowed to a mere 25, Klee was remarkably prolific: In the final two and a half years of his life, over 2000 works are recorded. Are we to conclude from this superabundance of creative energy and the enormity of his output at this time that the disease itself had little effect on Klee's art?

Serge Sabarsky, in the catalogue of the 1977 exhibition at his New York gallery devoted to Klee's late work, refers to the markedly simpler style of *A Super Sycophant* only as a shorthand demonstrative of the artist's maturity. So, too, Will Grohmann, long a respected interpreter (and close friend) of the painter, wrote of the paintings and drawings of this period with little regard for the ravaging effects of Klee's symptoms. The degenerative illness which would prove fatal to Klee in 1940 (he died of heart failure resulting from it) is not even indexed in Grohmann's most comprehensive study of the man and his work. Even Jürgen Glaesemer, the late Curator of the Paul Klee Foundation, cautioned that one could only speculate about the effects of the artist's physical symptoms and in his own writings focussed, rather, on the psychological effects of Klee's awareness of impending death.[1]

Similarly, Marcel Franciscono, among the most astute of Klee's contemporary interpreters, refuses to attribute the style of the late work, the "rough angularity" and the "flat patterning" of the late drawings, to the physical disabilities with which Klee was inflicted. Though Franciscono considers it probable that the mood of Klee's late work, its meaning and expression, reflects the psychological impact of his illness, and that Klee's great productivity in this period reflects an urgent sense of time, he does not attribute the marked evolution in style to the disease itself. He disqualifies the idea that any degree of digital constriction (scleroderma is rheumatological) determined the simplicity of the final paintings and drawings. "It is true," he argues, "that the handwriting of some of Klee's last inscriptions and in the final pages of his oeuvre catalogue is noticeably coarser and spikier, roughly paralleling the increased angularity of the final drawings." But this is not due to the illness, he claims, for "not even the very late handwriting is consistently coarse. Any number of inscriptions from late 1939 and 1940 show the fine, small characters we are used to seeing in Klee's earlier pictures, demonstrating, if demonstration were needed, an ample delicacy of control."[2]

While maintaining his position with regard to the psychological significance of the illness for Klee's late work, Franciscono notes a radical revision in recent critical assessments of the art of the painter's last years. It is now often said, he observes, that the late work results from an effort to meet market demands with a renewed style; that it is a response to the political atmosphere of Europe in the 1930s; or that it represents an overtly expressive or humanistic reaction to the modernist separation of art from life. Though Franciscono does not refute the validity of such claims, he chooses to emphasize, in addition to the artist's preoccupation with death, the affinities of Klee's late work with the art of its time, that of Matisse, Léger, Miró, Picasso, and others. The critic's valuation of the relation between, in particular, Picasso's aesthetic and Klee's own is well worth the reading. One can go further, though, and ask *why* this aesthetic so appealed to Klee. And would the appeal of these artists and their influence necessarily exclude a simultaneous effect of the organic disease on Klee's art?[3]

In the excellent catalogue he produced with Bridget Riley for the 2002 Klee exhibition at the Hayward Gallery in London, Robert Kudielka, unlike the others, does view the "coarsening of the line" that is the most obvious alteration in the late work as a direct outcome of the degenerative illness. Whereas Franciscono explicitly states that "The cause of this bolder and more simplified style, with its effect of childlike naiveté, has nothing to do with physical disability,"[4] Kudielka sees the stylistic evolution precisely as a result of the artist's restricted movement: "[T]his restriction would have remained an awkward limitation," Kudielka explains, "had he not balanced the nature of his work in a new way. With the 'bar-like stroke' came a structure in which disruption and elimination, removal and denial played a role equal to the positive plastic constituents."[5] Andrew Kagan, in an elegant essay for a Guggenheim Museum catalogue, similarly describes this very structure as it appears in the drawings made by the artist in the final three years of his life. Writing of a more "painterly" quality where the "wiry, etchinglike line" has given way to a "flat, thickly brushed quality," he too locates in the removal and elimination typical of the late work a shift from impediment to enhancement. But Kagan does not go as far as Kudielka in seeking its genesis. Though he terms the advent of what, for him, is an utterly new sensibility at a time of tremendous physical decline "almost miraculous," it is striking that Kagan does not pursue its source.[6]

Klee experimented with a variety of signs and symbols, sometimes letters of the alphabet, throughout the course of his career. "The word and the picture, that is, word-making and form-building, are one and the same," he told his students at the Bauhaus where he taught for some ten years.[7] Beginning in 1938, he altered his use of letters in his work. Their shape began to suggest more abbreviated representational forms (ancient pictographs seem to have inspired some of the pictures dating to 1938 and 1939) as they became increasingly poetic and magical. James Smith Pierce makes particular mention of this and offers an informative analysis of Klee's ideographic work of these years in his book *Paul Klee and Primitive Art*. Here again, however, the reasons for the more evocative use of line and space characteristic of the drawings and paintings of this period are insufficiently explored. In fact, Pierce takes up the highly important subject of dismemberment in Klee's work in the decade before his death without posing the question of its possible relation to the artist's disease at all. Rather, he confines his focus to purely aesthetic concerns and excludes any explanation of the reasons behind their appeal to Klee. In considering a disembodied pair of legs, for example, he merely argues that it was Klee's understanding of "the power of the simple diagonal" to suggest human movement that determined the choice of image.[8]

The seriousness that characterizes both thematically and formally the art of this period has been discussed by Werner Haftmann who links the economy of Klee's abstract hieroglyphic depictions, and the way they constitute meaning through analogy, to the overall solemnity of Klee's late oeuvre. Haftmann also relates the notable changes in Klee's choice of materials – from fine paper to a coarse parchment, from watercolor to poster paint, and so on – to Klee's growing ascetic sensibility.[9] But if he is eloquent in his humanistic interpretations and compassionate as he attributes the metamorphosis to the painter's psycho-spiritual preoccupations with death, Haftmann comes no closer than the others to the psychobiological contextualization I believe Klee's late creative impulse requires.

In addition to the far simpler compositions to which, I would argue, the muscular and vascular changes Klee suffered contributed, if only at times, the late work reveals, then, less of the gaiety (if no less of the irony) we associate with his art of the preceding years. More somber colors are also common in the last pictures and the preoccupation with death provokes many of the late images as well. Indeed, Klee's effort to master through his art emotional despair and the awareness of death is reflected in his celebrated series of angels (of which there are more than 50, two-thirds of which date to 1939–1940)[10] and in the well-known boat paintings in which death is depicted as a voyage. Much has been written on the symbolism of the late works, on the depiction of the transition from life to death as Klee was experiencing it, for death is prominently represented both figuratively and ideogramatically in this art. In *Death and Fire* from 1940, for instance, death appears in the title, in the twice painted letters t, o, and d (German for death), and as a white figure (a head) dominating the composition from its centered position. In the two series of drawings produced in the final month before Klee died, "Eidola" and "Passion in Detail", death is a consistently palpable motivation, whether for capturing human archetypes – *Eidola: Erstwhile Musician*, *Eidola: Erstwhile Actress*, *Eidola: Erstwhile Woman Drinker*, *Eidola: Erstwhile Cannibal* – or existential sufferings – *Want to Be in on It*, *Hard Parting*, *Centrally Affected*. As Esther Dreifuss-Kattan has noted, "Eidola" is used by Klee to depict a ghostly presence in each of the drawings of that grouping. In fact, in accordance with Glaesemer, she suggests that the creatures figured in this series move, like the artist, "in the borderland between life and death, not here any longer, not yet there."[11] Other drawings from this period, like *Prefers to Remain*, *Departs Reluctantly*, and *Endure!*, render all the more evident, both in content and title, the autobiographical source of the obsession.

But the thematic preoccupation does not tell the stylistic story. Why the works are often larger; why there was an increase in colors chromatically attuned; and why the pictorial forms overall are freer, a few simple marks suggestive of grand spaces rather than of the confinement of form, are questions not answered by the artist's psychological reaction to his illness. I have said that the changes in style are not wholly explainable by the mechanical limitations imposed by scleroderma and I also believe that we cannot reduce the work of the last years to a metaphorical transcription of anguish, fear, or loss. Despite the insistence on death and the circumscription of a transitional place between living and dying in which word and image interact more directly than before, in his late work Klee was never nostalgic or sentimental. As Franciscono says, Klee "can make us believe, at least for the moment, that death, too, wears a human face; that like everything fated in life, and a good many things inflicted by human beings, it is both tragic and ridiculous."[12] To what, then, do we owe the changes referred to above? To what do we owe the more dreamy quality of the late work and, more significant still, the simultaneous distancing from the gravity of its subject and its far greater intimacy? From where, in a word, does the sense of anonymity and detachment (inherent within the diminution of form and detail) and its concomitant deep pathos derive?

To answer we need to look at the *transformational potential* of Klee's late art. As I said in the few remarks preliminary to this section of the book, *we need to replace the paradigm of the past, as origin of a present reparative fantasy, with that of the present, as evidence of creativity's therapeutic efficacy*. This is to say that we need to view the sublimatory function of creativity not only in terms of defense, but as a new and innovative form of adaptation that is as much a physico-chemical compromise as a psychological one. To put it yet another way, we need to view creativity as being as much organic as psychological insofar as all mental functioning has to do with the functioning of the brain. If, as I maintain, it is at the interface of the psychological with the biological that we arrive at the crux of the matter, at what is truly innovative in the creative act, it is precisely because a kind of biological blueprint guides the growth, the psychic reorganization, creativity affords. Samuel Abrams has shown the therapeutic action of psychoanalysis to be comparable. In a recent paper Abrams wrote of the analyst as a "servant of creative adjustment" and explained that in reducing the therapeutic action in analytic treatment to structures of the past an opportunity for a creative transition to the future may be missed. It is not a matter of "resultants," Abrams observed, but of "emergents," moments in the treatment when the analyst "taps into the forward pull" of the patient's reorganizational capacity to give rise to a burst of creative adaptation. The "transformational potential" of an analytic interpretation, more precisely, is realized when the interpretation is made less in the interest of problem resolution (which implies a focus on the past) than in the interest of real change (that is, with an eye to the future). Analysis is especially creative, in other words, when the present–past orientation is supplanted by a distinctly present–future focus, though a biological blueprint actualizes the therapeutic effect.[13] What I am contending is that the very same process was operational in Klee's late art, that the paintings and drawings of, specifically, the years 1937 through 1940 differ from the earlier work in their display of a distinctly adaptational effect. This, however, was secondary to the profound transformation of the artist's inner representational world caused by the disease itself.

It is a commonplace to observe that each of us has an image of our self in our mind. A number of allegations may be made, though, about the constitution of that self-representation; allegations that bear on the question of the evolution of Klee's style:

1 A number of mechanisms of the central nervous system are important to the development of one's self-representation. Visual, auditory, tactile, and kinaesthetic sensory impressions all contribute to the constitution of the body schema inherent within it.
2 These organic processes are inseparable from psychic function and personality.
3 Human beings have strong feelings about their bodies that may be narcissistic, ambivalent, aversive, and so on.
4 In addition to its physiological and psychological bases, the self-representation is discharge oriented; that is, it is normally cathected (invested) with libidinal (and even, at times, aggressive) drive energy.
5 One's self-representation is not fixed or static, but in perpetual reconstruction.
6 Every healthy individual is responsive to how he or she is perceived by others.

It follows from these assertions that traumatic disturbance in bodily function, such as that suffered by Klee, cannot but affect one's self-representation and sense of bodily integrity. Insofar as creativity, viewed in the service of homeostasis, is fundamentally psychobiological, the deep relation between Klee's illness and the art of his last years seems to me undeniable. By this, once again, I mean a relation other than that reducible to the emotions that would be expected to accompany his acute awareness of nearing death and I mean a relation other than that reducible solely to the diminution in the range of movement in his hands. Just how, though, did the psychobiological connection play out in Klee's late work? This is the question that, in my opinion, has been sorely neglected in the literature referred to above.

All creativity, as Joyce McDougall rightly puts it, "springs originally from the body and the way in which its instinctual drives are represented and structured from the earliest beginnings of psychic life."[14] With this as our point of departure, I would suggest that any profound alteration in bodily function and appearance – in bearing specifically on body image and more broadly on the mental representation of self – would bear heavily on the creative act. This, I believe, is readily apparent in *how* Klee manifested his threatened sense of agency and the intolerability of his diminished self state in his late art. At the same time, however, while I contend that a shift in emphasis in Klee's inner representational world, a result of his illness, effected a change in his work, I am also suggesting that change in his work, in allowing for adaptation, was homeostatically useful. For I believe that both the change in style and the artist's enormous productivity in his last years had something to do with the potential of art to accommodate, to adjust an individual's internal environment in support of the constancy required for psychobiological health. To illustrate my argument that the deepest connection between Klee's illness and his art resides in a transformation of his inner representational world we need to consider, first, the precise nature of his affliction and, then, its manifestation in the figurations dating to the period in which he was ill. This will also allow for the investigation of my hypothesis concerning the marked increase in production in the late phase of the disease.

Klee was diagnosed with *vasomotorisch-trophische Neurose* (vasomotor neurosis) in 1936 after a prolonged period of illness in the preceding year. By most accounts the initial malady was misdiagnosed as a severe case of measles from which he was said to have recovered slowly and which was thought to have given way to pneumonia and other respiratory ailments prior to the correct diagnosis of scleroderma. Some, however, speculate that he did have measles, that the rash was not simply an early symptom of the subsequent disorder, and that the scleroderma, now known to have an autoimmune component, was actually initiated or exacerbated by that virus.[15] Either way, it was complications of the degenerative illness of the body's connective tissue that, in 1940, would prove fatal to the 60-year-old painter.

Vasomotor neurosis is a term that indicates neuro-circulatory instability. It refers to what Thomas G. Benedek, a rheumatologist and medical historian, describes as "subnormal or erratic control of blood vessel tone by the autonomic nervous system."[16] Interestingly, this was presumably the only diagnosis given Klee and his family, as there is no mention of "scleroderma" (or of skleroderma or sclerodermie) in his correspondence or in that of his wife Lily. The first to use the word was Grohmann and this was not until 1954. (It then appeared in the "Recollections" of Klee's son Felix following *The Diaries of Paul Klee*, published in 1957.) And yet, according to Benedek, the term, introduced in 1847, was standard nomenclature in Europe in the 1930s.

In part for this reason, the now widely accepted diagnosis of Klee's illness as scleroderma has recently been thrown into question by Gabriele Castenholz who believes it more accurate to speak simply of a complex of rheumatic diseases. Castenholz further claims that the diagnosis is uncertain because the evidence of Klee's having had Raynaud's phenomenon, a condition that usually precedes scleroderma, is inconclusive. The indication of myocarditis on Klee's death certificate, she argues, also complicates the diagnosis insofar as kidney dysfunction is the more usual cause of death in patients with scleroderma.[17] The situation is more definitive, however, than she believes. In the first place, as Benedek affirms, while the association of scleroderma with Raynaud's phenomenon does occur in about 90 percent of cases, it is not always present. And myocarditis provides no stronger evidence against the diagnosis. While myocarditis today is defined as inflammation of the heart muscle and there is typically no sign of inflammation of the heart in scleroderma, the term "fibrous trabecular myocarditis" does appear in a German case report from 1876. In fact, Benedek notes that "a few such cases were published prior to 1943 when, based on a clinico-pathologic study of a number of cases, 'scleroderma heart disease' became recognized as a specific type of heart disease." More important, though, photographs of the artist taken in his last years (in particular, one from 1939 and another from 1940 that closely reveal the shiny skin, thinly stretched lips, and general rigidity of his face) leave no room for doubt. Letters descriptive of Klee's symptoms, the history of medicine, and photographs of the artist oblige us, then, to accept the irony that Klee, whose entire "creative credo" was built on the idea of figuration as movement, was afflicted with an illness that progressively imprisoned him in his own ever tightening skin.

Details of Klee's illness are not available as a fire at the Swiss hospital (Sant'Agnes in Locarno-Muralto) where he died destroyed his medical records. We do not know, therefore, exactly how his illness was managed or exactly what provoked the heart failure to which he succumbed. (Renal crisis, pulmonary hypertension, or injury directly to the heart are all possible, with a pericarditis the least likely of the three.) We do know, though (mostly from Lily's letters and the testimony of Felix), that he suffered from fatigue and dyspnoea beginning in the summer of 1935 and from symptoms (suggestive of Raynaud's phenomenon?) as early as 1933. We also know that, while there were periods of greater and lesser affliction (he even had somewhat of a remission in 1938), he endured throughout those years arthritic pain in his hands, stiff and swollen joints, difficulties in swallowing owing to esophageal involvement, and a feeling of general ill health. Undoubtedly most important, however, was the physical and psychological discomfort of his increasingly taut skin.

Ordinarily, scleroderma advances over some 15 to 30 years with the skin of the hands and face, and later the inner organs, thickening from the intensifying obstruction of the blood vessels. What Klee would have had, though, was not the circumscribed but the far rarer, diffuse form of the disease afflicting only about 5 percent of patients and generally proving fatal in only three to five years. In this form of the illness the appearance of the face is dramatically altered, but not that of the hands, a situation corroborated by Felix who affirmed that his father's fingers were not remarkably changed and that their mobility remained unimpaired until the end.[18] This is meaningful in that the origin of the stylistic changes with which we are concerned here would not appear primarily attributable to physical deterioration caused by the disease. I would venture, in disagreement with Franciscono and others cited above, that some degree of swelling and stiffness in Klee's hands contributed to the characteristically broad lines and sparseness of his late works. I think it a reasonable assumption that it was easier for him, at times, to hold larger brushes and crayons than thin brushes and pens. Even if this was not consistently so (as Franciscono says, "fine, small characters" in some of the last works demonstrate a "delicacy of control"), given the vascular and muscular atrophy endemic to the disease there is certainly reason to think it caused sufficient discomfort to affect, however minimally, his art. My point, though, is that the notable modifications in style are not primarily the result of this physical degeneration. Nor, as I have said, do they primarily derive from Klee's affective reactions to it.

One is obliged to consider whether any of the medical treatments that the artist received may have played even a peripheral role. From necessarily limited, if nonetheless informative studies of Klee's symptoms and their management (such as those by Brigitta Danuser-Nideröst, Hans Suter, Gunter Wolf, and Gabriele Castenholz), we get a sense of what treatments were tried. From medical historians, however, we ascertain how little they could have affected his art. Thyroid and other hormones, arsenic and iron, liver injections, special diets, and warm baths (a reference, in all likelihood, to the spas of Tarasp, Montano, and Ascona, which Klee visited in 1936 and 1937) appear to have been administered to the artist. Of the hormone therapies, thyroid extract was by far the most commonly tried at the time. (It was recommended, in addition to the warm baths, by William Osler in his highly regarded medical textbook of 1920. And a 1939 volume on diseases of the skin notes that it was "serviceable in a small percentage of instances, and is worthy of a trial in all extensive cases of the disease.")[19] The motivation for the use of arsenical drugs, introduced in 1910, was a few cases of coincidental syphilis and/or false Wasserman tests and, by the 1930s, iron was used as a supportive measure. So too were vitamin supplements and diets. (B-12, for example, was discovered as a cure for pernicious anemia as result of research, begun around 1925, on the effect of liver on debility. Thus it may also have been administered.) Other treatments in the 1930s included various tonics, massage, and endocrine medications, but only the thyroid therapy could have caused any sort of relevant side effect: In large doses it could produce a tremor. Typically, though, small doses were given over a longer time, so it seems reasonable to conclude, as does Benedek, that Klee's medical treatment had no far-reaching consequences.[20] Certainly, it would have had less bearing on his art than the mechanical restrictions of the disease itself.

The pathogenesis of scleroderma remains unknown today. Hyperfunction of the parathyroid gland, bacteria, abnormal enzyme action, and nervous factors have all been implicated at one time or another.[21] Some have sought to link the outbreak of the illness in Klee to external stressors: for example, his abrupt dismissal from the Düsseldorf Academy in 1933 (the Nazis considered him a "cultural Bolshevist") and his forced departure from Germany. The thought here centers on the vulnerability of a weakened immune system. Others have looked to materials related to Klee's work, such as glue and paint (Felix speculated that the colors with which he experimented may have had a deleterious effect),[22] and to the possible inhalation of fumes while he applied finish to airplanes during his time in the military. Then there are those who favor a psychosomatic explanation and speculate, for instance, that the thickening of the skin in scleroderma served Klee as a somatic means of insulating himself from the world. Biologist Christoph Morscher has gone so far as to suggest the relevance of the hypothesis of morphogenetic fields and morphic resonance (the New Age metaphysical theory of Rupert Sheldrake) to the psychosomatic point of view. In a 1994 article Morscher proposes that condensation and displacement, two characteristics of primary-process mentation, are somatically valid outside the psychoanalytic context of conversion. To make his point and validate the possibility that Klee was psychologically ill with scleroderma before it manifested itself physically, he focusses both on what he considers an ambivalent relationship of the artist to his body and a tendency to somatize emotional difficulties. He also identifies the strong emphasis on certain parts of the body evident in Klee's work long before he fell ill as the very same body parts (the face, lungs, hands, and windpipe) affected by the disease to which Klee would later succumb.[23] And he links Klee's recurrent motif of the dead (as in the 1934 drawing *Lonely End*, for instance) with the artist's own self-representation considering it a precursor of the ultimate dessication which the illness would cause. However much one eschews the notion that the genesis of Klee's somatic disease resided in his psychic function, that a disease that made him resemble the dead derived from an internal image of his self as more dead than alive, it is uncanny that as early as 1905 Klee wrote in his diary: "If I had to paint a perfectly truthful self-portrait, I would show a peculiar shell. And inside – it would have to be made clear to everyone – I sit like a kernel in a nut. This work might also be named: allegory of incrustation."[24]

I turn now to the substantial stylistic changes in Klee's art that I believe were effected by his disease and will aim to demonstrate my two primary points: First, that the alteration in style was determined by more than the symbolic and allegoric expression of a preoccupation with mortality. Beyond that, it reveals a change in self-representation that culminated in a withdrawal of libidinal investment from the body (and from the world). And, second, insofar as libido originates in the body and, furthermore, insofar as the physical and emotional suffering that produced the divestment must be considered as a unit, the late art served an adaptive purpose and was homeostatically useful. That is, the aesthetic of abstraction and the disavowal of libidinal investment that contributed to it were means of preserving some sense of body integrity that rendered the creative act itself a stabilizing force.

Jacob Arlow reminded us some 30-odd years ago that the individual's identity is composed of many different self-representations and that the impact of conflict may cause it to disintegrate into its constituent parts.[25] Klee's late work reveals that the impact of trauma, at once somatic and psychic, may produce the same result. Klee was well aware of the multiplicity of self-representations and the coherent sense of self to which they give rise when, in 1905, he wrote in his diary: "Individuality is not an elementary sort of thing, but an organism. Elementary things of different sorts coexist in it, inseparably. If one tried to separate them, the components would die. My self, for instance, is a dramatic ensemble."[26] Arlow also made the point, however, that the balance between drive (what he called "cathectic potential") and repression ("counter cathectic force") determines the accessibility of mental representation to consciousness.[27] If Klee's work was radically different in his last years, if it became exceedingly abstract in ways it had not been before he became ill, it was in some measure due to an alteration of this balance. The evolution of Klee's self-portraits illustrates the point.

Klee's self-images, the great many acknowledged as such by the artist and the numerous others easily identifiable as him, reflect a tendency toward distancing and withdrawal from the start. In each of the three versions of *The Comedian*, for instance, etchings of himself that Klee made in 1903 and 1904, the artist's face appears from behind a menacing mask. One senses in the first two the transformational objective served by the mask: It is meant to convert his passive image to an image of (however exaggerated) self-assertiveness. Masks serve not only to disguise, however, but to conceal and given the forlorn, depressive even, affect of the artist's self-portrait, it would appear that that was the self-image he sought to hide. Numerous passages of Klee's *Diaries* attest to a not infrequent depressive (and at times suicidal) state. Not long after *The Comedian* he wrote to Lily, "Ich schaffe pour ne pas pleurer, das ist der letze und erste Grund" ("I create in order not to cry, that is the first and last reason").[28] In the third etching one notes a less depressed facial expression and greater independence from the mask. It has been said that the similarity between the bearded mask in that version and Klee's father, Hans, is suggestive of the artist's emergence from the domination of the paternal imago.[29] Interestingly, though, in his diary Klee defines the mask as art: "The mask as work of art; behind it, the man."[30] However we choose to interpret it, at play in this motif of disguise – which extended to a great many other of Klee's works – is the accessibility of the self.

In 1919 Klee made a group of five self-images. Their titles are indicative of his purpose, the analysis of the relation between the artist and his work: *Thinking Artist*, *Feeling Artist*, *Pondering Artist*, *Artist Forming*, and *Absorption*. The last of these is a pencil drawing in which the artist is shown without ears. Michele Vishny claims Klee eliminated the ears because "they would distract attention from the face."[31] I find this unlikely. In the first place, other caricature-like drawings show the artist without ears: *The Sultry Garden*, *Dance You Monster to My Soft Song!*, and *Pipe Bowl and Overturned Antique: Sketch for a Still Life*, from 1919, 1922, and 1924 respectively, come first to mind. The repetition alone is enough to indicate the importance of the phenomenon. Furthermore, *Absorption* also depicts the artist's eyes as closed. The image is clearly of one who neither hears nor sees and what is evident already in this work is the withdrawal from the world that would predominate – formally, if not anecdotally as in this drawing – in the late art.

In 1916 Klee wrote a lengthy description of the painter Franz Marc who had died in the war. Distinguishing Marc from himself, he described his friend as one in whom "the bond with the earth takes precedence over the bond with the universe." Marc, Klee goes on to say, "was still a real member of the human race, not a neutral creature." In fact, Klee sees his own art very much in terms of this "neutrality," this distancing whose absence he admires in Marc:

> What my art probably lacks, is a kind of passionate humanity. I don't love animals and every sort of creature with an earthly warmth. I don't descend to them or raise them to myself. I tend rather to dissolve into the whole of creation [. . .] The earth-idea gives way to the world-idea. My love is distant and religious. [. . .] There is no sensuous relationship, not even the noblest, between myself and the many. In my work I do not belong to the species, but am a cosmic point of reference. My earthly eye is too far-sighted and sees through and beyond the most beautiful things.[32]

Even in his artistic credo we see evidence of this remove, of the pull toward dissolution of the self into the "whole of creation," a tendency of which Klee was keenly (and at times painfully) aware. In his *Pedagogical Sketchbook*, his *Notebooks*, and various lectures, Klee developed a consistent theory of how art is to be made. Based not on any subjective intention, but on movement itself as agent, on the impulse that moves "from point to line," Klee's theory decreed form the result of an impetus inherent within the line: "It goes out for a walk, so to speak, aimlessly for the sake of the walk."[33] He conceived of his vision as cosmic: "Abstract formal elements are put together like numbers and letters to make concrete beings or abstract things; in the end a formal cosmos is achieved" and he thought art the culmination of "an interplay of movements in the universe."[34] Thus with respect to the human figure, what Klee required of his portraits (including those of himself) was far less the replication of external appearance than the revelation of the figure's "function" within the greater scope of the world.

His technique of creating what he called "individual" out of "dividual" form was not unrelated. Defining it as the articulation of matter in space, he accounted for the growth of the work by unveiling the rhythm, shape, and unity/disunity of its structure, its attunement with the natural order. In so doing he exposed the truth value of the image which, despite the variability of its interpretations, derives from the commonality of experience. What Klee was after, in other words, was "the maximum 'alienation' [. . .] of artistic value in a maximum of quality and purity," as Jürg Spiller put it, while also the capacity of the image "to associate itself with everyday life."[35] Franciscono refers similarly to Klee's metaphysical theory of the production of form. He describes the artist's writings during his years of teaching at the Bauhaus (1921–1931) in terms of a "growing vision of a world in which the commonplace is in some sense in union with the transcendental, or at least displays the ideal basis of its existence."[36] Dynamically speaking, however, I believe what was already operative in Klee's Platonism of the twenties was the repressive force that would manifest itself in the play with anonymity, with latent figuration, and with undetermined space and scale that characterizes the style of his work near the end of his life.

To return to the self-portraits, the proclivity to disengagement, then, is evident in the mask motif and in the withdrawal into the self implied by the sensory inhibition in several images of the artist from the early and middle years. Yet the balance between "cathectic potential" and "counter cathectic force" is maintained throughout these periods by the direct display of affect (mostly depressive) and the preponderance of descriptive or narrative elements in these works. It is also maintained by the determinedly erotic quality of many of these pictures. Looking again at *Absorption* we see that the nose is clearly phallic and that both the mouth and the closed eyes resemble pudenda. (This transposition of sex organs onto the head is also found in a number of other works of the late teens and twenties, such as *Portrait of an Artist* [1919], *Drawing for Barbarian Venus* [1920], *The Wild Man* [1922], and *Strange Garden* [1923]. And the reverse – the attribution of facial features to the body, breasts as eyes or pudenda as mouth – is not infrequent.)[37] The however subtle expression of impulse and desire in *Absorption's* sexual imagery, in fact, contrasts dramatically with the vacuity we find in many of the later self-images.

Klee saw his portraits as "truer" than the real figures they were meant to depict. Similarly, his self-images indicate not how he optically saw his own outward appearance, but how he saw his inner self in his mind: "There are some who will not acknowledge the truth of my mirror. They should bear in mind that I am not here to reflect the surface (a photographic plate can do that), but must look within."[38] In fact, the self-portraits helped him define the parameters of his identity; that is, articulating his inner self-representations helped him apprehend who he was: "I begin logically with chaos, it is the most natural start. In so doing, I feel at rest because I may, at first, be chaos myself."[39]

In *The Comedian* Klee displayed a ruggedly masculine self-image. (A 1903 entry in his diary reads "Striving toward the purification and the isolation of the masculine type in me.")[40] Yet in *Menacing Head* [1905], among the earliest of Klee's extant self-portraits and the final etching in the "Inventions" series, we find a very different sort of depiction. The image of a human head with a rat-like creature posed on top, it is striking for its surreal content, its harshly symmetrical composition, and the "overwhelming sense of foreboding as expressed by the hard lines of the frowning brow, hypnotic stare, and downturned mouth," to cite Vishny's succinct description. What is also remarkable, however, is the androgynous cast given the face. A seemingly latent femininity in the features offsets the otherwise male physiognomy that Klee termed "for the most part resigned."[41] A more overtly androgynous self-portrait is the 1908 ink drawing *The Father: Two Nudes*, where the artist appears, carrying his infant, with long hair and an enlarged, apparently pregnant belly. Klee was responsible at the time for running the household and caring for young Felix while Lily supported the family. (She gave piano lessons in Munich where the family resided.) His ambivalence with respect to the more laborious tasks of fatherhood, to say nothing of a persistent negative attitude toward pregnant women, has been documented.[42] However overburdened he may have felt, though, that he chose (albeit satirically) to depict himself as long-haired and pregnant, and with male genitalia as well, is curious. What Klee seems to be grappling with in these works is an awareness of the coexistence in his psychic structure of masculine and feminine elements and their relation to his creative potential.

Let me emphasize that I am not suggesting that Klee struggled with conflict around gender identification. Such speculation would be wholly unfounded. Rather, what I allude to is the projection in certain of his works of an interest in the subjectivity of gender as it relates to the primordial sense of self. Klee's investigation of masculine and feminine self-representations, in fact, appears congruent with the notion of a fundamental bisexual disposition that has been termed "a quality of the self" by Fausta Ferraro and acknowledged by Joyce McDougall as a universal hermaphroditic longing.[43] Not only the androgyny of the works in question, but also Klee's preoccupation with procreativity and his oft-cited identification of art with the Creation itself lend credence to this idea. Two 1914 entries from the *Diaries* are particularly relevant here:

> Genesis as formal motion is the essential thing in a work. In the beginning the motif, insertion of energy, sperm. Works as shaping of form in the material sense: the primitive female component.
>
> Works as form-determining sperm: the primitive male component. My drawings belong to the male realm.
>
> The shaping of form is weak in energy in comparison with the determining of form. The final consequence of both ways of forming is form. From the ways to the end. From activity to the accomplished. From the genuinely living thing to the objective thing.
>
> In the beginning the male speciality, the energetic stimulus. Then the fleshly growth of the egg. Or: first the bright flash of lightning, then the raining cloud.

And several others are comparable: As early as 1898, for example, Klee wrote: "Feminine impression connected with yearning for artistic form" and five years later, "As if I were pregnant with things needing form, and dead sure of a miscarriage!"[44]

Klee's many depictions of angels, at least some of which are clearly self-referential, are also revealing in this regard. Mark Luprecht has discussed the potentially autobiographical nature of Klee's 1920 watercolor *Angelus Novus* viewing the accentuation of the angel's left side (Klee was left-handed) and strikingly large eyes (organs consistently privileged by the artist) as noteworthy indications. Luprecht observes more subtle evidence of the self-referentiality of this and all Klee's other angels in their pointed construction: "Most of the artist's angels are formed by facets, like crystals, and 'crystals' is a key-word in Klee's *Diaries*" where, indeed, he describes himself as a crystal.[45] I would add to this the striking similarity of the shape of the face of the *Angelus Novus* to other works known to be self-images: Its exceedingly oblong contour appears in the 1922 watercolor and oil transfer drawing *Dance You Monster to My Soft Song!* and in the oil on burlap *Mask of Fear*, dated ten years later, to name but two. Further, the delineation of the nose is remarkably reminiscent of that in *Absorption* and other self-portraits catalogued as such by Klee. But here is the point: Klee's angels, most often interpreted in terms of what they reveal of the influence of writers (primarily Rilke for his angel imagery in the *Duino Elegies*, but also Baudelaire and others) on the painter, are significant in their depiction of aspects of the artist himself. And it is in the angels perhaps more than in any other motif that Klee articulates the convergence of masculine and feminine traits (Figure 4.1).

A certain ambiguity is, in fact, fundamental to Klee's angels: Though not on earth but in a cloud, the angel in *Angelus Novus* has distinctly human qualities, as do many of the angels by Klee. More to the point, though, this is a hermaphroditic angel clothed and coiffed like a woman with a phallic-nosed

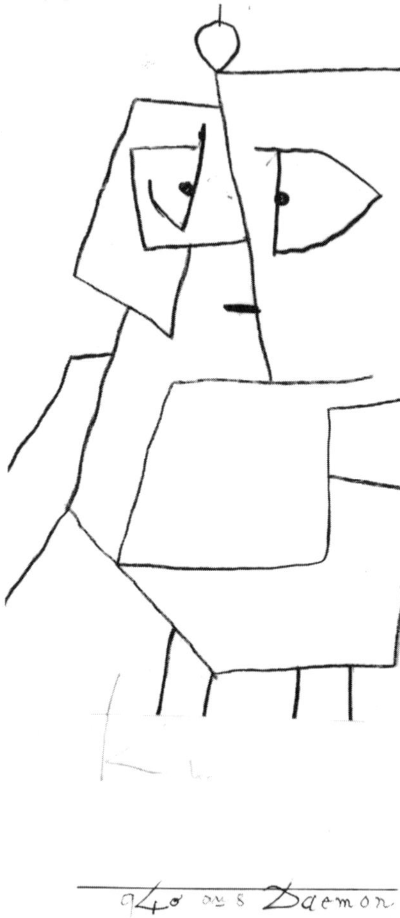

Figure 4.1 Daemon, 1940, 188 (Qu 8) Demon. Kreide auf Papier auf Karton; 29.6 × 21 cm.

face, as just noted, resembling that of Klee's self-portraits. In *Angel, Still Ugly* and also *Demon* (Figure 4.1), both from 1940, we are faced with the possibility that the figure we are viewing is really two, not one.[46] But, again, of relevance here is the conflation of masculine and feminine: Within a shape recalling a skirt there is an ambiguous form like a phallus. Interestingly, when *Angel, Still Ugly* was copied into the bottom left-hand corner of another work, the artist's final painting known as *Untitled* (*Last Still Life*), a vertical line was made to cross the short horizontal dash that is part of the seemingly phallic form. Luprecht offers two possible explanations: the substitution of a plus (+) for a minus (–) sign and a Greek cross that would be in keeping with a religious interpretation of the painting.[47] I would offer another, though, and that is a discrete disavowal of the phallic form, a cancellation of the masculine within a feminine frame, so to speak. This would leave us viewing an unambiguously female angel (in a skirt resembling a liturgical garment) as though, after years of an admitted "[d]istaste for procreation,"[48] a testimony to woman as procreator could finally be paid. Such an interpretation finds support in an earlier oil painting, *The Creator*, that dates to 1934 (but was probably begun in 1930.)[49] Here masculine and feminine are conflated in the focus on flight, a theme much discussed by Klee's interpreters and deconstructed by Franciscono as "a wry symbol of artistic aspiration."[50] A bent left wrist and ballet dancer-like fingers on the right hand are clearly meant to be feminine. If it is the artist himself who is aloft, a notion to which many subscribe and one that I believe warranted by Klee's thinking on art as comparable to the Creation, the feminine attribution becomes all the more compelling.

That men and women each have male and female features is hardly a new idea. I have said that Klee's self-images served him in the discovery of these components within himself and that they helped him achieve a deeper sense of his "function" in relation to others and the world. But the progression from the early to the late self-images shows a distinct change in this pursuit: In his years of illness Klee's references to himself are significantly less concerned with male and female traits. This is not only that in much of the late work Klee's play with ambiguity as it relates to content and meaning has yielded more fully to an essential ambiguity of form. In the late representations of himself, as in his non-self-referential pictures, rather, there is simply no longer the same libidinous charge.

Angel Serves a Small Breakfast is an amusing lithograph from 1920 (a preliminary pen and ink drawing predates it by five years) with watercolor additions. It pictures a long-haired and winged reference to the artist as homemaker. A heart situated in the center of the composition is set off from the rest by its placement, large size, and color whose intensity contrasts with the subtlety of the delicate inked lines and the work's overall paler tones. Klee has inscribed his name very close to the angel and encircled it in red to create a warm rapport with the heart in this way identified as his own. *Angel, Still Female*, in contrast, is a late work (from 1939, in crayon and colored paste on paper) whose starkness is both riveting and rendered all the more bleak by comparison. But most astonishing is that, despite two semi-circular breasts, highlighted and the focus of one seemingly apprehensive eye,[51] it retains almost nothing of the human, let alone the personal constituents of the early work.

It is true that personal references to home and family gave way to a greater emphasis on the transcendental, to cosmic distancing, well before the artist was ill and that the self-images were becoming increasingly anonymous already in the preceding decade. If the mask motif infiltrated his work over many years (and several hundred pictures, and also puppets, inspired by the theater relate closely to this motif), disguise also took other forms in the self-images of the early 1920s. As Vishny summarizes them, Klee "appears as a magician, alchemist, pseudo-scientist, mechanized ghost, expressionist artist, puppet, musician, and even as his own pipe!"[52] By the 1930s, though, disguise is no longer necessary so extensive is the artist's remove. In *Scholar*, a highly textured, but spare and affectless bust-like image executed in 1933 in oil on canvas on wood, to cite but one more example, there is nothing left in the shape of the head or in the facial features to identify Klee. It is, rather, a generic depiction (human, but not in any way particularized), though he calls it a self-portrait.

Nonetheless, the shift in balance between the investment of drive and its repression (between "cathectic potential" and "counter cathectic force") is not fully realized until Klee's last years. This is to say that notwithstanding the earlier proclivity to libidinal withdrawal the more extreme depersonalization that would be its result is not truly emblematic of Klee's work before his was seriously ill with scleroderma. Franciscono writes: "From the very beginning of his career Klee had tended to use as subjects his physical disturbances and those of others close to him." Though the late work often deals with the most unsettling of subjects, from the direct representation of his illness to the immanence of death, it differs from what came before in its dissociative quality or impassivity. I do not mean that it lacks pathos or that the late works are not poignant; on the contrary, they are deeply moving. What has changed is that they are no longer "confessional" (the term is Franciscono's): "Their allegorical language, their precise structures, and most of all, perhaps, their carefully rendered and stylized forms (however rapidly and 'spontaneously' they may have been drawn) objectify their content too much for that."[53] But the question remains: Why?

Esther Dreifuss-Kattan offers this explanation: "Th[e] confrontation with death led Klee to momentous inner changes. On a narcissistic level, Klee mourned the lost integrity of his own body, which continually changed. Since earliest development of the ego is closely connected with the image of an intact body ego, Klee must have been threatened by a feeling of diminished self-worth when his body disintegrated, fostering strong emotions of shame and anger." This forced him "to withdraw all libidinal cathexis from his body and thus from most of his drive wishes."[54] A number of things support this thinking: I have spoken of the thematic preoccupation with death and argued that this in itself is insufficient to account for the change in style. Yet the many figurations done between 1938 and 1940 of death and dying are certainly indicative of the artist's anguished state that was a contributing factor. In this context must be cited the late angel pictures, the two series "The Inferner Park" (1939) and "Passion in Detail" (1940), and the best known of the paintings where death is personified, *Insula Dulcamara* (1938), *Timpanist*

(1940),[55] and *Death and Fire* (1940). Not only do the late pictures themselves attest to the distress of the "confrontation," moreover, but the estrangement and indeterminacy of many of Klee's titles testify to the decathexis Dreifuss-Kattan describes: Those of the 1939 series of 29 drawings Klee called "Approximations" lack any reference to an agent; the 16 drawings of "The Inferner Park" series have subtitles indicative of unlocalizable places; and those of the "Eidola" series are mostly archetypal. Finally, the idea that the abstract and simplified figurations of his last years originated in Klee's "mourn[ing] the lost integrity of his body" is supported by what we know of how Klee subjectively experienced the creative act.

Initially, making art had a defining quality for Klee. As we saw in *The Comedian* and other early self-portraits, expressing his struggle with autonomy (inhibited first by his dominating father and later by his role as principal caretaker of his son) helped him achieve a greater sense of self. "[T]he main thing now," he wrote in 1902 in his *Diaries*, "is [. . .] to be or, at least, to become an individual." And eight years later he would again stress the urgency of self-delineation: "[T]o adapt oneself to the contents of the paint-box is more important than nature and its study." Making art was first and foremost a means of enriching his inner representational image. It also gave him a sense of dominion over himself and his environs – "I wanted to render things that could be controlled," he wrote in 1901 – but mostly art provided a protection against the threat of dissolution. In one passage of his *Diaries* he describes "dangerous moments" when he might be devoured by nature and admits to feeling at such times that he is "annihilated." In another, he defends himself against the dry recording of his surroundings: "Amidst such surroundings I must not settle in the long run. Or else I shall lose myself." In still another, from 1911, he reviewed the preceding years as follows: "In lucid moments, I now have a clear view of twelve years of the history of my inner self. First the cramped self, that self with the big blinkers, then the disappearance of the blinkers and the self, now gradually the reemergence of a self without blinkers." This last citation is perhaps the most telling: It reveals the struggle against detachment and the increase in libidinal investment in the artist's internal self-representation that, if only for a time, took precedence over it. In fact, the word "blinkers" may be linked to the "devastating self-criticism" explicitly referred to in an earlier entry for a clue to the source of the dissolution that threatened him.[56] But any real speculation regarding its origin cannot be justified.

I have noted above the protective function of the mask that Klee acknowledged as a symbol of art. Marta Schneider Brody has likened this to a secondary skin formation and I myself am reminded of Didier Anzieu's concept of the *Moi-peau*, a primordial fantasy of an enveloping "ego-skin." Brody explains that in *The Comedian*, for instance, "The surfaces of the forms (the skin of the figures) are rendered by the repetitive (rhythmic) use of countless minute dots and fine lines." And, as Margaret Plant has observed, in these images "The mask is joined to the head so that it has grown to become part of the brain and skin, physically attached." The resemblance between these masks and the "skin merging masks of Goya," whom Klee greatly admired, is also noted by Plant and Brody. Additional confirmation that art served Klee as a second skin formation is found by Brody in his choice of materials: "As a response to the death and destruction surrounding him during World War I, Klee used pieces of coarse canvas that he removed from the debris of the crashed airplanes as a painting surface. In this way Klee was able to use the 'skin' of the airplane to process and express primitive forms of anxiety through his art."[57]

In *Le Moi-peau*, Anzieu describes "the fantasy of a skin surface common to mother and child,"[58] a primordial fantasy of symbiotic fusion generated to protect against the anxiety of separation from the mother. It is tempting to seek an explanation for Klee's fear of "annihilation" in this anxiety. And even, perhaps, to view the androgyny (considered above as an expression of Klee's preoccupation with "function" and the natural order) as an expression of the fantasy that defends against it. But nothing in Klee's writings or in the personal recollections of those who have written about him sanctions such assumptions. Very little is known of Klee's psychic life (he was always emotionally reserved and remained very private even in his correspondence). Where Anzieu's notion of the "ego-skin" *can* be useful to our understanding of Klee's relation to his art, however, is simply in the fantasy's function of reinforcing a sense of invulnerability. McDougall has described a characteristic fantasy of the artist as merging with his or her medium.[59] Several entries in the *Diaries* affirm its applicability to Klee. Here is one that is particularly apt:

> A flying man! I force the third dimension into the flat plane.
> Disposition of the arms, paired legs, absence of foreshortening.
> I even dream about it. I dream of myself. I dream that I become
> my model. Projected self. Upon wakening, I realize the truth of it.
> I lie in a complicated position, but flat, attached to the
> linen surface. I am my style.[60]

Klee, moreover, considered the picture organic: "Pictures have their skeleton, muscles, and skin like human beings." Reading his *Diaries* one is struck by the way in which he speaks of seeing through art as an organic entity and he articulately defines the necessity for "discipline" in generating art's revelatory power. It is in this context that he explicated in 1902 a "principle of economy": The artist must be "frugal" to achieve "firmly restraining linear boundaries." To execute his "relief style," as he called it, Klee described "economically" projecting "on the surface [. . .] the essence of a subject" in "a single act." The concepts of art as a secondary skin formation or an "ego-skin" that would render him invulnerable to the threat of "annihilation" go a long way toward explaining Klee's "small and tight work" (as he himself referred to it). For this was the art typical of his early and mid-career when he was most vulnerable to his own self-criticism, the art so distinguishable from what would come later, and it was against what he termed his "poetic enthusiasm," against excess, chaos, and vulnerability that art served as a protection.[61]

But the notion of a second skin formation or that of an "ego-skin" are compelling with regard to the late style too. As previously mentioned, Klee's late forms are generally larger (some of his paintings from 1938 are longer than five feet)[62] and freer. Nonetheless, his pictures from 1937 to 1940 reveal a greater intensity; and most obvious in many of his paintings from this period are the thicker and far denser contours. Even in the more narrow-lined drawings, particularly those from 1939 and 1940, there is a firmness to his line not present before. Some of these late works are defined by an unrelenting angularity; others by forceful curves – all have a weight that sets them apart from the work of the preceding years. It is as though the feeling of being in a hardened and thickened skin was transposed to the density and coarseness of his line. It is also as though the protective service rendered by the more narrative, generally smaller, and tighter art gave way to something more expansive but also more form conscious when Klee's own skin tightened from scleroderma. The withdrawal of libidinal investment from the artist's body schema as manifested above all in the drawings of the late years, in other words, seems to have given rise to a new preoccupation with the very process of figuration itself.

Returning to Dreifuss-Kattan's remarks about Klee's "momentous inner changes," her points, in sum, are well taken. But we need to consider whence these changes derive. The remove to which we bear witness from the start of Klee's career and that culminated in the extreme decathexis we see in his late art cannot be viewed as independent of the neurobiological underpinnings of this psychic defense. Indeed, as it is the purpose of this chapter to show, a combined neuroscientific and psychodynamic perspective on the late style renders its interplay with Klee's disease eminently clearer.

Because the brain does not have much connective tissue, scleroderma does not directly affect that part of the anatomy. Nevertheless, because our internal representations (Freud's *Vorstellung*) result from multiple brain systems its significance for brain function may be considered no less real. Representations in the mind are composed of associative patterns resulting from the earliest continuous meanings established by the body. Distress (primarily hunger) in the infant and the subsequent satisfaction of need, for example, lead to the internalization, first, of the part object (the breast) and, then, of the whole object (the mother) whose representations foster a sense of constancy. It is precisely the creation of internal representations that lets us tolerate the absence of the real object and, increasingly over time, delay the need for gratification. Yet the network of the patterns set by the transfer across numerous synapses of the original sensory input is rendered malleable by the plasticity of the brain. This is to say that the brain allows for changes in the neural systems so that, with the activation of any of these patterns through life experience, new groupings of neurons are stimulated and changes in associations are triggered. Thus any profoundly dynamic experience necessarily affects brain function. Were this not so psychoanalysis itself could not be therapeutic: As Charles Brenner has put it, "When an analyst speaks to an analysand physicochemical events are initiated in the analysand's brain: in the cochlea, in the geniculate bodies, in the temporal cortex, and elsewhere. One can say of psychoanalysis, just as one does of the administration of psychotropic drugs, that it affects the functioning of the brain."[63]

It goes without saying that, dynamically speaking, Klee's illness was of great magnitude for several reasons, not least of which was his increasing awareness that it was life threatening. We can also appreciate, however, the dynamic effects produced by perception. Joseph Sandler has described the importance to the inner representational world of the "many organized schemata that the individual constructs during the course of his development and that form the background frame of reference to all current processes of perception, imagining, remembering, feeling and thinking."[64] Different kinds of stimuli – those arising from within the body and those arising from outside it – influence the organization of these schemata. And the registering of stimuli having a degree of constancy, as in prolonged illness, can dramatically modify them. Given the visual alteration wrought by scleroderma on his self-perception, there had to be change in the artist's psychic schemata. His body image, for one, had to be affected by the perception of his depreciating physical capacities; that is, by the perception from within of his waning strength, independent of the affective response it provoked. Add to this the alteration in sensations perceived through the skin. Then there is the incongruity between the current input from his primary sensory modalities and his perceptual and emotional self "memories" in the past. Take, for example, the visual perception of change in his appearance. Not only did he have to contend with being seen as disfigured but to struggle with seeing himself in a way incongruent with his earlier self-image. The dynamic consequences of all were no doubt significant.

The impact of the psyche on brain function is multifaceted. Without delving too deeply into the different memory systems that exist within the brain, suffice it to say that our representations of self and world are complex precisely because they combine the perceptual and conceptual processing of space and time with an emotional memory system. This system is housed in the amygdala and related areas and may be aroused by the activation of consciously or unconsciously processed stimuli. Klee's representations had to evolve with his illness insofar as it stimulated implicit emotional memory traces. And it is the incongruity between these implicit emotional memories with the actuality of perceptual input that would have disrupted his inner representational world. But there is also the effect of prolonged stress (such as would stem from severe organic illness) on brain function to consider:

Recent studies have shown that continuous stress may result in degeneration within the hippocampus. This would account for disturbances in explicit or declarative memory. More to the point, though, stress may also intensify the reactivation of emotional memories, while not otherwise interfering with amygdala function, a finding of importance with regard to the fluidity of the inner representational world.[65]

I think it apparent from the art Klee made in the last years of his life that, as the integrated structure that was his body image became more uncertain and *dis*integrated with the advance of his disease, he sought to cope in two distinct ways. He worked more intensely with the very process of figuration itself, with the transition from formlessness to form, so as to assimilate or metabolize over time the changes to his body pictorially. (The discussion below of some of his drawings from 1939 and 1940, principally those of dismemberment and swollen hands and feet, shows this to be so.) And he sought to fend off the threat to his self-representation and autonomy through a hypercathexis of the creative act. That is to say, he instinctually redirected his libidinal drive away from his body as the source of distress. Klee's astonishing output from 1937 on is not, to my thinking, only to be viewed as a feverish fight against time and his mortality. That he produced 1654 works in 1939 and 1940 alone was also, and perhaps mostly, an effort to retrieve a sense of internal constancy when the mutability of his own self-image, and thus that of the world and his position within it, was most apparent.

I have said that scleroderma does not act on the brain directly insofar as it is a disease of connective tissue, of which the brain has little, and that it would rather have impacted the brain indirectly through an alteration in Klee's inner self-representation. I substantiated this by saying that a modified self-image would have resulted from his altered appearance (photos attest to the hardening of his facial skin), a change in tactile stimuli, and his perception of the progressive diminishment of his capacities. The disease would necessarily have dealt a blow to his healthy if narcissistic regard for his body's integrity if only because one's self-representation, neurobiologically constituted, is libidinal in structure. That is, it emanates from a primary concern with the body as a need-driven unit even before the regard for regions of erogenic significance becomes paramount. The biology of self-representation is such that it reflects the homeostatic tendency of every living organism. This, then, is the essential point: What has heretofore been considered solely the province of the interrelation of psychology and aesthetics – Klee's emotional response to facing death as manifested in his art – is inseparable from the physiology of the brain. My argument derives primarily from what recent advances in neuroscience tell us of the neurobiology of drive and its significance for creative function.

Consider that the midbrain, through which the brainstem and the cerebral hemispheres are joined, is crucial for instinctual drive regulation and that its many connections to the cerebral cortex are important, among other things, for motivating us to perform cortical tasks. It is to these connections that we owe both metaphoric thinking and the inspiration to create. The temporal lobes that are contained within the cortex, for instance, are of singular importance to the creative mind insofar as they are vital both to memory and emotional response (primarily through the hippocampus and the amygdala respectively) and to visual recognition as well. Temporal lobe activity may be triggered by activity in the limbic system (the emotional control network) through which the midbrain and the cerebral cortex interact. Suffering (such as Klee certainly did in the last five years of his life) is a good example: As Alice Flaherty has eloquently related, it can produce an increase in the desire to communicate, whether verbally or in some other way. A number of compulsive painters and writers, in fact, are known to have had temporal lobe epilepsy and, remarkably, as Flaherty reports, one even stopped painting when, in the effort to control his seizures, doctors removed his temporal lobe altogether. Studies, like those of Allan Snyder at The Center for the Mind in Australia, have also shown that transcranial magnetic stimulation to the left temporal lobe promotes both qualitative and quantitative change. Snyder's subjects ceased making childlike drawings and their renderings of reality became more naturalistic when that lobe was magnetically stimulated only to revert to the former caricature-like style shortly after the end of the trial. Klee himself did not have a seizure disorder. But it is extremely interesting that there is an association between epilepsy (of which 70 percent is temporal lobe) and a subtype of scleroderma (called linear scleroderma), and that this type of scleroderma may have as its only symptom intermittent dissociated states. One can only wonder whether the dream-like quality notable in much of Klee's late art (and to which I will return in a moment) and even the excessive withdrawal of libido from his bodily self were in some way linked to the dissociation produced by cerebral neuron dysfunction. One wonders as well whether Klee's hyper-productivity at the end of his life was connected to some temporal lobe abnormality, as was the hypergraphia of several well-known writers.[66]

More important, though, is that instinctual drives, whose generation in the brain Freud knew would one day be proved, exist to reduce "unpleasure," the feeling of disharmony within the body's internal environment that originates in the region of the brainstem known as the periaqueductal gray (or PAG). That the instinct toward the reduction of "unpleasure" induces life-enhancing activities and that cerebral structures, such as the PAG, are what monitor the homeostatic systems regulating our internal milieu would indicate that Klee's incredible productivity from 1937 on represented something much more profound than a fight against time.[67] Let me explain how I arrived at that conclusion.

In the tradition of Darwin many modern theorists have distinguished a number of basic emotions that are universally identifiable and believed to be "hardwired" in the brain.[68] These emotions are linked to motivation mainly through the cingulate gyrus, a subcortical structure that processes sensory information and reflects the body's internal states. With connections to areas important for memory, motor reaction, and physiological arousal, the cingulate is able to determine motivational priorities.[69] Now Howard Shevrin argues that human activities are in themselves motivational, that they render the emotional system operative and exert thereby a motivational pressure.[70] Because the making or viewing of art, for example, is for some an intrinsic source of pleasure, it can make one "feel good" and motivate continuance. This, in fact, is precisely what Freud had in mind when, in *Civilization and Its Discontents*, he gave what is perhaps his most comprehensive energic description of creative activity as a displacement of libidinal drive.[71]

In outlining what he terms "the laws of art" that account for the good feeling exploited by the artist, V. S. Ramachandran seemingly supports Shevrin's Freudian-based thinking. Included in these laws that constitute the neurological foundation of artistic universals are "grouping," "contrast," "symmetry," "balance," "metaphor," and others. An illustration of what is meant by the neurology of the first of these laws goes like this:

> Little does the salesgirl at Nordstrom realize that when she picks the "matching" red scarf for your red skirt, she is tapping into a deep principle underlying brain organization, and that she's taking advantage of the fact that your brain evolved to detect lions seen behind the foliage – so grouping "feels good." Of course the red scarf and red skirt are *not* one object, so logically they shouldn't be grouped, but that doesn't stop her from exploiting the "grouping law" anyway, to create an attractive combination. The same holds true for paintings and mattes, or even blobs of similar color on different objects within a painting.

But how does the brain accomplish the task of grouping when fragments are dispersed throughout the visual field? The answer has to do with the excitation of nerve cells (either separate cells or small clusters) in the visual cortex and color areas of the brain. And it is the synchronization of these nerve-cell firings that allows for the "pleasure" of whole object recognition. As Ramachandran explains it, they are "encoded in such a way that a coherent output emerges which is relayed to the emotional ('limbic') core of the brain, creating an 'Aha! Look here – it's an object!' jolt in you. This jolt 'arouses' you and makes you swivel your eyeballs and head towards the object. So you can pay attention to it, identify it, and take action."[72] The "aha" signal is precisely what is exploited by the artist when he makes use of grouping and it is this that presumably accounts, at least in part, for the motivational theory to which Shevrin subscribes.

Of course, aesthetic pleasure is irreducible to object recognition; the neurology of grouping pertains to associations as well as to the object as an autonomous entity, as we saw in the example of the red scarf and red skirt.

Indeed, resemblance extends beyond what is structurally united. Furthermore, grouping is but one contributory factor. It is, though, an important precipitant of the pleasure Klee himself referred to when he famously said "Art does not reproduce the visible but makes visible."[73] As the painter Bridget Riley has noted, Klee alludes in this statement not to the rendering of something previously unseen, but to the satisfaction derived from "the opening up of our vision to the greater and fuller span of the generative force of life." So it is that when all recognizable imagery is absent, such as in abstract art, the joy of "making visible" is in no way diminished.[74]

Klee left copious notes (more than 2500 notebook pages) from his many years of teaching at the Bauhaus and then the Düsseldorf Academy. These provide insight into his theory of form and the pleasurable aim of visual art. "The picture has no particular purpose. It only has the purpose of making us happy," he wrote in his notes from 1922.[75] How it achieves this purpose is by allowing artist and viewer to co-create, to participate together in the creative revelation of the life-giving force that renders art and nature analogous. In his *Pedagogical Sketchbook*, the Bauhaus lectures he published in 1925, Klee defines the dependence of this revelation upon the symbolic function of form and content. Two components of the symbolic order that "makes visible" the harmony between art and nature are balance and movement, with the former disclosing the latter in the "reciprocal motion" circumscribed by left–right, above–below rotations of the center. It is by virtue of the earth's terrestrial tension, moreover, that the rhythms of color (its gradations and contrasts) and of figuration (the inherent musicality of plastic form) relate to nature's dynamic forces. What Klee was making explicit for his students in his theoretical analyses of the pleasure of art, defined as perceiving the congruence between human and natural creation, were exactly those neurobiological foundations of aesthetics for which researchers would find empirical evidence more than three-quarters of a century later.

Balance, for instance, has been shown to be an intrinsic organizing principle of compositional approach. In fact, pictorial centricity (the physical center of the pictorial field) and visual equilibrium (the distribution and duration of eye movement fixations) coincide in the comprehensive transmission of aesthetic meaning. And it has been demonstrated that the perceptual salience of pictorial features (like the weight and positioning of shapes and colors) – in other words, the "visual rightness" of art – is independent of knowledge and experience in the aesthetic arena.[76] The rhythm of art, moreover, what Klee considered its movement, may well be a property shared by the frequency of brain organization. Shevrin, for one, believes this to be the case. In a recent paper he cites the role of functional resonating frequencies ("brain melodies") in the formation of visual and motor systems.[77] Attempting to discover whether these brain processes also carry affect information, he transformed sequences of time-frequency features into audible brain melodies and had them ranked according to their degree of unpleasantness.

The results led him to suspect a relation between negative affective signaling and inhibitory defenses. Shevrin has additionally considered the possibility that rhythmic patterns in the brain integrate diverse brain regions to instantiate unconscious conflict in much the same way that the synchronous firing of various visual systems allows for the perception of a whole object and even the grouping referred to above. The implications of this for the understanding of aesthetic experience, and Klee's in particular, are enormous: The expressive manifestations of our internal frequency patterns would be not only the rhythmic organizations perceptible in speech tones, gestures, and the like. They would be, as Shevrin notes, the transmission of affect states in art, whatever the medium. Shevrin's work is of the utmost importance insofar as conceiving of an inherent relation between the rhythm of art and brain frequency tells us much about the "pleasure" of aesthetic experience. It bridges the well-worn gap between mental events (whether conscious or unconscious) and neurobiological processes.[78] And it lends considerable credence both to the very assumptions intuited by Klee in his cosmological vision of art and to the idea that his disease played a highly significant role in the transformation of his style.

Balance and movement, as primary constituents of art's symbolic link to nature, were understood by Klee to be motivational of human function insofar as any disturbance in psychic or physical equilibrium provokes a compensatory impulse. It was this principle that guided his art even in his late style. In his final period, for instance, Klee preferred colors close to each other on the chromatic circle. Haftmann explains that this was because "such colors blend without a struggle, support each other, and thus contribute to the final colour." At times, though, he offset the tension posed by too great a span between colors by transposing them, as in the 1937 pastel *Harmonized Struggle* where he sought to balance the strife between orange and violet by transposing them into a generalized neutral tone of light gold.[79]

Mostly, though, in his last years Klee cultivated a linear art that was less preoccupied with color. Now more than ever the need to counterbalance tension and to attain a degree of serenity was compelling, but it was increasingly conveyed in the freeing of form and the considerable enlarging of the overall picture. Klee began at this time to dramatically simplify the ideograms and hieroglyphics of his art to the point of abstraction and thick marks gave his expressive signs even greater anonymity and remove. What had typically been fine, thin lines were now often thickened black bar strokes (as in the 1939 oil and watercolor *Destroyed Labyrinth* which is exemplary in this regard). As noted previously, he frequently turned from the richness of watercolor to the far coarser poster paint, thereby simplifying and enhancing the intensity of his line and from fine paper to a coarse parchment and fine canvas to coarse sacking. The 1937 work *Animals Perform a Comedy* was even painted on an old tablecloth and *Vigilant Angel*, also from 1939, on newspaper.[80] The result of this transformation was an asceticism that gave his aesthetic ideals of balance and movement new meaning.

The starkness of his late style has provoked many a critic to write of the metaphysical quality of Klee's late art. The late drawings, in particular, underscore his statement that art has a "salutary effect." For their unique combination of pathos and remoteness drives home the idea that, as Klee said, "imagination, borne on the wings of instinctual stimuli, conjures up states of being that are somehow more encouraging and more inspiring than those we know on earth or in our conscious dreams." Symbols, he also wrote, console the mind "by showing it that there is something more than the earthly and its possible intensifications."[81] Of course, the transcendental element is no more restricted to the power of symbols to free us from the terrestrial arena than it is to the thematic preoccupations with death as seen in the series of angels and boat paintings. Many of the drawings from Klee's last two years reveal a purposeful lack of detail and substance so persistent and powerful that one is obliged to look beyond their symbolic or metaphorical meaning, and even beyond the aesthetic valuation of minimalism, to locate its source. Indeed, just as the copious production of the last period stemmed from something more than the race against time, the transcendental quality of the late style derived from something more than either narrative purpose or aesthetic device.

We might consider that by partaking of the supernatural through its depiction in his work Klee felt he regained a measure of control. That is, by sharing in the omniscience of a creature not of this world (the angel) and imaging the journey beyond the here and now (the boat), he recovered some command over his life. But there is also the artist's profoundly visual thinking that itself contributed to the otherworldly quality of his late style. What I refer to is the very process of figuration that became even more important to Klee in his last years than in the preceding periods when his greatest preoccupation was color. Christian Geelhaar claims in his biography of the artist that the angels in the late work represent a proximity to God as much as an awareness of death. Critic Gottfried Boehm, however, maintains that neither Christian iconography nor, for that matter, literary references (to Rilke, for instance) explain the angel theme. In claiming that the angel symbolizes (as both human and deity) the transition not from life to death but from formlessness to form,[82] Boehm throws into question narrative and aesthetic strategies at once. Similarly, Kudielka has noted that the late work pays "homage to the pleasures of a yet unformed life" in diverting "our attention to a primal state of formation [. . .] where the potential of face, vessel or figure is as yet unresolved." With a once again thinner and suppler line, the drawings of the last two years of Klee's life are said to yield "to a vast luminous whiteness as the impalpable matrix of formation."[83] To this I would add that, in so doing, they reveal the power inherent within the balance and movement of form even before they are made explicit in the constitution of recognizable shapes.

This newly defined focus on figuration, in other words, more than the metaphorical potential of the narrative content, reveals the value of art to enhance a sense of wholeness and respond thereby to the instinctual pull of the life drive.[84]

Throughout the enormous quantity of drawings from Klee's last few years and some of the late paintings as well, however, disintegration is a recurrent motif. In the anonymity of faces, the fragmentation of bodies, and the disproportion of human extremities (Klee often depicted swellings as would be caused by his disease), decomposition and an overall feeling of dissolution subtend the transcendental quality of the work whose emphasis is on figuration. Just how this concern with giving form to deformation is compatible with my view of Klee's late creative impulse as life enhancing becomes clearer when we recognize that beyond the focus on impairment and mortality Klee's final vision of balance and movement was in the service of adjustment. What the defensive mechanism of decathexis afforded him was a means of protection against the continued mourning of a lost self-representation.

Felix Klee commented that throughout his life his father was "intensely interested in people's faces. In innumerable drawings he sought to catch the grimaces and mimicry of an actor, the good and evil, humanness and inhumanness of facial expression. Even his fish wear human expressions [. . .]."[85] Though faceless figurations do appear before he fell ill, the migration from this overt physiognomy, characteristic of the work preceding the creative upsurge of 1937, to the latent physiognomy of the dissociated figurations typical of the late period is worthy of note. As early as 1909, for instance, Klee depicted himself as faceless in the watercolor *The Draughtsman at the Window*. What changed some 30 years later, however, was that the face no longer typically appeared hidden, present but shaded by brush strokes. Instead, the anonymity arose from only subtle suggestions of a visage, as in the "Approximation" series of 1939, or from the radical decomposition of facial features. In *Love Song by the New Moon*, a 1939 watercolor on burlap, the face, like the rest of the body, appears disjointed ("broken up and reconstituted" is how Grohmann describes it). *Enclose*, from the same year, is a semicircular head within which there are only two black circles for eyes. It rests on an abstract torso flanked by two black heavenly bodies on the upper left and a sign lower right that balance the composition. A lyrical movement emanates from the thick lines of the bar strokes containing the marks of a dry brush rhythmic in themselves.[86] In *Hand and Little Hand*, also from 1939, the artist's faceless head is separated from his disease-ridden body with its swollen extremities (Figure 4.2).

Stick figures were for Klee an additional means of psychically decathecting body and world and they, like the blank faces, provide another dimension to the metaphysical quality of the late work. In a series of paintings in 1935, Klee was already reducing to child-like primitivism figures having the

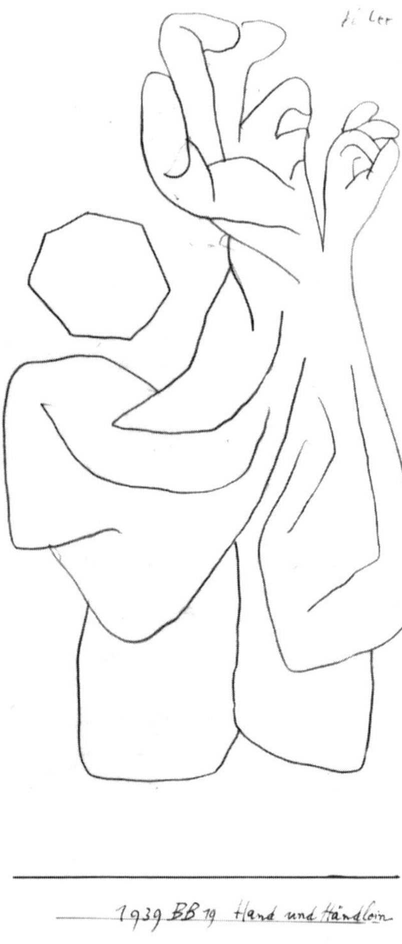

Figure 4.2 Hand und Händlein, 1939, 539 (BB19). Bleistift auf Papier auf Karton; 29.7 × 20.9 cm.

unadorned line as their only source of balance and movement. But it is in the stick figures from 1937 and after, and in other figurations that are not properly stick figures but geometric forms exhibiting the same striving for harmony and order, that we find the impetus toward well-being defined as the primary motivation for this art. And it is this drive, rather than the focus on nostalgia or loss, which prevents the late style from giving way to morbidity despite the artist's awareness of impending death.

In the 1938 pencil on paper drawing *Repair*, the artist, pen in hand, observes his own body parts strewn before him. In *Princess of the Shadows*,

Poisonous Apples, and *Demon*, deeply moving drawings from 1940, eyes on utterly expressionless faces are focussed on the swelling and rigid contours of the robotic bodies to which they belong. Another drawing from the same year, *Alack-a-day!*, bears but a hint of sadness in a slightly downturned mouth adorning a head horizontally posed on a conspicuously immobile body. The open spaces, disjointed facial features, and disconnected limbs of the extraordinary *Outbreak of Fear* (1939) or of the often capricious "Eidola" series similarly confer on the late works what Kudielka calls "a new dynamism and scale."[87] If Klee could write, "I create in order not to cry, that is the first and last reason," it is because as an alternative to weeping his work clarified the reality of his situation and provided a means of adaptation. Such was the function, late in his life, of the drawings of dismemberment and fragmentation, those, for instance, of the 1939 "The Inferner Park" series where the play of rounded and angular forms projects diverse rhythms onto a universe without depth, if not without longing.

Klee wrote to Felix in 1939 that one result of his illness was that "a certain adaptation" was taking place in the preponderance of drawing.[88] The eradication of any semblance of a world order, the almost total elimination of associations to his personal environs, the affectless forms, and the emptiness of the spaces between them are all evidence of the withdrawal of libidinal investment characteristic of the work of this period. And it is precisely this disengagement that reveals that the "adaptation" of which he wrote to his son consisted in something more profound than a physical accommodation of his hardening skin.

The non-material universe of Klee's late art, in sum, with its withdrawal of libidinal investment in the body and its derealization of the exterior world, had a therapeutic function not to be overlooked. A century ago Freud wrote of the "psycho-physical relation to conditions of stability and instability" – of the constancy-seeking instinctual efforts of the mind/brain – in *Beyond the Pleasure Principle* and elsewhere. He targeted homeostasis when he described the endeavor of mental apparatus "to keep the quantity of excitation present in it as low as possible or at least to keep it constant." Indeed, in an 1893 lecture he very explicitly stated: "If a person experiences a psychical impression, something in his nervous system which we will for the moment call the 'sum of excitation' is increased. Now in every individual there exists a tendency to diminish this sum of excitation once more, in order to preserve his health."[89] The neurobiology of drive and the link between subjective feeling states and homeostasis was not scientifically demonstrable then. But, as the underlying principle of mind/brain organization, it comes to the fore in all that Solms, Panksepp, Shevrin, and others engaged in neuro-psychoanalytic research are now undertaking. Of course, the notion of a redistribution of drive as a consequence of changes in the ego, such as Freud conceived of it and such as I have tried to show in Klee's work, is still disputed. But I believe that over time we will come to appreciate the value of such knowledge for our understanding of a variety of humanistic endeavors, for it provides far more than a mechanistic view of the pleasure derived from them.

I have suggested the need to view Klee's late style in the context of the life force reflected in the motivational drive or pleasure-seeking aims (that, after all, are the very reason our internal representations exist). I have claimed that, when viewed in the context of the biological tendency toward self-preservation, the metaphysical quality that defines Klee's style at the end of his life was not limited to a metaphorical expression of a preoccupation with mortality. And I have argued that Klee's voluminous output late in his life (1654 works in a period of 16 months!) emanated from the need to retrieve a sense of internal constancy when he was coping with the loss of body integrity to which his disease gave rise. What is illustrated by the compulsive redirecting of his libidinal energy away from the source of distress and onto his art is precisely that creativity has a regulatory bearing on existence, that as a search for meaning it performs a fundamentally homeostatic role. Jaak Panksepp has demonstrated that the human brain contains a basic impulse to make sense of the environment in which we live. This is the "foraging/exploration/investigation/curiosity/interest/expectancy/SEEKING" system that both "*drives* and *energizes* [. . .] the search for higher meaning" and "responds unconditionally to homeostatic imbalances" as well.[90] I have aimed to show in this chapter that aesthetic experience may provide a way into that drive-motivated system and that by inducing subjective feeling states it taps into the deepest neural networks ensuring homeostasis.

We have seen that the remove of Klee's late style was evident from the start (especially in the self-portraits), but that the balance between "cathectic potential" and "counter cathectic force" shifted toward the end of his life. In *Wandering Artist: A Poster* (1940) the artist represented himself as totally without expression; only black dots for eyes remain on his face. In fact, all that indicates his presence in the picture is his name homonymically situated (clé) within the image so complete is his withdrawal.[91] Given that drives are biologically rooted and, as we shall see in the next chapter, that the self has neurological referents, it is insufficient, simplistic even, to view Klee's late work (both its style and its profusion) as unrelated to his disease. Similarly, it is reductive to account for the stylistic change merely by citing the influence on him of the modernist aesthetic. The significance for Klee of Matisse's lyricism, the surrealists' automatism, and Picasso's expressive qualities is undeniable. And I do not wish to minimize what Franciscono, for one, has argued so convincingly and elegantly with regard to the meaning these and other artists who were roughly Klee's contemporaries had for him.[92] But I do believe the attraction of this aesthetic was due to its resonance with viscerally altered schemata that were externalized in the effort to mediate aesthetically a rapidly diminishing self-representation and recover the integrity of an internal self and object world.

Chapter 5

The shape of process

Martha Graham's journey into the self

Early in this book I took a new look at an old question. I considered what recent findings on the brain bring to the once popular but as yet unresolved matter of the "feminine" in art. For several decades women have been seeking to refine the meaning of what it is to be and even to create as a woman. However defined – psychodynamically, culturally, or biologically – the "feminine" has come to be seen as a locality whence the self, the inner person, may make or view creative work. What neuroscience brings to this is an understanding of how, specifically, the parameters of this site are constituted and, more generally, what constitutes body awareness and the mental representation of self.

Exploring Beckett's metaphoric depiction of extreme ego weakness and the anxiety of dissolution associated with frail psychic boundaries, I aimed to show how a preoccupation with mental illness provoked an experience of creativity discernible as a stabilizing force. Focussing primarily on the disembodied characterization of the playwright's masterful *Not I*, I was again concerned with imaginative expression as it relates to the mind/brain's representation of a primordial self. The conflated visual and verbal projection of the impaired self/non-self differentiation in Beckett's play revealed how both the most primitive sensations connected with the formation of the body-ego and the ego's difficulties in coping with surexcitation and a barrage of internal stimuli may be recalled in the literary work of art.

Creativity in the service of equilibration took a different turn in the chapter on Klee where real as opposed to metaphoric illness was the point of departure for consideration of the interplay between perception and the dynamic representations of self. In the context of a disfiguring disease, one that not only distorted his outward appearance but how he felt, quite literally, within his skin, it may be said that Klee's creative objective was redefined. Within the framework of his scleroderma, the dramatic stylistic changes of Klee's late art and the extraordinarily prolific creative outpouring of the last years of his life were thus seen in that chapter as originating primarily in the loss of integrity of his inner representational world. There, too, inquiry into the nature of creative experience and into the specificity of its function within the context of an individual's life was impelled by the belief that the "pleasure" of art is related to the need for constancy in the internal environment of the self.

I would like now to consider how another art form, dance, may relate to homeodynamic stability in ways that literature and painting do not. Why one expressive medium as opposed to any other is the choice of a given artist cannot, of course, be addressed outside the context of that individual's psychic life. What can be generically assessed, though, are differences in the physiological resonance of the arts – differences in the ways that the arts not only reflect but also act on the artist or spectator's internal states – a matter far more complex than the dichotomies of verbal/non-verbal and visual/non-visual would have us believe. Indeed, such taxonomy is of little use in the effort to understand these differences for two principal reasons: The first is that, just as a single mental task implicates multiple brain functions, one brain function may be implicated in a variety of mental tasks. Visual imagery alone, for instance, is involved in memory and reasoning as well as in visual perception. We know from neuroimaging studies that the visual imaging structures of the brain are even activated when no overt visual perception is taking place. Likewise, motor structures may be activated when only the visual imagery of motor behavior, not the overt motor task, is tested.[1] The second is simply the considerable overlap in all the arts, particularly in the modern and postmodern eras, of expressive media. Klee, for example, used words in his paintings that, like his titles, bear semantically, syntactically, and paradigmatically on the meaning we visually perceive in or project onto his art. Moreover, it was through music (he was an accomplished violinist born of a musician father and married to a pianist) that he found the means to understand both color and form. So, too, *Not I* is a literary text; written for the theater, however, it is also and perhaps most significantly a visual work of art.

Beckett, in fact, stretched the dramatic genre well beyond its conventional limits. If *Waiting for Godot* (1952) revolutionized the theater it was precisely because the waiting that the play was about was the waiting the audience was made to endure. *Endgame* (1957) is, similarly, a wait for the finish: From the first spoken line – "Finished, it's finished, it must be nearly finished" – to the last – "You . . . remain" – what is said and what the audience experiences are merged. *Play* (1964) begins with a character's response to the faint spot that lights her: "Yes, strange, darkness best, and the darker the worse, till all dark, then all well, for the time, but it will come, the time will come, the thing is there, you'll see it, get off me, keep off me, all dark, all still, all over, wiped out –." In *Breath* (1970), synchronized light and recorded breath controlled by two identical cries of a newborn are all that is left of the dialogue, character, and action that normally make up the theater event, rendering congruent the content of the fiction and the theatrical experience.[2] Many of the playwright's other works exhibit this "theatereality" (as Ruby Cohn famously called it): Krapp's time, in *Krapp's Last Tape*, like that of the woman in *Rockaby*, is our time in the theater as much as any other. And in *Not I*, as we saw in Chapter 3,

Mouth emerges as this "tiny little girl" projected "before her time" into this "godforsaken hole" that is, simultaneously, the orifice constituting this unusual dramatis persona and the darkened world of the theater itself.

In the same way, dance, like music, takes place in (and thereby articulates) real time. Whereas the literary text and the plastic arts transport reader and viewer into virtual worlds, both dance and music are based in the actuality of performance. As such, they differ ontologically from the nonperformance-based arts, meaning that they are dissimilar for creator and spectator on multiple levels inclusive of perception, cognition, and the transmission and arousal of affect. Undoubtedly, they impact both the performer and perceiver in many of the same ways as, say, a novel or painting, for the neurophysiological determinants of feeling, though particular to each individual, are intrinsic to the brain's emotional operating systems. But the mechanisms of communication are not the same: Expression in real time bypasses the external referent. As Susanne Langer noted, musical notes, unlike words, have no innate meanings. Their significance derives purely from the relationship between them. Though in a sense grammatical and syntactical, they do not signify by sign and symbol, as language does.[3] The same is true of the movements choreographed into a ballet or modern dance. The only reality is that of the dancer's body, which cannot designate any other reality existing a priori outside it. This is not to say that the narrative content of a dance work is not referential, but that the instrument of its expression is devoid of connotation. As inherently temporal arts, dance and music are meaningful reflections of their own signifying process; in revealing something of the world, they necessarily reveal their unique self-referentiality as well.

Dance and music are also alike in that they signify through motion. Rhythm, motion's primary structure, shapes music from a succession of auditory tones, just as it shapes dance from a succession of physical movements. In truth, though, it is not that music itself moves – it does not occupy space in the same way as dance – but rather that we project the illusion of movement onto it.[4] How we do so has been studied by many throughout history and it is not my intent to enter the centuries-long debate on this art's expressivity. My interest lies, rather, in the relation between real movement, that of the dance it comprises, and somatopsychic constancy, for dance differs from all other art forms, including music, in transforming – through the body's energic configuration of space – subjectivity. Indeed, it is the inseparability of bodily movements from modes of being in dance that makes it an art as opposed to a sport. Though music, kinesthetically speaking, is the medium to which dance is most closely connected, the neurophysiological workings of the body and the subjectivity they support render dance, in a sense, prior to music. Because music as pure form is illusory movement, we might even say, with one philosopher, that "what singers and players of instruments do is already to dance, in that they perform the dance that will embody the form that the music identifies."[5] In fact, the physicality of dance, its consonance with bodily function, serves consciousness (and thus homeostasis) in a way that no other art can: Dance training and performance inform the self – directly through the moving body – of what and how it feels.

In a word, then, the idea I will develop in this chapter is that dance is unique in transposing the dancer, precisely through the movement of his or her body, into an altered state of being. That is to say that the dancer's relation to time, space, and the world at large is changed through a kind of "bodily consciousness" (to borrow a term from Francis Sparshott)[6] and that this transformation is subjectively perceived as self-knowledge or, more precisely, a reinforced sense of self. To make the point I will focus on a dancer for whom this self-enhancement was framed by the relation of the individual to the whole of humanity and for whom the aesthetic, as a consequence, was deeply entwined with the mythological and with the psychological symbolism that mythology unveils.

Among the most important creative geniuses of the twentieth century (she is often compared with Stravinsky, Joyce, and Picasso), Martha Graham used to say "You should *be* the beat, not *follow* the beat"[7] and she created a technique and styled a choreography that accentuated this orientation to self *within* rhythm. In one of her many letters to the lay psychoanalyst Frances Wickes – who, as we shall see, would have a great influence on her creative activity as well as on her daily life – Graham speaks of her preliminary meetings with the composer for her 1962 *Legend of Judith*. What she describes is how these meetings were responsible for the emergence of a company work from what had previously been a solo (*Judith*, 1950) and, in alluding to the significant broadening of the scope of the dance, Graham acknowledges that music always radically affected her in this way. Similarly, in another letter to Wickes she finds fault with George Balanchine (for whom she undertook a depiction of Mary, Queen of Scots, in the 1959 combined choreographic effort *Episodes*) for sacrificing dance, as she saw it, to his passion for music. Graham believed that, insofar as dance has its own dynamic, music must remain separate from the vitality and necessity of movement; in other words, it must not carry the dance or the dancer. In fact, one of her last works, *Night Chant* (1988) was to have music composed by Pierre Boulez. While the score was "exciting," she told a *New York Times* reporter, it was too "dominant" and lacked "that intrinsic let-it-aloneness that music should have."[8] Graham had no interest in interpreting music through movement and she resisted the seductive power of audible rhythm, at least in the early part of her career, by beginning a work in silence, seeking first the rhythm that would be perceptible to the eye rather than the ear.[9] When later she added the musical composition, there was a renewed source of inspiration which enriched the choreography without compromising its organic purpose. Dance, for her, always had a fundamental reason for being, a sense of urgency that she called in yet another letter the "livingness" at its root; without this, one does little more than display the result of moving at the expense of its cause. When dance is not emptied of meaning, either by subservience to music, a "bleakness of spirit," or some other means, it could have for Graham a distinctly liberating effect. The creation of *Episodes*, in fact, freed her by putting her once again "in circulation with [her] inner self" after a period she described as a "limbo of lethargy or negativism or emotional fatigue."[10]

Graham's view of dance – from the use of training to discipline and release the energy of the nervous system to the freeing of the body into a deepened awareness of self – says much about the physiological relation between that art and music. In another of her letters to the analyst/friend she mostly addressed as "Mrs. Wickes," Graham writes of her need to achieve "a closer association" between dance and music than she had had of late. She terms what she is seeking a "breath association" – as opposed to an "intellectual association" – and she explains it in terms of a Beethoven quartet she had recently heard in concert. This music, she tells Wickes, "used silence and the suspension of stop in just the way I hope to use it someday in dance with music. The deep internal, eternal rhythm does not stop, is in no way broken, but is enhanced by an ability to wait, to hold, to listen to the inner breathing of life."[11] (This was in 1953. Matt Turney, who danced in the Graham company through the 1950s and 1960s, would relate in an interview many years later how the choreographer worked to coordinate the musical with the movement accents: "Don't anticipate," Graham would say, ". . . don't even out the dynamics.")[12] What she was after was not only the preservation of the primary inspiration for the work, the movement's reason for being, but the *drama* of the interplay between dance and music's rhythmic structures. Graham intensified the theatrical value of her choreography precisely by not allowing the affective dimension of the movement's rhythm to be governed by the affective dimension of the rhythm of the music. But to better understand Graham's theatrical aesthetic and the meaning both dancing and the creation of dances had for her as an individual, we need to look more closely at the physiology of affect as it is transmitted through sound and movement. This should allow us to better appreciate both the phenomenology of dance in its difference from music, a difference that is profound despite the kinesthetic affinity, and the psychological implications of the mythological undercurrents of Graham's artistic vision.

* * *

That aesthetic experience elicits the perceptual response we feel as emotion because it is in sync with the dynamic of tension and release at the core of affect is the thesis Gilbert Rose has maintained throughout his writings. In his most recent book, *Between Couch and Piano*, Rose situates more precisely in relation to the nervous system the congruence between music's rhythmic structures and this dynamic structure of affect noting that the nervous system "functions by way of periodicity: it sends out intermittent firings which result in a continuous movement, sensation or state." He is right, of course, to observe that there are also "non-nervous system organs that contribute rhythmic information that is integrated by the nervous system." And he is right that there are processes, chemical and metabolic, also underlying "the time sense of human beings." Why then, I wonder, does he emphasize the idea that music is "a *transformation* of [an] *inter*personal system of affect regulation to an *intra*psychic, abstract level" evocative of "early internalizations"?[13] Why not see the *intra*psychic processes of affect arousal and regulation by the brain's innate emotional systems – the activation of those brain structures that respond to homeostatic disturbance or physiological disequilibrium with desire and affectively motivated behavior – as primary in the making of and listening to music? Viewing our affective resonance with the rhythmic structures of sound, and also of movement, as emerging from the complex interaction of our innate emotional systems with our neurally based developmental perceptions of self and reality would certainly be consonant with the most recent advances in neuroscientific thinking. And it would also be in keeping with the psychoanalytic thinking that resists reducing to the matrix of attachments formed early in life the innate affective motivation of the brain's instinctual mechanisms.

The suggestion, however, that the pleasure of music springs from the emotional quality of the interrelational experience of the infant–mother dyad is not new. Sarah Nettleton tells us that "The tensions and resolutions present in even the simplest of tunes will resonate [. . .] with the infant's experience – of waiting for and then receiving the breast, of transient discomfort or of brief maternal absences." And, certainly, this is true (despite the no doubt unintended implication that music resonates only with those having had significant early attachments or "good-enough" mothering). But the point is that there is a deeper connection that is not interrelational: the resonance with and indeed stimulation of the meter of music in the dynamic sensations of the body. This, as Nettleton notes, is what is echoed as we rock a baby to sleep. That it can also develop into compulsive rocking or head banging suggests, as she puts it, "that rhythm exists prior to the split between good and bad, before we imbue it with a particular emotional quality; it is a basic ingredient of our psychic experience."[14] There is, in other words, an intrapsychic experience of rhythm – one associated with physiological equilibrium and disequilibrium – whose primacy renders it more relevant to the rhythmic structure of both music and dance than the interpsychic relation emphasized by Rose. Listen to the late music theorist David Epstein:

> It is but a small and logical step from the dynamic buildup and release of tensions [. . .] to the factor of motion, as it operates in music as the carrier of these tensions and as the means through which tensions are controlled, modulated, and ultimately resolved. For our sense of musical motion is in part felt physically (muscularly) and psychologically in terms

> of tension and release. Tension/release may indeed be the essential factor, conveying the sensation of movement, of motion, in the absence of true physical motion in space.[15]

That our physiological rhythms, those of our very organicity, are similar or even identical in form to the auditory patterns of music has long been noted, but only now are we beginning to understand the curious intimacy between them. Only now are we beginning to grasp the psychodynamic significance of the analogy and that what accounts for the emotional meaning of a rhythmic pattern, whether rendered in sound or in movement, is something rhythmic about the brain itself. If emotion were not rhythmically rooted in the brain's organization, particular rhythmic patterns would not project anger or gaiety, for instance, in virtually every culture throughout the world. Moreover, it is only now that we are beginning to conceive of the evolutionary and survival benefits that undoubtedly derived from the arousal of emotion and other bodily responses to sound.[16] Damasio, among others, has lamented the disregard on the part of modern science for both the homeostatic and evolutionary gains that stem from the architecture and operation of the mind–brain. It is not that scientists were not preoccupied throughout the twentieth century with the neurophysiology of homeostasis, with its neuroanatomical and neurochemical components and with those systems (endocrine, immune, and nervous) upon which it depends. They were. But emotion as a key ingredient has, until recently, been neglected in their work. As Damasio and others have demonstrated, the emotions play an important regulatory role in the life of the human being; they are based on biological processes having a long evolutionary history. With their origin in subcortical structures that access the higher brain regions to represent and coordinate bodily states, what they are fundamentally about is the body and their expression in art has thus not only served us culturally but as a means of adaptation as well.[17]

As though to illustrate the point, Jaak Panksepp and Günther Bernatzky have noted the interaction of arousal control systems, such as those based on the chemical control (by norepinephrine and serotonin) of emotional response, with music. Indicating the importance of a generalized motivational system for the intra-cerebral estimation of time flow, they have hypothesized a mechanism generating "various musical expectancies, especially those related to the rhythmic movements of the body." These, in turn, appear as a kind of "ancestral pre-adaptation for the emotional components of music."[18] The substantiation of Damasio cum Panksepp and Bernatzky's evolutionary perspective is alone evidence of a connection between human physiology and rhythm more primary than that between rhythm and early interpsychic experience. In fact, the one seemingly explains the other: Insofar as it is our intra-cerebral emotional brain circuitry – the relay systems that transmit information from the internal and external environment into the regions responsible for motivated behavior – that allows for the dyadic attachment in the first place, is it not logical that the primary level of the emotional resonance of rhythmic sound and movement would be that of these deep (subcortical) systems?

Rose is most successful, to my way of thinking, when he bridges the arousal of affect by art with the perception of the internal world. Citing Mark Solms and Edward Nersessian, he writes: "Contemporary psychoanalysis and neuroscience agree that when an external event evokes affects, 'the felt emotion is a perception of the *subjective response* to that event; it is not a perception of the external event itself.'" His point is that the power of aesthetic form lies in its enhancement of self-recognition – which I would qualify as the brain's recognition of diverse feeling states within the body – for an increased sense of self is the outcome of the "subjective response" in question. In concluding that it is the "*kinesthetic* experience of rhythmic motion" that is the most significant element of self-recognition he brings us, in fact, to the very crux of the matter: Music and dance bear on affect and its regulation precisely by eliciting an emotional response that is constructed on body representation.[19] In other words, *the link between the sensory experience of rhythm and the structural pattern of affect is the physical self schema, the awareness of one's bodily self in the kinesthetic quality of music and dance.*

Sensory information is transmitted from the surface of the body to its representation in the brain (that is, to the representation of our physical selves known as the homunculus) by way of synaptic connections and their relay to neurons in the cerebral cortex. Thus a sensory map is established that is both structurally universal (the body's right side, for example, is represented in the left hemisphere and vice versa) and distinctive. It is distinctive in part because it is modifiable by the usage of the sensory pathways over time. Indeed, studies have shown the brains of musicians to be different from those of non-musicians. In one, where professional musicians were matched for age, sex, and handedness with non-musician controls, the anterior half of the corpus callosum was considerably increased in those musicians who had begun training before the age of seven. Comparative analysis with previous studies showing a positive anatomic correlation between the groups indicated that the disparity in size was due to interhemispheric communication and perhaps also to hemispheric asymmetry in the sensorimotor areas. In another study the cortical representation of the fingers of the left hand of violinists, the hand that requires persistent digital manipulation, was seen on imaging to be larger than that of the right. Still other research has shown a significant asymmetry in a region of the brain associated with language and auditory processing (the planum temporale) in musicians with absolute pitch. While this may be genetic and determined in utero, there has been speculation that it is the result of an early exposure to music. One study which looked at differences in the way in which the various patterns of neural connections are bound together in the brains of musicians and non-musicians led to the hypothesis that they owed to the cognitive and motor effects of continuous musical training throughout childhood and adolescence.[20]

More relevant to our present purposes, however, is a region of the brain known to be involved in the mediation of affect, the inferior colliculus, which Panksepp and Bernatzky refer to as "an obligatory brainstem way-station for auditory processing." Not only may this region "mediate attachments we develop to certain sounds (e.g. the voices of those we love) and hence [. . .] to certain types of music," but it is "adjacent to the PAG where all emotional systems converge upon a coherent self-representation of the organism, a primordial core consciousness."[21] Panksepp has written elsewhere on the affective nature of this primal awareness and on the influence of the primal emotional circuits on self-recognition. Of particular interest is the following in which he cites not only the stabilizing effects of the self-schema, but the regulatory influence of certain kinds of input on self-awareness; that is, the modification of affective consciousness precisely by the input that is sensory-motor rhythm:

> [T]he self-schema provides input into many sensory analyzers, and it is also strongly influenced by the primal emotional circuits [. . .] This foundation process – the primordial self-schema – [. . .] not only helps guide many higher perceptual processes, by promoting attentional focus and perceptual sensitivity, but also may provide a fundamental stability for the psychological "binding" that is characteristic of our perceptual field. Presumably, this foundation process [. . .] may be strongly and automatically modified by various other influences – by conditioned emotional "triggers," by meditation, by music, dance, and probably a variety of other rhythmic sensory-motor inputs and activities.[22]

What I am getting at here are these two points: First, music, like dance, bears on somatopsychic equilibrium through the subservience of psychic conceptualization to sensorimotor experience. And, second, the constitution and perception of rhythmic structures in sound and movement emerge from the neurobiological generation of and impact on emotion. With regard to the first, that we perceive through the body yet conceive through the mind has been proven erroneous by, among others, Lakoff and Johnson with their illustrations of the shaping of conceptual structures by bodily projections. In *Philosophy in the Flesh*, they showed how spatial relations and various other image schemas are neurally modeled on, which is to say comprehended through, the body. (The notion is not incompatible with Freudian drive theory and the idea that reality is tested and the ego integrated though the dominance of bodily urges.) Neuroscientists, like Damasio, have demonstrated how information about the body is relayed via pathways throughout the central nervous system to the brain where it is acted upon in the service of equilibrium. Neuropsychologists, like Solms and Turnbull, have shown how we "know" if this information is succeeding in maintaining the balance. Simply put, we "know" through consciousness whose primary function is to evaluate how we feel and to monitor our homeostatic systems. What this has to do with music and dance is that these time-based art forms are unifying experiences: In ways that differ from those arts that do not create time through rhythm (ways about which I will say more shortly), they influence the body's regulatory capacities and enhance the harmonious integration of self and world.

Concerning the second point, any investigation of the expressive foundation of art (à la Langer) has necessarily, today, to look at the origin of affect and its neurobiological sources. Indeed, if anything can deconstruct the weary association of psychopathology to creativity, it is a better understanding of how art, rather than being merely symptomatic of feelings, both emanates from and stimulates them. That is to say that the well-worn link between creativity and madness is undone by the recognition that brain circuits are not uni-directional; that, rather, they are like two-way streets with a constant flow of traffic in both directions. Our chemico-physiological makeup, moreover, is such that emotions (from which feelings derive) affect our bodies: Sadness or joy may produce tears, or changes in bodily states, like the quickening or slowing of breathing or the raising or lowering of blood pressure, pulse, and heart rate. Though many brain functions are related to motion, specific structures responsible for the control of the body's physical movement (the basal ganglia and cerebellum) are located right next to the limbic system, which (as noted earlier) accounts for the close connection of certain body movement disorders to emotion.[23] But what this may also explain is the bodily urge to move to music. It increasingly looks as though music and dance not only arise from but also stimulate feelings precisely by tapping into the brain's emotional systems. In fact, music's ability to generate affect and its impact on the brain systems controlling movement are why music and dance may be said to share an ancestral relationship. As Panksepp and Bernatzky see it, these two art forms may well have co-evolved precisely from the dynamics of emotional arousal.[24] That emotions are both expressible in and generated by rhythmic movements of the body, in other words, may have been the very impetus for their cultural evolution.

The specificity of dance, however, lies elsewhere. Without going further into the complexities of sensory perception and its relation to the structural and chemical emotional systems of the brain that stimulate and are stimulated by it, we can distinguish a psychodynamics of motility, movement's own rhythmic constitution of affect, from the affective temporality of music. Dance creates time through what one theorist calls the "projectional quality of force," the manner or way in which force is released.[25] Its intensity, its prolongation and discharge of tension, determines the ebb and flow of phrasing in movement. In so doing, force (or the flow of energy) evokes affective meaning in choreography. The qualitative aspect of rhythm is thus directly associated with sensations within the body, with the detection of tension by receptors in the body's muscular sectors and with the information conveyed by them to the central nervous system. And the aesthetic dimension of dance is precisely the affective signification of this control of energy. When dancers speak of the "need" to move, they are recognizing a motor impulse that is deeply somatic. Indeed, the somatic senses, including proprioception (the ability to sense balance, position, location, and movement of the body) and kinesthesia (the ability to feel the body's muscular tensions), are mediated by pathways that convey information to the brain; information that may become conscious or not. This relay of information – this "bodily consciousness" – serves the purposes of perception, arousal, and motor control.

A drive in its own right, moreover, the motor impulse is multidetermined: In the first years of life rhythmic motor patterns overtly display their affective relation to oral, anal, and genital urges; in the second and third years, in fact, the motor drive dominates all others. As a component of the sexual instinct, a means of aggression, a way of overcoming anxiety, and so on, the motility urge may retain a profound psychological significance for the individual and may derive from deep within his or her earliest psychic organization.[26] For this reason, though studies reveal the enhancement of cognitive capacities in the highly trained dancer, cortical indications of changes induced by the discipline of motor functions do not fully account for the homeodynamic influence of dance movement.

Dancers generally begin training while very young so as to develop the musculature required for this art. But what is also derived from the early practice of rigorous movement, and this owing to the younger brain's having greater plasticity than the older one, is the development of more finely tuned synaptic connections and thus a more finely tuned representation of the body and the bodily component of the self-schema. In the writer or painter activity-based modification may occur in the areas involving language, spatial, and other skills related to the higher brain regions, and the strengthening of neural connections in one area of the brain probably benefits others. But the sensorimotor input of dance singularly acts on somatopsychic stability through a "continuity of reference" (the term is Damasio's) that bodily movement is unique in supporting as it does. As ordered motion, dance reflects the functionally rhythmic tensions of our organicity, the pulsation of brain patterns, of respiration, and even of what Damasio describes as the "pulses" of core consciousness. These are the "many singular units of consciousness occurring one after the other" at intervals so small and with "the amount of parallel pulses so abundant" that they are registered only as a "continuous, whirring blur."[27] At the same time, though, there is a level of bodily experience that, however intertwined with it, is irreducible to neurobiology.

Indeed, the body has what Maxine Sheets-Johnstone calls "an individual kinetic history." As she so rightly describes it, the body is "rich in movement memories, expectations, and values" and "has in consequence developed certain kinetic dispositions, habits, and ways of responding."[28] Martha Graham was acutely aware of this and if she knew how to get the best from her dancers, particularly in the "golden era" of the Graham company, the 1950s and 1960s, it was precisely that she spoke to their special qualities as individuals. She choreographed in function of *their* strengths and *their* personalities. I do not refer here simply to the dancers' technical virtuosity but to their identities and Graham's means of bolstering their sense of self in even the simplest of movements. "Martha was able to develop with any class she worked with – but particularly with the company – a way of walking, with such dignity, quietness and a sense of self," Jane Dudley, who joined the Graham company in the mid-1930s, has said. Helen McGehee, who became a company member a decade later, has also noted Graham's encouraging of "the individual quest" through dance and she too has spoken of the realization of her own identity through the very act of moving. Similarly, Robert Cohan, with Graham from 1946 through the early 1970s, observed how successful the choreographer was at "bringing out your own personality" and Terese Capucilli, who joined the company in 1979, reiterated the point: "Martha allowed *me* to live in each role. This is something that has become uniquely mine, that no one can ever know in the same way or ever take away from me. This was Martha's gift to each of us." Speaking of Graham's way of moving, Capucilli added, "Technically, the movement can stand by itself. But you must be able to add something dramatically – *your* inner dialogue." And, further, "I feel what is important is not whether a step is this way or that way, but to continually hold onto what Martha has given me, molded on me and created *in* me."[29] Others have also said stressed how much Graham made them realize their own identity, not just as artists but as men and women.

Dancers speak of the kind of sensory experience derived from deep muscle tensions stimulated by movement as "body memory." This bodily record increases the sense of self by registering one's bearings and deepening one's perception of reality; it does so through the integration of physical sensations that the trained and well-rehearsed body has come to understand and recognize, not intellectually but kinetically, over time. The dancer's choice of one technique or movement style over another is significant in this regard. Needless to say, classical ballet training differs greatly from training in modern dance and within the modern idiom itself, a number of techniques – principally those of Graham, José Limón (whose technique was developed in association with Doris Humphrey and Charles Weidman), and Merce Cunningham may be distinguished. Why one selects Graham, say, reflects a kinetic sensibility, a physical compatibility even, more profound than one might suspect. Paul Taylor, for instance, has said that he preferred the Graham technique to Limón's "not because of what it meant or the content, but because of the movement itself"; it "made sense physically, to my body, and I naturally gravitated towards it."[30] Some, however, feel a deeper congruence with the pure movement style and lyricism associated with Limón, with the principle of fall and recovery, imbalance and balance, that defines that approach to movement, than with the more angular, percussive, and also emotive character of Graham's technique and choreography. A dancer may, of course, move from one technique to another as he or she grows. Certainly, one dances with more than one company over the span of a career and ballet dancers, Margot Fonteyn, Rudolf Nureyev, and Mikhail Baryshnikov not least among them, have danced with modern dance companies just as the reverse has sometimes been true. But one is primarily drawn to a way of moving that is consonant with one's own physical (and emotional) self and that is where, as one dancer put it, you "learn to play your own physical instrument in the most eloquent, most efficient way."[31] Thus if the act of dancing intensifies one's sense of identity it is through the body's detection of a kind of familiarity or aptness intrinsic to a particular way of moving. Something in the dancer's neuromuscular system, in other words, resonates with a technique, with its emotional quality certainly, but more directly with the physicality of its movement.

A kinesthetic sensibility is also significant in the experience of the spectator who is responsive to the tensions, the play of forces, created by the dancer. Graham saw awakening this sensibility, arousing a visceral response, as her creative mission:

> My dancing is just dancing. It is not an attempt to interpret life in a literary sense. It is not the affirmation of life through movement. Its only aim is to impart the sensation of living – to energize the spectator into keener awareness of the vigor, of the mystery, the humor, the variety, and the wonder of life – to send the spectator away with a fuller sense of his own potentialities and the power of realizing them, whatever the medium of his activity.[32]

What I am suggesting is that dance, like all forms of aesthetic experience, contributes to the maintenance of harmony in the internal milieu of the individual. But it does so in a way that other art forms do not precisely because of its spatiotemporal constitution, which is to say its rhythm and real movement of the body in space. Dance acts on circulation, metabolism, and the overall efficiency of the body. Its rigorous discipline is physically significant and therefore psychologically valuable as well. Yet the real value of dance for somatopsychic stability is more profound. Rose is right to speak of the intensification of self-recognition that is the sine qua non of all aesthetic experience, but his use of the term requires qualification. For it is not self-recognition – which implies either a narcissistic projection of self into the art work or a kind of neo-Kantian empathic identification with it – as much as self-knowledge. Dance, in particular, consists in a somatic consciousness of the self; more precisely, it consists in an awareness of how the self is feeling that comes from articulating the rhythmic structures of its bodily relation to space and time. As an art that employs the body, dance imparts that knowledge more directly than any other art.

* * *

I have maintained in this chapter that, for the dancer, the "continuity of reference" at the heart of the apperception of self is realized through the kinesthetic experience of motion and that the connection, in rhythm, between dance and the life forces of the body is deep precisely because the body is that art's only tool of expression. In fact, respiration itself is what determines the integrity of dance's rhythmic execution. Every young dancer is told from the start of his or her training not to "forget" to breathe; the struggle to execute difficult movements, though it sometimes feels that it will be, is never eased by holding one's breath. On the contrary; the flow of movement is improved, the passage from one movement to the next is rendered more harmonious, as the dancer learns to breathe more fully. The reasons are twofold: On the one hand, there is the body's need for synchrony in the release of one breath and the taking of another. Without it, the physical exertion exhausts the dancer's need for oxygen. On the other, what the rhythmic continuity of respiration intensifies in the aesthetic experience is what Susanne Langer called its "organic unity."[33]

For Martha Graham the natural movements of the body and also their relation to gravitational force, both of which classical ballet ardently strove to oppose, determined the aesthetics of dance. If, as she said, her aim was to energize and "impart the sensation of living," she did so by basing her technique and choreography on breathing and on the earth's pull of the body, its weight. Her choreographic style and training process were, in fact, created primarily from two kinds of movement: On the one hand, there are the "contraction" and "release" that derive from exhalation and inhalation; on the other, the spiraling of the torso and head on the spinal axis. The "spiral" is the dramatic consequence of a natural opposition in the body. A tension or resistant force that comes from the body's "need to balance movement on one side with reverse movement on the other," as Stuart Hodes explains it, it was the basis for a great many movements within the Graham vocabulary.[34] Breathing, of course, is the basis of life – it is not for nothing that "breath" in Greek and numerous other languages is the word for "life force"[35] – and Graham was motivated by this sine qua non of the body's physicality. This is to say that unlike ballet, which she saw as artificial in aiming above all to be pretty, her way of moving reveals the physiological, and by extension emotional, legitimacy of dance. Graham often commented, "Movement never lies," an observation she acquired from her physician father, who said, "That which you are comes out in your movement. [. . .] It tells you what the person feels and how immediately that person is in the instant."[36] Graham's choreography and technique are wholly consonant with this belief precisely because of their kinetic honesty: Whereas ballet dancers are trained to find the impulse to move in the upper torso and even in the arms and legs, the body's periphery, the Graham dancer is taught to move from the very center of the body. The impulse to contract and release is found deep within the pelvis and extends from there to the torso and the body's extremities.

Pearl Lang, a soloist with the company from 1942 to 1952 who returned in Graham's later years to dance seven of her roles, has explained the sequence of exercises the dancer repeats each day in a Graham technique class as follows:

> The breath in the body goes way down from the genitals up through the waist, through the throat, and through the top of the head, and then down again. These exercises are repeated each day. In the next development the head goes all the way back and the gaze is turned upward. The back arches and then the energy returns. The dancer works always from the base of the spine all the way up though the center of the body, the navel, the heart, the mouth, the head. Graham carried it further, so that not an arm was lifted without the rising energy of the breath, on the life impulse. Only after the energy has risen to its highest level does the arm lift, very like the bud of a blossom opening. The force comes through the center of the body and finally bursts out.[37]

Graham began to develop her revolutionary way of moving in the mid-1920s after leaving the Denishawn School and Company, where she had spent the first part of her career under the strong influence of Ruth St. Denis and Ted Shawn, the founders. "The artist in me was born in Denishawn," she acknowledged in a 1923 letter to Shawn, "and because that is fundamentally the *me* – I was born there."[38] Others, most notably Doris Humphrey and Charles Weidman, also came out of Denishawn in the early part of the last century and established their own kind of dancing. What "Miss Ruth" and Shawn gave Graham, though, was a profound regard for the spiritual inspiration of Eastern philosophy and for the exoticism of Hindu dance, and this would bestow upon her way of moving a very different sort of intensity. In the first breathing exercises of the Graham class that Lang describes above the dancer is seated on the floor with legs crossed in a Yoga-like position. More important, these exercises and indeed much of the Graham class is based on the Yoga principles of the deep breathing and flow of energy through the spine that allow the body to function as what has been called "the gateway to higher forms of consciousness."[39] I will return in a moment to the growth of this initial inspiration into a keen interest in both ancient mythology and Jungian psychoanalysis and their significance for the restorative (or stabilizing) power that Graham's creative work had for her personally. What I wish to stress here, however, is her intuition, from the very start of her career, of the transformative value of dance for an individual's sense of well-being. In her 1941 text "A Modern Dancer's Primer for Action" Graham defined constancy within the spontaneity of bodily movement as a liberating agent: "Training, technique, is important; but it is always [. . .] only the means to an end. Its importance is that it frees the body to become its ultimate self." What dancing meant to Graham and why, late in her life, she felt compelled to continue dancing when no longer physically able is largely revealed in the idea that dance was synonymous for her with the spontaneity of movement which, in turn, was synonymous with the vitality of living. That she had great difficulty relinquishing her roles to others in her company – that stopping to dance at age 75 sent her into a period of physical and psychological decline from which she and her company would recover only by virtue of her will – is to be understood in this way. "Training and technique are means to strength, to freedom, to spontaneity," she wrote in that early text. "Contrary to popular belief, spontaneity [. . .] is not wholly dependent on emotion at that instant. [. . .] It is not essentially intellectual or emotional, but is nerve reaction. That is why art is not to be *understood*, as we use the term, but is to be *experienced*."[40]

Defining the ontology of dance as a transformation of the mode of being of the dancer, and of the spectator whose own self-state is acted upon by the dancer's rhythmic motion, implies a flaw in the conventional view of dance as fundamentally expressive of emotion. Francis Sparshott is correct to observe that, for example, "A mourning dance may be congruous with what mourners conventionally are supposed to feel, and people who are actually mourning may, in performing such a dance, find their actual feelings endorsed, or normalized, or stimulated – but equally they may not. [. . .] Of course, it may happen that a particular dancer or a choreographer is unable to dance or to compose without first being in some emotional condition; but that is far from saying that, even for such people, the function of the dance is to give their inner feeling an outward form."[41] Indeed, the premise of this book – that neurobiology is of the utmost significance for our psychodynamic understanding of mind and vice versa, and that creativity is one domain in which this is particularly evident – is rooted in a quite different view; namely, that inner feeling is not externalized or objectified by aesthetic experience. Rather, it is *altered* by it. Were this not so, the awareness of feeling as determinative of homeostasis would not be subject to the effects of creative process.

Now Graham's intuition of movement as a modification of being and a significant (not to say superior) source of self-knowledge was based on the idea of, as she titled her 1991 autobiography, "blood memory." As she explained, "There are always ancestral footsteps behind me, pushing me, when I am creating a new dance, and gestures are flowing through me. Whether good or bad, they are ancestral." If she experienced an ontological transformation as she moved and set her movements choreographically, it was that she perceived her bodily self as accommodating the totality of its heritage. "You get to the point where your body is something else," she wrote in *Blood Memory*, "and it takes on a world of cultures from the past."[42] A number of influences contributed to this thinking beginning with that of the Oriental dance styles, Eastern philosophies, and Central American cultures to which she was exposed via her training and performances with Denishawn.

Though Ted Shawn, who had a great interest in the Mayan, Aztec, and Toltec civilizations, was certainly a presence in Graham's life while she was at the Denishawn School, it was Miss Ruth, as she was known, who engaged her young students in long discussions of Eastern philosophy, mysticism, religion, and the meaning of dance in the Orient as well as in ancient cultures more generally. Located not far from the large Oriental communities of Los Angeles, the school additionally gave its dancers firsthand knowledge of its spiritual affinities by offering invited lectures and demonstrations, and photographs from these formative years of Graham's career show her in a variety of ethnic costumes ranging from Egyptian and Greek to Spanish and Indian. (Perhaps her best-known role of this period was that of the beautiful Aztec maiden Xochitl in Ted Shawn's ambitious choreography about the Indian princess.)[43]

The next significant influence on Graham's ancestral view of dance (and, indeed, of all art) was Joseph Campbell, the professor of and prolific writer on mythology whose passion for knowledge was comparable to her own. Graham met Campbell in the mid-1930s when she began teaching monthly classes at Sarah Lawrence College in Bronxville, New York. (He taught mythology and classical literature there and one of his students, Jean Erdman, would eventually join Graham's company and also become Campbell's wife.) It was at Bennington College, however, where modern dance in this country took form over the course of several summers that Graham would really get to know Campbell. Indeed, she saw him regularly at Bennington and it is said that on one occasion, during a discussion of the Brontë sisters (whose lives would become the subject of Graham's 1943 *Deaths and Entrances*), the choreographer said something, as Agnes de Mille relates it, of "their kinship to the world spirits of the moors, the *sidh* of Celtic folklore, the fairy folk." Campbell replied, "When you talk about fairy folk you are really entering the world of the unconscious, and these creatures that come out of the fairy hills are manifestations of the psyche. You are now tapping the unconscious memories of the race."[44] While Graham had already been exploring through movement the biographical reservoirs of the unconscious to which Freud had brought much attention, she now added to the heavily psychoanalytical orientation of her artistic vision the evolutionary pre-figurations of the mind as well. These, in fact, stimulated the explorations of biblical stories and mythological themes that would increasingly come to dominate her work.

Campbell supported Graham's forays into the moral quagmires of mythology and also helped develop her understanding of the complexities of their psychological import. Though he was well-versed in Freud's concepts of the relation between spirituality and culture (*The Interpretation of Dreams*, *Totem and Taboo*, and *Moses and Monotheism* were of particular interest to him), it was Jung's Platonic and universal approach to the myth that made the Swiss analyst appeal to him more.[45] Jung's thinking was also more in keeping with Campbell's aesthetic preoccupations which were rooted in the idea of the artist, not as reproducer, but as transformer of the universe, one through whom cosmic energy poured. As Campbell explained, he himself had "a theory about the relationship of myth to aesthetic form and psychological structures. Myth, psychology, and aesthetics – this triangle; and that certain movements in the dance had psychological implications – which they certainly do when they have mythological ones." Campbell, moreover, believed that to achieve authenticity art had to reveal more than technical or formal proficiency. It had also to unveil the "sinister" in life, evil and human weakness.[46]

Pearl Lang has gone so far as to claim that "Martha would not do a piece without consulting Joseph Campbell"[47] and Graham expected of her dancers themselves a certain familiarity with the mythological figures that intrigued her. (It was not unusual for her to direct their readings.) But it was not scholarship she was after; what really interested her, what she sought in her own voracious reading, and what informed her choreography was insight of a different kind. Her interest in the human being had too much to do with "body consciousness" to be limited to intellectual knowledge. It is true that Campbell would go on to emphasize later in his career the somatic encoding of myth, the relation of myth to the body. (He offered week-long annual workshops with Stanley Keleman, the developer of a method of somatic therapy, over a 15-year period.[48]) What Graham was seeking, though, was how movement could aesthetically express the body's psycho-ontological heritage. Consider what Robert Cohan has described as Graham's "rediscovery" of ballet's "third," "fourth," and "fifth" positions: "[O]ne never got excited doing fourth position in ballet class," he explained, but it was extremely exciting when, in the late 1940s, Graham added these positions to her modern dance technique because she based them on a physical and historical legitimacy: the body's spiral, its turn around the spinal center. From the one- and two-dimensional bas-relief, she had the body emerge "into walking out of an archaic past."[49] Graham's choreography, like her technique, developed from an ancestral presence. If she sought verification of her interpretations or a deepening of inspiration in her readings and in her discussions with Campbell, it was to justify her intuition of the psychological implications of the textual material. It is understandable, therefore, that the most significant influence on her understanding of the self as not only the organizing principle of personality but the central archetype of the collective unconscious was not a scholar but a Jungian analyst.

Frances Wickes was a New York social worker (she is often erroneously referred to in print as "Dr. Wickes") who trained as an analyst with Carl Jung and who was also analyzed by him. In addition to teaching (at the Jung Institute in Zurich, where she held seminars, as well as in London and New York), she authored three seminal books in analytical psychology, *The Inner World of Man* (1938), *The Inner World of Choice* (1963), and *The Inner World of Childhood* (1966), several professional papers, a novel, and stories for children. Wickes was a founding member of the Analytical Psychology Club of New York and of the Association for Analytical Psychology and both friend and caregiver to many highly creative people. Her love of art and her interest in creativity combined with an uncommon warmth and remarkably intuitive nature to draw people to her from a variety of professions. One patient, who himself became a Jungian analyst, recounted stories recently of his two years in treatment with Wickes. What he remembered most vividly was the very "real dialogue" she had with her patients. Not of the non-directive tradition of psychoanalysts, he explained, she was "an introverted intuitive" (a Jungian personality type) especially gifted in the analysis of dreams and their symbolism. Like other early Jungians, she tended to be generous to those in her care both with advice and with friendship. Indeed, not having much personal training and supervision, "Wickes may not have realized the phenomenon and power of transference and counter transference between patient and analyst."[50] Her relationship with Muriel Rukeyser is a case in point: From the early 1950s to her death in 1967, Wickes maintained with the poet a kind of "barter arrangement," the one serving as analyst the other as literary assistant and editor.[51] An accurate assessment of her relationship to Graham, therefore, is exceedingly difficult to make and, unfortunately, errors proliferate in the literature. One thing, however, is certain: From Graham's letters to her (and this is confirmed by interviews with several of her mid-century company members), the attachment was exceedingly strong. Graham longed for her meetings with the analyst when she was on tour with her company (she even expresses gratitude in the correspondence for the miseries that brought her to Wickes) and it was the one she referred to as a "magnificent eagle" or "radiant hen" who both inspired her thinking and saw her through many an emotional crisis. Of course, the question that fascinates is the extent of Wickes's influence on Graham's creative process.

Helen McGehee has said that she herself, not Graham, choreographed most of her role as Electra in *Clytemnestra* (1958) and that, later, when the choreographer was unable successfully to complete a work she and others did so for her. (Alcoholism got the better of Graham at various points in her career and she became seriously depressed when she stopped dancing in 1969.) So, too, Pearl Lang maintains that throughout her career Graham had the female soloists create their own dances. "She didn't take any chances, though," Lang explained. After so many years (and many of them on tour where she watched again and again every detail of Graham's moving), Lang "knew physically" exactly what the impulses were and how they needed to be executed. But what Lang also revealed is the importance of what she, not without irony, referred to as Graham's "committee": Whenever she was doing a new work, Joseph Campbell and Louis Horst, the pianist/composer, musical director of Graham's early group, and noted teacher of dance composition, had input into it. "Nothing went out of the studio, particularly in the years before it was relocated to East 63rd Street from 66 Fifth Avenue," Lang said, "without Campbell and Horst having looked at it." And with Graham seeing Wickes at least four times a week, as Lang recollects, the triumvirate was completed.[52] Clearly Wickes shared not only in the turmoil of the dancer's daily life but in her creative moments. The 14-year-long correspondence, with Graham's numerous references to her own understanding of her work and its allusions to the analyst's input, corroborates this. So do the lengthy descriptions of the evolution of certain of her dances and Graham's mailing to Wickes, while she was working on the dance, the typewritten script of *Visionary Recital* (which premiered in 1961 and was revised as *Samson Agonistes* the following year).

The reasons for Graham's close relationship with Wickes are considerably more complicated than those of any of her other associations. Over and above his early romantic involvement with her, Horst mentored Graham, disciplined her to work through periods of despondency, and was deeply supportive of her and her dancers in myriad ways over decades. (He held her tendency to all kinds of extravagance very much in check, as Bertram Ross, Graham's partner in the great majority of her dances, put it.)[53] Horst's musical expertise and knowledge of dance composition, to say nothing of his loyalty, were certainly exceptional and her reliance on him has nothing enigmatic about it. Indeed, his presence in the studio was critical. The relationship with Campbell is just as comprehensible. Though Horst deepened Graham's awareness of and respect for the organic nature of dance – the idea that movement and its choreographic design must never be gratuitously conceived but dictated by the body – it cannot be said that he enriched the ancestral perspective of her work as did the mythologist. This was Campbell's province. But what are we to make of the relationship with Wickes? Was this simply a matter of a prolonged unanalyzed transference? Something more socially intimate? And why is it of singular importance? Graham had been engaged with Jung's writing before she began treatment. (It was her turbulent relationship with Erick Hawkins – who had become the first male dancer in her company in 1938, whom she married a decade later, and from whom she ultimately separated in 1950 – that brought her to analysis.) But it was through the relationship with Wickes that Jung came alive for her. As it is only through the assimilation of Jung's thinking into Graham's technique and choreography that we can understand in what way her creative work was restorative, I believe our consideration of the relationship warranted.

The letters from Graham to Wickes unquestionably reveal a depth of caring that not many thought Graham capable of feeling. Stuart Hodes, among Graham's leading male dancers from 1947 to 1958, hypothesizes that Graham's feelings for Wickes stemmed largely from the fact that the analyst, given both her professional role and her personality, did not parasitize the dancer.[54] While many of Graham's relationships were characterized by the other's quasi-parental need of her, Wickes was not only wise but not needy. In her analyst, moreover, Graham had less a masterful interpreter of her thinking than an influential soul mate and the writings of the two women demonstrate a remarkable congruence of metaphorical expression and artistic credo. In the unused notes for a text called "The Creative Process," Wickes wrote of the need to know when to yield "to the moment of creativity and when to wait patiently for the idea to germinate, so giving it time to develop within the womb of the unconscious." She claimed that "The creative person must have within him a little touch of the broody hen. There is the precious germ contained within the original idea, – the egg, – [that] must be brooded over, kept warm while it germinates." A 1957 mailing from Graham to Wickes is something of a poem, a playful communication in which "Miserable Duckling craves opinion of RADIANT HEN" (Graham's typography), and in other letters both the germination and "broody hen" metaphors are exploited to the fullest. In a paper presented in New York in the late 1940s titled "Creative Awareness," the analyst spoke of the demand by creative process for "emotional acceptance." In a letter dated August 1, 1952, Graham wrote that she was beginning "to know" what Wickes told her about acceptance. And, though she alludes to the difference between "living in or with sorrow," thus placing the acceptance in a somewhat different context, one senses the scope of the analyst's use of the concept. In fact, Jung himself was explicit in emphasizing acceptance (specifically, that of the contents of the unconscious) as requisite to the renewal or rebirth so prevalent in myth and dream symbolism. This was a theme, as we shall see below, that already dominated Graham's choreography by the time she came to Wickes, yet it was reinforced both by her experience of analysis and by her analyst's distinctly Jungian approach. In yet another letter, the choreographer referred to "our Judith," the 1950 solo portrayal of the biblical heroine, assuring Wickes that though she was considering expanding the piece to a work for the company, it was still the Judith *they found* and who spoke through *them*. Throughout the letters, moreover, there are references to Graham's readings. When reported in relation to particular images of which Wickes had spoken (as in Graham's discussion of *The Sea Around Us* by Rachel Carson), the measure of Wickes' decisively Jungian influence is definitive.

In "Creative Awareness" Wickes described, as had Jung, the reanimation in modern thought of the ancient image: "An act of true creation is an original experience and yet it partakes of and is closely allied to re-creation for all that is new contains a living germ bequeathed from the old." Creative joy, she believed, came from the discovery of "a pure form in an ancient design" that, in "the spirit of reverence," is made "available in some new combination suited to present need." This is the contribution of the individual to the "collective creative heritage," a donation made only by the self, which is to say never by the ego. Similarly, though somewhat earlier, Graham had written eloquently of her fear of "being sucked into a vortex . . . of anonymity" and related it to the Jungian notion of individuation. In a letter of August 4, 1953 (Wickes's talk dates to 1948) in which she refers to her new work *Voyage*, Graham told her analyst that she was reading again the *Essays on a Science of Mythology* by Jung and Kerenyi. Whereas it had only been an interest for her before, this time it "came alive" for her and she felt it applied both to her and to *Voyage*.[55]

Martha Graham was an intensely visual thinker. Among her most effective means of instructing her students was asking them to visualize. Sometimes it was the heavens, whose viewing allowed the ever-deepening contraction of the pelvis to extend upward into the chest causing the head to pitch backward. Other times it was Michelangelo's *Pietà* or the *Ecstasy of St. Theresa* by Bernini which suggest the technique's exaltation of the head and body. The image of a light-reflecting diamond-studded collarbone was used for the demi-plié and that of the endless stirring of the cauldron by the three witches of *Macbeth* invigorated the movement referred to in Graham terminology as the "knee vibrations."[56] There is no doubt that Wickes's Jungian thought appealed to her for the pivotal role analytical psychology assigned to images. Jung's central concept of the archetype is itself meaningful metaphorically and images constituted for this psychoanalyst the dominant structure of the instinct-driven, symbol-forming psyche. Graham's letters to Wickes are illuminating for their visual depictions of feeling, but their richness lies even more in their disclosure of the imagistic origins of her creative process. In one, she writes of an idea for a dance whose working title was "Point of the Wolves" or "Promontory of the Wolves." "I think of Point Lobos and those lovely twisted trees," she revealed. "It is a night or a year or a lifetime . . . but it is crisis and the wolves are the hungry ones who tear at the heart with that cruel hunger that only wolves have."

Her visualization, however subtle its expression, is remarkably Jungian in its perception of the self's relation to cosmic order. Though the dance was to involve the entire company, it was to be primarily about "one woman and her tide-pool at night where driftwood and dead things float after the surge up of the sea." She imaged a sequence of storm at dark: "moon-rise and moon-set, deep dark" and also dawn: "a luminous bathed essence of new day," the "lovely instant of pervasive green which marks the return to color and life [. . .]." She conjectured that she had "not yet reached the instant of deep dark which precedes the dawn," that she might be living still "with the curious strange fantasies of the moon world, the images beautiful and terrifying but less so than the reality of the actual which would release me into the lovely anonymity which is dawn."

A subsequent letter, written some six weeks later, details the continuation of the dance's germination and makes clear a connection with Wickes's own thinking: "I had been thinking of the Cypress Tree . . . the Cedar of Lebannon [sic] of which you had spoken and I knew that image of constancy in face of the elements was [. . .] deep within me also." Graham had truly assimilated the Jungian notion of the individual's embodiment of the wholeness of humanity as is illustrated by the degree to which it informed her thinking while the plans for the dance evolved. Referring to the process of individuation as analogous to the regeneration of the primordial patterns of nature (what in a later letter she calls "the deep symbol of continuity"), she wrote of seeing in the "Twilight movement" a solo and, in the "Moon sequence" a group dance with solo overtones, this being a sequence where "all is strange and eternal and yet fantastic as all universal things seem to be." She wrote of a trio, for two men and herself, "in the Deep Dark," where the "struggle is as in a dream between these two instants in life" and then there is the dawn, like "the first recognition." She described emphasizing "the deliberate universality of recognition, not as prelude to tragedy or isolation, not as act of exclusion, but as an identification with other through a commonness of experience."

Equally telling are Graham's epistolary commentaries on another dance, *Voyage* (a company work that premiered in New York in 1953 with a set by Isamu Noguchi and music by William Schuman). Her affinity with Jungian psychology is evident where she speaks of her interpretation of the work's psychological meaning and its significance within the overall frame of her creative process. In fact, writing of how she came to understand what *Voyage* is about (after a dream of cats), she explicitly states that the Jung and Kerenyi text noted above applies to herself and this dance. Frances Wickes had not introduced Graham to Jung's thinking but clearly the analyst, the analysis, and the friendship between the two women solidified its impact.[57]

Jungian thought was, of course, very much in the air at the time and Graham had read Jung's *Psychology of the Unconscious* (today titled *Symbols of Transformation*), *Psychological Types*, and *The Archetypes of the Collective Unconscious*. She was also well acquainted with those critics who were then using the analyst's understanding of the psyche – with its tripartite division between consciousness, the personal unconscious, and the collective unconscious – for the interpretation of literature. F. M. Cornford, J. L. Weston, and J. A. Stewart may all be cited for their influence on Graham, but the critic whose literary explorations of Jungian archetypes were of greatest interest to her was Maud Bodkin, the author of *Archetypal Patterns in Poetry*. Graham concentrated mostly on two chapters in Bodkin's book, one on the archetypal image of women and thc other on the myth of rebirth.[58] Both aided her in her investigations of the ancestral qualities so deftly captured in her characterizations of legendary female figures. From Medea,

Jocasta, Clytemnestra, Phaedra, and Judith to Mary Queen of Scots, Héloïse, Joan of Arc, the Brontë sisters, and Emily Dickinson, the choreographer's heroines were sculpted from the archaic images of the female as temptress, martyr, saint, earth mother, and virgin. And behind all these images loomed that embodied by Martha Graham herself: the female as creator, the female as Goddess.

Numerous other archetypes, however, also provided significant choreographic foci. Those that Jung himself had singled out as particularly notable with respect to behavior and character type supplied Graham with enormously diverse avenues of creative exploration: The persona (one's public façade), the anima and animus (the feminine and masculine feelings and qualities projected onto male and female personalities respectively), the shadow (the animalistic side of human nature), and the self (the organizing principle of personality) all feature prominently in her dances. As she strove to resolve the philosophical conundrum that underlies her choreography – namely, whether there is a secular faith, a way to believe in something not religious[59] – Graham found in Jung, particularly during World War II and the post-war period, symbols, images, and themes that spoke strongly to her own preoccupations.

I do not mean to imply that Graham's effort was a deliberate depiction of the prototypical contents identified by Jung within the collective unconscious. Rather, it is simply that she believed in the power of the potentialities and predispositions Jung maintained were engraved over time in all our psyches. But why was their universal significance so important to her choreographically? To what is owed the substantial role played by mythology in her oeuvre? And, perhaps most important, what kind of identification motivated the selection of the women she danced? Of the many archetypes described by Jung, it is interesting that it was renewal or rebirth that resonated most deeply with the choreographer. Indeed, a clue to the answers to these questions resides therein, for her depiction of this inherently theatrical archetype as a dramatic voyage through the darkness of the unconscious to the enlightenment of consciousness is her most persistent image. In fact, it is emblematic of the salutary effect of the creative act. In other words, Graham's insistence on the metaphorical transcription of this archetype into a mythic journey into the self is what justifies our viewing her creative use of the body as transformative, or at least as having a stabilizing effect. For in repeating in dance after dance the sense of renewal that accompanies awareness she revealed the meaning she subjectively gave to her art.

It is commonly recognized that Graham's extraordinarily large choreographic corpus (191 dances created over more than seven decades) is divisible into four primary periods. Of these, the two in the middle are the most easily delimited: From the early 1930s through the mid-1940s, the span roughly extending from *Primitive Mysteries* (which premiered in 1931) to *Appalachian Spring* (1944), Graham delved into the heart of Americana. Moving away from the abstraction of her earlier mood-oriented pieces (like the anguished *Lamentation* of 1930), she focussed in these two dances – and in others of this period, most notably *Frontier* (1935), *American Document* (1938) and *Letter to the World* (1940) – on the socio-cultural frame of religiosity, puritanism, and domestic joy. Emotion, though, was still her primary interest and she continued to investigate a range of feelings extending from loneliness to courageousness and desire. In other dances of this time, *Deaths and Entrances* (1943) for instance, she also scanned the psyche, specifically the emotional precipices to which passion may take us, but it wasn't until the following period that she found the inspiration for her psychological portraits that would significantly broaden the narrative scope of her work. This is when she created the majority of her mythological masterpieces, including *Dark Meadow* (1946), *Cave of the Heart* (1946), *Errand into the Maze* (1947), *Night Journey* (1947), *Judith* (1950), *Seraphic Dialogue* (1955), *Clytemnestra* (1958), *Embattled Garden* (1958), *Alcestis* (1960), *Phaedra* (1962), and *Circe* (1963). As the titles suggest, Graham had become intensely focussed on the drama intrinsic within ancient myth and biblical narrative and this is when the voyage into the unconscious truly became her dominant theme.

Martha Graham entered this third period of her creative evolution with *Dark Meadow*, an abstract dance for which Carlos Chàvez composed the music and Isamu Noguchi (who devised some 22 sets for Graham) created the few rock-like objects and phallic stakes inhabiting an otherwise sparse setting. The work, whose preliminary title was *Ancestral Footsteps* (after an unwritten tale by Nathaniel Hawthorne), is comprised of four sections entitled "Remembrance of Ancestral Footsteps," "Terror of Loss," "Ceaselessness of Love," and "Recurring Ecstasy of the Flowering Branch." These are linked by transitional dances performed by five men and four women, a chorus called, simply, They Who Dance Together. The three lead dancers are also named generically: One Who Seeks (Graham's role), She of the Ground (an imaging of the earth mother archetype), and He Who Summons (the archetypal leader originally danced by Erick Hawkins). In *Letter to the World*, Graham's highly successful choreographic treatment of the artist who sacrifices her personal life for her art, we had already witnessed the dramatic intensity of generic identification: One Who Dances and One Who Speaks were what Graham called the two figures representing the outer persona and the "inner landscape" (Graham's term) of Emily Dickinson, and the Ancestress was the name she gave the puritanical New England conscience repressive of the poet's desire. There she had shown how effectively, through the soul of another, she could delve into and gain a deeper sense of her own. Since the inception of her relationship with Hawkins, Graham had been preoccupied with how love could be combined with the total dedication demanded of the artist. The extraordinarily lyrical portrayal of her generic artist kin pre-figured the obsessive probing of the unconscious central to the dances to be created over the next several decades. "I am nobody, who are you?" – the Dickinson line spoken after the opening dance for the two women representing Emily – would prove a profoundly meaningful epigraph for the choreographic journey into the self that was now to come.

Interpretations of *Dark Meadow* differ considerably: Described by one critic as a meditation, a dance "of root causes and responses," its epic characters were said to be engaged in "a ritual designed to expiate or placate a disturbance in the deeper flow of movement – life." A second critic claimed that the work embraced "the eschatological doctrines of preexistence, penance, reincarnation, and final purification of the soul." Yet a third, while acknowledging the validity of the work's frequent evaluation as a "fertility ritual," stressed the importance of the disappearance (by rolling into the wings "like a dust ball") of the male lover who leaves She Who Seeks alone, center stage, "seemingly at the threshold of discovery." The work's blatant eroticism – continuous couplings by the chorus prefigure the lovers' own intoxicating consummation – was described by that critic as playing "a significant, even catalytic part in [the seeker's] self-realization, but not the principal one." As in *Letter to the World*, that is the role played by art, with She Who Seeks representing the artist. One thing, though, is not contested: Above all else, the dance is an exquisite progression toward awareness; it is the "subtle unfolding of a woman's consciousness," as Ernestine Stodelle said of it. We know from the program note that Graham herself saw the work as a stunning "re-enactment of the Mysteries which attend the eternal adventure of seeking." Powerfully underscoring the quest is a series of quasi-religious symbols, the most significant of which is a black cloth, the image of death and a symbol of the darkened meadow of the seeker's unconscious.[60]

"Who are the other Women who have made the Journey – the Pilgrimage – There must be some way of making this more specific; of narrowing it down to the scale of understanding, of self-identification," Martha Graham mused in her notebooks.[61] In Medea, Ariadne, Jocasta, Clytemnestra, Judith, St. Joan, and other epic and ageless women, she found vehicles for the "self-identification" she was seeking. *Cave of the Heart* (with music by Samuel Barber) premiered the same year as *Dark Meadow*, but based on the story of Euripedes' *Medea* it was far more explicit in its unveiling of the journey inward. Of all Graham's portrayals that of Medea is certainly among the most passionate: An implacable woman whose curse of jealousy renders her the incarnation of an unfathomable evil, she was ruthless and tireless in her drive for revenge when the young prince Jason prefers another to her. Graham's venom as the murderous sorceress was depicted in one of the most memorable solos of her career. Its percussive movements, preceded by serpentine crawls along the floor (the dance was originally titled "Serpent Heart"), were dominated by convulsive vibrations during which she appeared slowly to withdraw from her mouth a long red scarf (the snake). With pulsing hands and feet performing very rapid footwork ("bourrées") in place, Graham raised the metaphorical reptile over head, moving it frenetically from side to side. It was then strewn across her shoulder, coiled around her waist, and generally looped in and around her body before it was "eaten" and "spat out" in dramatic falls to and recoveries from the floor. "Spasm-like contraction[s]," as she described them in her notations, reveal the at once "possessive" and "destroying" nature of the unrequited love that "feeds upon itself like the serpent heart," to cite from an early program note.[62]

A year later, Graham would offer *Night Journey* (with music by William Schuman). The title of this work is alone indicative of the significance of the archaic for the choreographer and of the influence, seconded by the relationship with Wickes and the analytic experience generally, of Jungian thought. (Graham's published notebooks reveal numerous references to Jung's work, to the myths with which Jung was concerned, and to the concepts on which his analytical psychology was founded. The notes for *Dark Meadow*, for instance, frequently cite him and refer specifically to the archetype of rebirth.) The choreography of *Night Journey*, though, defines the nature of the preoccupation with mythology and with Jung: Under the guise of the Oedipus legend, it relates the journey to awareness and identification of the self. In *Psychology of the Unconscious* Jung had interpreted the mythic cosmogony of the sun's nocturnal journey as a universal yearning for renewal. More precisely, in the voyage to the other side of the sea, as Egyptian legend and other tales accounted for the solar setting at nightfall and rising at dawn, he had seen a longing to return to the womb and to be reborn. He had also outlined a number of implications of this "night sea journey" that, like those of every mythic shaping of an archetype, are very diverse. One derived from the regressive connotation of the return-to-the-womb fantasy: Analogous to the regressive journey of the psychoanalytic experience, it implied the renewal of the psyche that takes place through the revival of unconscious wishes and conflicts associated with the past and making them conscious. Another derived from a different sort of contact with the unconscious, a contact with one's creative energies. The "night sea journey" not only constituted a psychic rebirth, but a transformation to a higher level at which it is creativity itself that is nourished. Jung drew from the mythic representation of the rebirth or renewal archetype an additional implication as well: Insofar as individuation requires continual journeys to the depths of the unconscious, he saw a link between the "night sea journey" and the progressive realization of self. Every psychic upheaval, each suffering in life, is endured as a journey to hell and these provisional meetings with death are overcome precisely by insight, an increase in self-knowledge.[63] Graham's *Night Journey* plays on all these Jungian implications of the myth. Like her other Greek works, it is violent, as demanding psychically as it is physically (it is an emotionally wrenching work for both dancer and spectator), and transformative. But how?

Night Journey relates the Oedipus story from a distinctly feminine perspective; the tale is recounted from the viewpoint of the heroine, not (as is usual) from that of the hero. In another dance from 1947, *Errand into the Maze* (with music by Gian Carlo Menotti), Graham ventured a third time into Greek myth, which is to say into the envies, lustfulness, incest, and murder these legends put on the stage. This time she danced a female Theseus who slays the Minotaur, the half-man half-bull monster representing the darkest regions of the unconscious and the demon of fear that dwells therein (Figure 5.1). What accounts for these shifts? According to one writer, it is a fusion of Jocasta with the mother archetype as explored by Jung that explains the superimposing of the female on the traditionally male perspective in that dance.[64] It is true that Graham was troubled by the idea of motherhood (her letters to Wickes contain proof) and that during the time when she was making *Night Journey* she was fixated on this and other prototypes. But the notion that the Jungian mother archetype was a model for the Jocasta role, however accurate the observation, does not elucidate why. The question that remains with regard to *Night Journey*, to *Errand into the Maze*, and to all the other Graham works of similar inspiration where the female is made to occupy the centermost position of the legend is this: What need did the adaptation of a masculine-dominated tale to her female body and viewpoint fulfill? Why, in fact, was Graham's full-evening theatrical magnum opus, *Clytemnestra*, which is based on the trilogy that is Aeschuylus' *Orestia*, not given the name of any of the plays (*Agamemnon*, *The Libation Bearers*, *The Furies*) that make up that drama or named for the *Orestia* itself?

The answer, less obvious than egoism, is threefold: First, subsuming the masculine role rendered each of the women portrayed by Graham the true hero of the story, the one who accomplished the journey of epic proportions and achieved the heroic goal. If Graham identified with the likes of Joan of Arc, it was as a visionary, as an indefatigable woman of action. If she called her chorus of furies in *Night Journey* Daughters of the Night, it was that she delighted in the idea of Fate as a feminine force. This is why we can read in her notebooks, at the end of her notations for *Dark Meadow*, the following passage:

> I will not be released from this bondage until I have released myself. No man can do it for me. There is a cry against Fate when first we see her face. But then after the terror of recognition passes we can live with her as we are destined to do – forever – We can never escape her presence any more – ever – Then we can cultivate and know Joy because we must or go mad. For there is no hope – there is only what we do –[65]

Graham's heroines, moreover, all possess a measure of divinity that permits them, while standing in their moments of passion, rage, and ecstasy alongside all women, to prevail as unique.[66] More important, though, is that this divine quality is an assurance of immortality, not a negligible matter for one who very much equated dancing with being alive. In at least one prolonged period

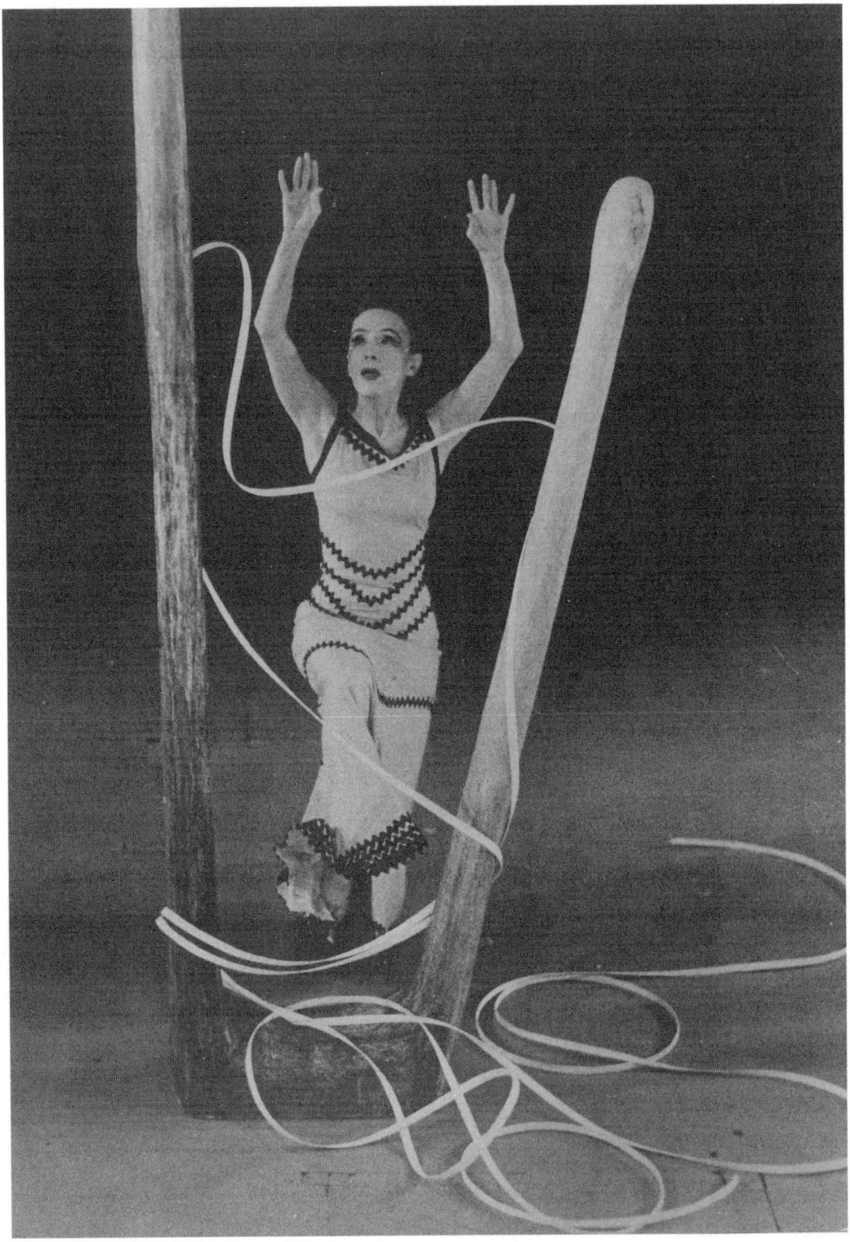

Figure 5.1 Martha Graham in *Errand into the Maze*. Jerome Robbins Dance Division, The New York Public Library for the Performing Arts, Astor, Lenox and Tilden Foundations

of deep depression she felt that if she could no longer dance she wanted to die. (Graham returned to choreography, however, at age 79 and created over 20 new works and revived 30 others!)

Third, through her feminine adaptation of a strong and direct body language, Graham was able to formalize – and thereby triumph over – the most primitive feelings universally experienced. This reason has in common with the first two a single need: to conquer the unknown by elucidating the unconscious, through a journey into the self, and revealing what motivates those schisms between desire and repression, sexuality and spirituality, and evil and goodness that make us neither men nor women, but human.

As mother, lover, and queen in *Night Journey* Graham was struggling with her own sense of identity which her turbulent relationship with Hawkins and the conflict between love and the committed life of the artist were continually at risk of undermining. As Agnes de Mille put it, *Night Journey* reflected Graham's "frantic cries for identification." De Mille explains: "At this moment Martha was at the apex of her creative powers, and just then her lover [Erick Hawkins] had begun to attempt to identify himself, to claim parity with her in her own company, on her own stage. In short, to threaten her very essence."[67] This is true. But it is also true that the meaning Graham made of her psychological portrayals, the self-identifying process they connoted, was a constant of her choreographic experience.

Self-identification, which is what she was seeking within the heroic, the divine, and the collective unconscious, was the reason for Graham's preoccupation with the archetype of renewal. Her expression of the "night sea journey," the symbolic voyage into the deepest motivations of which we are unaware, took many forms but it was always a means of rebirth and resolution. In *Lamentation* she surpassed the personal experience of despair by displaying anguish itself before us on the stage. In *Frontier* and *American Document* she again exceeded the arena of the private, this time by rendering a resurgence of spirit as a universal. Extending her own sense of increasing confidence as a pioneer in the world of dance to the adventurousness and hopefulness of a country in the post-Depression era, she explored a very different kind of human feeling. In the humorous *Every Soul is a Circus* (whose title was taken from a poem by Vachel Lindsay) she transcended her own eccentricities by poking fun at those of all mankind. In each of her dances, it was via the prototype that she was able to see the particular more clearly. This is not to say she always understood intellectually her own dances. It is clear from her letters to Wickes that she didn't. But through an investigation of the darkest corners of the souls of others she accessed on some level the identity and boundaries of her own. This was true of works like *Letter to the World* and *Deaths and Entrances*, but it became even more evident as the connection between her self-realization and the archetype of renewal intensified, as it did in *Dark Meadow* and in the many works of mythological inspiration that followed. Rebirth implies death and certainly the Greek dances privileged banishment, beheading, and similar brutalities. Former company member Peggy Lyman has said this of the murderous acts performed by the strong women Graham created: "As women we got to explore a huge range of vivid emotions by acting out our characters' angers and fears and ecstasies." But she is explicit in noting the purpose: Graham's choreographed aggressions were "Not just [for] experiencing [in movement] the turmoil of life, but creating a solution out of it. There is the stumbling block, the struggle and salvation."[68]

* * *

In Chapter 3 we saw how Beckett's theatrical characterizations resemble brain-damaged patients with deconstructed selves. Like the disembodied voices or partially buried characters of the playwright, patients with asomatognosia and similar neurological disorders deny (or misidentify) parts of their bodies with the result that their sense of self is fragmented. What dancers achieve through the engagement with their bodies is the reverse: They experience an increase in their self-representation, a clarification of their sense of boundaries. Just as there may be loss of self-identity and of a coherent and stable self-world relation in the patient with lesions (usually of the right hemisphere) in the brain, there may be expansion of both through the constant repetition of physical movements in time and space. (We saw above with respect to violinists that the repetitive use of parts of the body increases the size of its representation in the appropriate parts of cortical body maps.)[69]

I also suggested in the chapter on Beckett that his depersonalized characters resemble patients with frontal lobe damage by their persistent confabulations. In their use of fictional stories, their ceaseless outpouring of words, they sustain themselves, for in Beckett's universe language and existence are synonymous; words create the self that is lacking. In the wordlessness of dance, the body configures the boundaries of the self as it moves spatiotemporally. There are millions of neurons that compose the motor system and these are organized in such a way that they may function in unity. Neuroscientists are not in agreement as to how much the vestibular, visual, and proprioceptive systems each contribute to a dancer's movement.[70] Nor is it clear how much predictive input versus sensory feedback assists the dancer in balancing the body against the pull of gravity as it moves the body in space. What is known, however, is that there is no locus of an "inner I" commanding the body to move; there is no site where a "ghost in the machine" (as philosopher Gilbert Ryle famously called it) would be located.[71] What neuroscientists and psychoanalysts have learned from their exchange of empirical and clinical data is, rather, that the self is integrated in *meaning*. This is precisely why (as Arnold Modell, Todd Feinberg, and others have persuasively argued) the mind is irreducible to the brain. And this is precisely why I believe the subjective experience of creativity sheds light on our understanding of art.

Because its impulse is felt as a physical sensation of the body, movement acts on body image and identity to effect change that is perceptible psychobiologically. Indeed, dance is a means of deepening self boundaries. It does so through the musculoskeletal sensations derived from the phsyicality of movement, including the pain associated with the difficulty of its execution. Pain, in fact, serves self-definition as a distinct source of creative energy. The implications of this are many and varied, but what I wish to stress here is the primitive nature of choreography. Because choreography is not a cognitive endeavor, like any art it mediates affect and shapes self-awareness by acting on the brain's neural circuitry. More than other artists, however, the choreographer is responsive to bodily sensation and thereby to the intimacy between soma and psyche. Ernestine Stodelle eloquently observed that the practice of dance is "the dialogue between body and brain, when action meets reaction, force summons force, effort begets feeling, and movement, sure as an arrow in flight, takes off into space."[72] The same might be said of choreography. Not only dancing itself but the making of dances helped Martha Graham achieve self-realization and more stable boundary delineation. Creating dances, particularly those of her Greek period, renewed her sense of relatedness. Performing them was personally and profoundly restorative. I do not say this only because dancing and making dances were outlets for the aggressive behavior to which she was prone, or because the violent streak in her personality (to which many have attested) was tamed by the sublimatory processes. Rather, the evidence is found both in her correspondence and in her notebooks. More significant, though, is that no one who has witnessed the intensity of the "ripples" and "vibrations" of the Sorceress's solo in *Cave of the Heart* or the distillation of energy in St. Joan's exaltation in *Seraphic Dialogue* can question the transformative nature of Graham's choreography. No one who has experienced the "ecstatic inner tension" of a Graham contraction, the "dynamic eloquence" and "muscular depth, resonance and vibrato" that her technique produces in the dancer (the terms are Lang's) can question the transformative nature of Graham's technique.

Another celebrated choreographer, Alvin Ailey, once observed that dance is a condensation of one's personal experience: "Everything in dancing is style, allusion, the essence of many thoughts and feelings, the abstraction of many moments. Each movement is the sum total of moments and experiences." At the same time, however, "without the safety of mediating words," dance throws one back to "the most basic impulses and memories," as *New York Times* critic Jennifer Dunning has written. If Graham was drawn to the expression of mythological themes it was to reclaim within the frame of her Greek and Hebrew characters' individual psyches, but also those of all her heroes and heroines, the commonality of primal feelings. Dance, in fact, is the most universal of media: "Separate the movement from the music, costumes and sets," notes Dunning, "slow it down in the mind's eye, and dance can be clearly seen as first cousin to a walk."[73] It is not for nothing that over the years critics have continually highlighted the visceral quality of Graham's creative impulse and of the response it elicited in her audience. Walter Terry wrote of her "nerve-deep choreography" and John Martin wrote that it was "un-understandable through the usual organs of understanding," that it "slips in through sensory perceptions."[74] But the last word must be given to Graham herself, for her way of moving the body consists in an art conceived as rigorously as any science ("an absolute science" is how she described it) and it remains the most vital modern dance idiom in the world today:

> I can tell you what the shoulder means. [. . .] I can tell you where the arm comes from in the back and all of the excitement of where in the body it grows. I don't know how many years it took to learn certain things. But I enjoyed it. I enjoyed the physical engagement with myself.[75]

Epilogue

Since Freud's pathographic writings on Leonardo, Michelangelo, E. T. A. Hoffmann, and others, psychoanalysis has informed the study of art in a number of ways. It is sometimes used to expose an aspect (thematic, stylistic, or other) of the work itself or to reveal something of our collective psychology, our common experience of, say, the family romance or Oedipal longings. For the most part, though, the effort of the psychoanalytically informed critic has been to elucidate more narrowly the inner world of the artist. Whatever the point of departure – whether the vicissitudes of intrapsychic development demonstrable in the psychobiography of the artist or the reparation of interpsychic relations played out at the aesthetic site – all too often applied psychoanalysis has sought to reveal the artist's psychic life by perpetuating the dualistic legacy of Descartes. It tends to treat the mind, in other words, as though it were autonomous, with the result that the application of psychoanalytic concepts to art causes many an eyebrow to be raised in disdain. For the most part, the contempt originates in the belief that data obtained other than by free-floating attention are not appropriate for the kind of investigation psychoanalysis implies. Insofar as the work of art is incomparable to an associating patient, the application of psychoanalytic theory to a literary text or the plastic arts is often deemed of marginal interest at best. Moreover, applied psychoanalysis is by nature hypothetical; while the validity of clinical interpretations may be tested against the degree of change in the patient (however lacking in objective rigor that testing may be), no such gauge of legitimacy exists for the interpretation of literature or visual art.

Some years ago Charles Brenner pronounced the psychoanalysis of art "misdirected."[1] In a sense, I would agree: To the extent that it is wanting in criteria for validation and that, admittedly, it can be profoundly reductive of what the artist creates, it is not well conceived. To redirect applied psychoanalysis (perhaps a misnomer?) its point of departure must be rethought. Hence my emphasis in this book on creative experience as opposed to what is created in art. Taking the subjective experience of the creator (or co-creator) as the starting point (and not the work as a product separable from it) maintains the dynamic dimension of art at the fore. It legitimizes the analogy between artistic and psychoanalytic process underlying the practice of (what I prefer to call) interdisciplinary psychoanalysis and allows us to perceive that aesthetic experience accommodates the projection of fantasy and the workings of the unconscious in much the same way as the psychoanalytic transference itself. It even defeats the all-too-common assumption of a necessary kinship between pathology and art. (Was not the comparability of art and play the basis for Freud's and then Winnicott's insights into the *healthy* functioning of the child?) Thus focussing on the subjectivity of creative experience serves to protect against the very reductiveness for which "applied" psychoanalysis is disdained. In a word, it protects against the reification of art, for creativity, the sine qua non of fantasy, cannot be objectified any more than the interrelation between brain and mind in which it resides.

Those who persist in limiting the text or painting to a material reflection of the artist's (or even the reader/spectator's) own innermost world put not only the work of art but "applied" psychoanalysis itself in the position of having to come up short. When the aim of applying psychoanalytic theory is perceived to be the demonstration of some "hidden truth" (or, worse yet, pathology) there can only be distrust. What Emanuel Berman has referred to as "the pretence of objective knowledge and authoritative understanding of 'true deep meaning'"[2] can only vex further those tending toward disbelief from the start. Yet such has been the impetus for the "applied" psychoanalytic tradition. If we are to succeed in revitalizing and indeed validating the application of psychoanalysis to art, we need now to extend our focus beyond what, long ago, Heidegger called art's "thingly" concept and beyond the notion of art as symbolic of the mind that either makes or perceives it. We need to do away with the condescension lodged in that unilateral perspective, with the idea of revealing the "truth" of the work at hand. Enhancing the credibility of the dialogue between artist and the psychoanalytically oriented spectator or reader entails a reassessment of the very constitution of meaning. It entails looking for new avenues of investigation that reveal art – a fundamentally intersubjective, which is to say transferential and countertransferential phenomenon – as creative precisely in its function as an agent for insight and growth.[3]

Psychoanalysis itself developed from precisely the kind of dialectical thinking that such an extension of focus implies; it developed from within the very same philosophical frame that led Freud and others of his time, namely, Brentano and Husserl, to overcome the subject–object schism bequeathed the modern world by Descartes. Freud's initial concerns were with the very meaning of "mind" and at one time he intended to pursue a doctorate in philosophy. In his early work on aphasia he probed the relation between mind and brain attempting to determine how, if language is not mere sound, but meaningful sound, it extended from a neuro-physiological impulse in the ear to something comprehensible in the mind. What he was grappling with was the impasse addressed by Husserl but a few years later in his theory of intentionality. Indeed, if Husserl's phenomenology would unite subject and object in the spatiotemporal projection of consciousness, in what was termed an "intentional" relation, it was that he was deeply influenced by Brentano, with whom Freud also studied in his first year at the University of Vienna.

But it was to Immanuel Kant that Freud was most indebted for his neurologically framed resolution of the Cartesian dualism. In his *Critique of Pure Reason* (1781) Kant argued against the separation of mind and matter (the *res cogitans* and the *res extensa*) and, through the notion of transcendental schemata, he showed the mind to be actively involved in the objects of its experience. With his schema theory, in other words – the notion that "it is not images of objects, but schemata, which lie at the foundation of our pure sensible concepts"[4] – Kant was able to connect what is thought with what is apprehended by the senses. In a word, Freud was persuaded by Kant's view that the mind and its objects exist in a correlative relation. Indeed, when writing his posthumously published "Project for a Scientific Psychology," Freud discovered that mentation is not the result of events in the brain however dependent it may be upon them. That is, he understood that the mind–brain relation is not one of causality, that, rather, perception in the mind and perception by the brain are co-relational; in other words, they interconnect. His notion of an unconscious was incompatible with the phenomenological "act psychology" of Brentano and Husserl, wherein psychical perception necessarily referred to an external object. Nonetheless, the mind–matter or mind–brain juxtaposition was deflated for Freud, as it had been for these philosophers, as soon as he conceived of the dialectical, as opposed to causal, connection.

However ironically, what is now emerging within the psychoanalytic community as a result of new and better technology is verification of early Freudian thought. As Solms has outlined in a recent article, the "conventional wisdom" of Freud's conceptualizations is now being subjected, as it must be, "to an entirely new level of biological scrutiny" and clearly coming out on top. Panksepp put it this way: "[I]t is not a matter of proving Freud right or wrong, but of finishing the job."[5] As the neuro-psychoanalytic model of the mind/brain supplants its Cartesian forerunner, it seems to me that interdisciplinary psychoanalysis must account for the heretofore insufficiently recognized role of the body in all modes of psychic functioning, with that of creativity (imaginative thinking) near the top of the list.

Psychoanalysis is intimately connected with neuroscience in the decision-making process that defines the creative act: Why a painter, writer, or choreographer gives shape to a particular image and positions it in any given place on the canvas, in the text, or ballet is what we mean by "artistic sense." This is an intuitive faculty that projects the feeling of the perceptualizing self in relation to its inner and external worlds. How this feeling is operative in creativity is what neuro-psychoanalysis has to offer the interpretive domain. I have maintained throughout this book that, with the greater attention now being paid to both the somatic determination and recording of psychic events, our assumptions with regard to the parameters of homeostatic regulation must also be reassessed. This entails consideration of how creativity not only enriches our cultural experience of the world but modifies our ability to auto-regulate our most fundamental self-states.

In his celebrated paper of 1999, Nobel laureate Eric Kandel details the relevance of psychoanalysis to what he previously termed the "new intellectual framework" of psychiatry, that defined by the interest in psychopharmacology and, more generally, in the biological relationship of mind to brain so conspicuous in recent years. Noting the need to maintain "the rich insights that have come from psychoanalysis" as psychiatry draws ever closer to biology, Kandel cites a number of focal points shared by neuroscience and psychoanalysis: These include, among others, unconscious processing, autobiographical memory, dreaming, affect, and motivation.[6] If I would add to this list the creative disposition of the mind/brain, it is precisely because, in elucidating these areas of investigation, neuro-psychoanalysis enhances ipso facto our understanding of the imagination itself. In fact, at the very interface of neuroscience and psychoanalysis, where the molecular mechanisms of cognition and feeling are shown to meet the psychodynamic processes of mentation and affect, creative thinking is revealed as an essential feature of human life.

Initially, Freud approached the "mental apparatus" (his term) that apprehends the self by conceptualizing its relation to three coordinates that he described as dynamic, topographical, and economic. Even after he divided it into its component parts of ego, id, and superego in what subsequently became known as the structural model (1923), he never abandoned the metapsychological approach that had framed his earlier speculations. It remained a means of conceiving of what is operative in every sort of psychic event: the cathexes (or economic investments) stimulated endogenously by the body's instinctual needs, the ideational representatives that (dynamically) discharge them, and the (topographical) situating of these representatives in the mind. The psychic event itself was understood by Freud to be regulated by the pleasure principle, the notion that the mind seeks automatically to lower the quantity of tension-producing excitation the body instills within it. Equating this regulatory operation with the production of pleasure, Freud was hypothesizing that the mental apparatus, in aiming to maintain as low a level of excitation as possible or at least to maintain its level constant, is in constant pursuit of the pleasure derived from stability within the internal environment.

Neuroscientists have since confirmed the metapsychological premises of Freud's thinking and shown that the mind/brain does, in fact, function according to the pleasure principle Freud envisaged. By observing patients with damage to the inhibitory (frontal limbic) region of the brain, they have demonstrated the influence of unconscious wishful thinking on perception and memory, among other neurologically based mechanisms of cognition, to prove the validity of Freud's theory.[7] If, as I have claimed, the measure of creativity in art is its impact on the creator (or on the recipient as co-creator of the work), it is precisely that true innovation lies in the redirecting of the self toward the feeling of harmony, the pleasure that equilibration affords. To the extent that the primary goal of the mind/brain is a sense of well-being and that art is a means of achieving it, we can see how creativity may be said to fulfill a broadly defined homeostatic function.

Of course, the clinico-anatomical method employed by the neuro-psychoanalyst is very far removed from the practice of the aesthetician or critic. Consisting in examining alterations (neurological and/or chemical) in the brain for the purpose of uncovering and treating the mental function of the region concerned, it reveals the ways in which brain function impacts psychic function and vice versa. The neuro-physiological substantiation of clinical psychoanalytic concepts to which it is equally devoted, however, bears significantly on the study of creative process, the subjective experience of the artist, and the reception of the artwork as well. As psychoanalysis, in conjunction with neuroscience, departs from the hermeneutic ideal of a "philosophy of mind" to become a "science of mind" (as Kandel put it), we need to think how it might be used more exactingly by those seeking to account for the dynamics of imaginative function. What do the neurobiology of emotion and feeling and the neurophysiology of mental representation have to tell us about the creative experience of an individual? What are the consequences of a better understanding of the mind/brain for our understanding of the creation and reception of art? What might constitute a "neuro-psychoanalytic aesthetics" involves our continually seeking answers to these and related questions whatever the subjective context of the aesthetic experience at hand.

Notes

Introduction

1 S. Freud, "Leonardo da Vinci and a Memory of His Childhood," SE Vol. 11, London, Random House, 2001, p. 136.
2 In psychoanalytic parlance the "object" refers to a person. Object relations theories vary considerably with some viewing the relational model it presupposes as juxtaposed to classical drive theory and others viewing it as supplementary to the instinctual model. Self psychology refers to the movement initiated by Heinz Kohut who emphasized the structural development of the self over ego formation.
3 This notion has been admirably substantiated by Joel Whitebook in "Sublimation – a frontier concept," *The Spectrum of Psychoanalysis*, eds. A. K. Richards and A. D. Richards, Madison, CT, International Universities Press, 1994, pp. 321–336.
4 D. Winnicott, *Playing and Reality*, London, Tavistock, 1971; rpt. New York, Routledge, 1989, p. 106.
5 Kris, E. (1955) "Neutralization and sublimation: observations on young children," *Psychoanalytic Study of the Child* 10, 30.
6 H. Loewald, *Sublimation: Inquiries into Theoretical Psychoanalysis, The Essential Loewald: Collected Papers and Monographs*, Hagerstown, MD, University Publishing Group, 2000, p. 453.
7 See Solms, M. (1997) "Review of *Affect Regulation and the Origin of the Self: The Neurobiology of Emotional Development*", by Allan N. Schore, *Journal of the American Psychoanalytic Association* 54(3), 968.
8 G. Rose, "From dreams to creative vision: toward affect theory," *The Spectrum of Psychoanalysis*, Richards, R. K. and Richards, A. D. (eds). Madison, CT, International Universities Press, 1994, p. 343.
9 Hartman posed this question to the Psychoanalysis and Literature discussion group of the American Psychoanalytic Association at their annual meeting in New York in December 2001.
10 A. Damasio, *The Feeling of What Happens: Body and Emotion in the Making of Consciousness*, New York, Harcourt, 1999, pp. 188–189.
11 Damasio, *The Feeling of What Happens*, p. 188.
12 P. B. Neubauer and A. Neubauer, *Nature's Thumbprint*, New York, Columbia University Press, 1996, p. 47.
13 J. J. Ratey, *A User's Guide to the Brain*, New York, Vintage Books, 2002, pp. 162 and 174.
14 Damasio, *The Feeling of What Happens*, p. 22.
15 A. M. Cooper, "The Chaning psychoanalytic model of the mind," *Whose Freud?*, eds P. Brooks and A. Woloch, New Haven, Yale University Press, 2000, pp. 275–280; A. H. Modell, *Imagination and the Meaningful Brain*, Cambridge, MA,

MIT Press, 2003; and Damasio, paper presented at the Arnold Pfeffer Center for Neuro-Psychoanalysis at the New York Psychoanalytic Institute, March 2, 2002.

16 See E. Gellhorn, *Physiological Foundations of Neurology and Psychiatry*, Minneapolis, University of Minneapolis Press, 1953, p. 389.

1 Creativity and biology

1 H. Gardner, *Creating Minds*, NewYork, Basic Books, 1993, pp. 7–9.

2 Simonton, D. K. (2003) "Scientific creativity as constrained stochastic behavior: the integration of product, person, and process perspectives," *Psychological Bulletin* 129, 484. I am grateful to Leon Hoffman for bringing Simonton's work to my attention.

3 Simonton, p. 486.

4 Simonton, p. 490.

5 M. Reiser, "Relationship of psychoanalysis to neuroscience," *Textbook of Psychoanalysis*, eds E. Nersessian and R. Kopff, Washington, DC and London, American Psychiatric Press, 1996, p. 625.

6 See Reiser, "Relationship of psychoanalysis to neuroscience," in particular, pp. 625–628.

7 E. Jacobson, *The Self and The Object World*, New York: International Universities Press, 1964, p. 81–84.

8 P. Dunn, e-mail communication to L.O. of October 3, 2004. I am grateful to Dr. Dunn for his comments on differences in Kris and Brenner's points of view.

9 Brenner, "Creativity and psychodynamics," pp. 514 and 512.

10 A. Flaherty, "Mood and creative state influences on temporal perception: how the brain minds the time," paper presented at the International Psychoanalytical Biennial Meeting, New Orleans, March 11, 2004.

11 Heilman has studied the relation of stress and stress-reducing drugs to creative problem solving in, for example, "Noradrenergic modulation of cognitive flexibility in problem solving," *NeuroReport* 10, 2763–2767.

12 N. Holland, "What is creativity?" in *Your Mind On Media*, available on-line at http://www.clas.ufl.edu/users/nnh/, October 10, 2004, pp. 23, 25, 31.

13 S. Zeki, *Inner Vision: An Exploration of Art and the Brain*, Oxford, Oxford University Press, 1999, pp. 3 and 22.

14 S. Freud, "Dostoevsky and parricide," cited by P. Gay, *The Freud Reader*, New York, Norton, 1989, p. 444.

15 Van der Kolk, B. A. (2000) "Neuroscience and the etiology of hysteria: an exploration of the relevance of Breuer and Freud's 1893 article in light of modern neuroscience," *Journal of the American Academy of Neuroscience* 28(2), 248–249.

16 Greenacre, P. (1957) "Play in relation to creative imagination," *Psychoanalytic Study of the Child* 14, 77.

17 Mayes, L. C. and Cohen, D. J. (1992) "The development of a capacity for imagination in early childhood," *Psychoanalytic Study of the Child* 47, 23.

18 A. Freud, "Foreword" to Marion Milner, *On Not Being Able to Paint*, New York, Penguin, 1957, p. xv.

19 Freud, A. "Sublimation as a factor in upbringing," *Health Education Journal* 6, n.p.; cited by E. Young-Bruehl in *Anna Freud: A Biography*, New York, Norton, 1988, p. 319.

20 J. E. Gedo, *The Artist and the Emotional World*, New York, Columbia University Press, 1996, pp. 29 and 31.

21 Panksepp and Solms' remarks were part of a discussion that took place on July 27, 2003, at the 4th annual Neuro-Psychoanalysis Congress in New York.

22 R. Pally, *The Mind–Brain Relationship*, London, Karnac, 2000, p. 6.

23 See, for instance, Urrila et al. (2003) "Metabolic imaging of human cognition: an fMRI/1H-MRS study of brain lactate response to silent word generation," *Journal of Cerebral Blood Flow Metabolism* 8, 942–948. The authors of this recent paper on metabolism and cognition found by using spectroscopic imaging (proton magnetic resonance spectroscopy or 1H MRS) that the lactate level in a particular region of the brain, the left inferior frontal gyrus, is significantly raised in subjects performing a silent word-generation task.

24 Levin, F. (1997) "Integrating some mind and brain views of transference: the phenomena," *Journal of the American Psychoanalytic Association* 45, 1129–1130.

25 Schore, A. (2001) "Effects of a secure attachment relationship on right brain development, affect regulation, and infant mental health," *Infant Mental Health Journal* 22, 7–66. Andreason's work is cited by David V. Forrest, in "Freud's neuromental model: analytic structures and local habitations," *Whose Freud?*, eds P. Brooks and A. Woloch, New Haven, Yale University Press, 2000, p. 258.

26. Shulman and Rothman discuss Solms's view, as expressed in "What is consciousness?" (*Journal of the American Psychoanalytic Association* 45 [1997], 681–703), in "Freud's theory of the mind and modern functional imaging experiments," *Whose Freud?*, pp. 267–274.

27 Cited by David V. Forrest in "Freud's neuromental model: analytic structures and local habitations," *Whose Freud?*, p. 259.

28 M. Solms and O. Turnbull, *The Brain and the Inner World*, NewYork, Other Press, 2002, p. 310 (emphasis mine).

29 Turnbull, O. (2001) "Cognitive neuropsychology comes of age," *Cortex* 37, 446.

30 See Reiser, M. "Can psychoanalysis and cognitive-emotional neuroscience collaborate in remodelling our concept of mind brain?," *Whose Freud?*, p. 249.

31 Solms, M. (1997) "What is consciousness?," *Journal of the American Psychoanalytic Association* 45, 681–703.

32 See, for example, the debate between Panksepp and Damasio as referred to in Panksepp's review of Damasio's book, *The Feeling of What Happens*, in *Neuro-Psychoanalysis* 2, 86.

33 Schore, A. (1997) "A century after Freud's project: is a rapprochement between psychoanalysis and neurobiology at hand?," *Journal of the American Psychoanalytic Association* 45, 827–829 and 822.

34 See G. Lakoff and M. Johnson, *Philosophy in the Flesh*, NewYork, Basic Books, 1999, in particular pp. 54–59.

35 A. Modell, *The Private Self*, Cambridge, MA, Harvard University Press, 1993, pp. 48 and 163.

36 Cited by Modell, from his then unpublished *Imagination and the Meaningful Brain*, in an e-mail communication to L.O. of April 12, 2002.

37 Modell, *The Private Self*, p. 164.

38 Modell, A. "Reflections on metaphor and affects," *PsyArt: A Hyperlink Journal for the Psychological Study of the Arts*, article 000906. September 6, 2000, n.p. http://www.clas.ufl.edu/ipsa/journal/articles/psyart2000/modell01.htm, available April 12, 2002.

39 Modell, "Reflections on metaphor and affects," n.p.

40 Ramachandran, V. S. with S. Blakeslee, *Phantoms in the Brain*, NewYork, William Morrow, 1998, p. 112. Ramachandran goes on to mention Charles Bonnet syndrome, a common disorder of sight pathways between eye and brain in which the brain provides as hallucinations whatever visual data may be missing.

41 This has been noted by Garry Kennard in "The uses of paradox: brain function and the arts," *PsyArt: A Hyperlink Journal for Psychological Study of the Arts*, article 010214. February 14, 2001. http://www.clas.ufl.edu/ipsa/journal/articles/psyart2001/kennar01.htm, available April 12, 2002.

42 K. Burke, *A Grammar of Motives*, Berkeley and Los Angeles, University of California Press, 1969, p. 503. Sidney Feshbach is to be thanked for bringing Burke's writings on metaphor to my attention.
43 Pally, *The Mind–Brain Relationship*, p. 132.
44 Damasio, *The Feeling of What Happens*, pp. 315–316.
45 Freud, *The Ego and the Id*, SE 1923, New York and London, Norton, 1960, p. 8.
46 Freud, *The Freud Reader*, ed. Peter Gay, NewYork, Norton, 1989, p. 625.
47 G. J. Rose, *The Power of Form*, Madison, CT, International Universities Press, 1980, p. 15.
48 Rose, *The Power of Form*, p.10.
49 Rose, *The Power of Form*, p. 21.
50 G. Rose, "From dreams to creative vision: toward affect theory," *The Spectrum of Psychoanalysis*, p. 346.
51 Rose, "From dreams to creative vision," p. 345.
52 Rose, "From dreams to creative vision," p. 346.
53 Rose, *The Power of Form*, p. 201.
54 G. Rose, *Trauma and Mastery in Life and Art*, Madison, CT, International Universities Press, 1987, p. 210 (emphasis mine).
55 Rose, *Between Couch and Piano*, London, Routledge, 2004, pp. 159–160.
56 See Schore, A. (2002) "Dysregulation of the right brain: a fundamental mechanism of traumatic attachment and the psychopathogenesis of post-traumatic stress disorder," *Australian and New Zealand Journal of Psychiatry* 36, 9–30.
57 Levin, "Integrating some mind and brain views of transference, p. 1129.
58 Holland, "What is creativity?," p. 17.

2 Redressing the question: Neuroscience and the "feminine" in art

1 Cf. S. Felman, *Writing and Madness*, Palo Alto, Stanford University Press, 2003, p. 278.
2 J. K. Gardiner, "On female identity and writing by women," *Writing and Sexual Difference*, ed. E. Abel, Chicago, University of Chicago Press, 1982, pp. 190–191.
3 Cited by M. R. Witzling in "Through the flower: Judy Chicago's conflict between a woman-centered vision and the male artist hero," *Writing the Woman Artist: Essays on Poetics, Politics, and Portraiture*, ed. S. W. Jones, Philadelphia, University of Pennsyvania, 1991, p. xiv.
4 J. Chicago, *The Birth Project*, New York, Doubleday, 1985, p. 224.
5 Chicago, *The Birth Project*, p. 12.
6 Chicago, *The Birth Project*, p. 13.
7 G. Rose, "The artist as child: roots of human creativity," paper presented on April 27, 2002, at a one-day conference on creativity organized in New York by the Lucy Daniels Foundation. I thank Dr. Rose for making the text of his talk available to me.
8 Chicago, *The Birth Project*, p. 13.
9 Chicago, *The Birth Project*, p. 78.
10 Cited by J. Gallop in *Thinking Through the Body*, NewYork, Columbia University Press, 1988, p. 1.
11 D. Stanton, in *Feminist Literary Theory*, 2nd edn, ed. M. Eagleton, Oxford, Blackwell, 1996, pp. 335–336.
12 E. O. Wilson, *Consilience: The Unity of Knowledge*, New York, Knopf, 1998, p. 214.
13 S. R. Suleiman, "Introduction" to Hélène Cixous *"Coming to Writing" and Other Essays*, Cambridge, Harvard University Press, 1991, pp. vii–viii.
14 Greenacre, P. (1960) "Woman as artist," *Psychoanalytic Quarterly* 29, 210.
15 Greenacre, "Woman as artist," p. 211.

16 Greenacre, "Woman as artist," p. 218.
17 Showalter, E. (1981) "Feminist criticism in the wilderness," *Critical Inquiry* 8; rpt. *Feminist Criticism: Essays on Women, Literature, Theory*, ed. E. Showalter, New York, Pantheon Books, 1985, p. 250.
18 Cixous, H. (1976) "The laugh of the Medusa," *Signs*, rpt. *New French Feminisms*, eds E. Marks and I. de Courtivron, Amherst, University of Massachusetts Press, 1980, pp. 246, 251–252. Quotation translated by K. Cohen and P. Cohen.
19 H. Cixous, interview with Conley, in V. A. Conley, *Hélène Cixous: Writing the Feminine*, Lincoln, University of Nebraska Press, 1984, p. 129.
20 Cixous, interview with Conley, p. 158.
21 V. A. Conley, "The Feminine and ecology," *On the Feminine*, ed. M. Calle, trans. C. McGann, Atlantic Highlands, NJ, Humanities Press, 1996, pp. 42–44.
22 L. Irigaray, *Thinking the Difference*, trans. Karin Montin, NewYork, Routledge, 1994, pp. 24–26 and 29.
23 L. Irigaray, "This sex which is not one," cited in *Luce Irigaray: Philosophy in the Feminine*, ed. M. Witford, London, Routledge, 1991, p. 46.
24 Gauthier, X. (1974) "Existe-t-il une écriture de femme?," *Tel Quel*; rpt. in trans. by M. A. August, *New French Feminisms*, p. 163.
25 N. Sarraute, *Three Decades of the French New Novel*, ed. L. Oppenheim, trans. L. Oppenheim and E. Costa de Beauregard, Urbana, University of Illinois Press, 1986, p. 122.
26 Michèle Montrelay makes this point in "Inquiry into femininity," *French Feminist Thought*, ed. T. Moi, Cambridge, MA, Basil Blackwell, 1987, p. 239.
27 L. Irigaray, "Sexual difference," *French Feminist Thought*, p. 120.
28 Leon Roudiez reminds us of this in his introduction to Julia Kristeva, *Desire in Language*, New York, Columbia University Press, 1980, p. 16.
29 Kristeva, *French Feminist Thought*, pp. 114 and 111.
30 Kristeva, *New French Feminisms*, p. 137.
31 Freud, "The Neuro-Psychoses of Defence," SE Vol. 3, p. 60.
32 Freud, "Three Essays on Sexuality," SE Vol. 7, p. 219.
33 Freud, "New Introductory Lectures on Psycho-Analysis," SE Vol. 22, p. 131 (italics mine).
34 Freud, "New Introductory Lectures on Psycho-Analysis," p. 131.
35 Personal e-mail communication to L.O. dated October 18, 2004.
36 Kristeva has named in this regard Mallarmé, Lautréamont, Joyce, and Artaud. See, for example, Kristeva, J. (2000) "From symbols to flesh: the polymorphous destiny of narration," *International Journal of Psychoanalysis* 81, 772.
37 E. Young-Bruehl, *Freud on Women: A Reader*, New York and London, Norton, 1990, p. 19. It should be noted, though, that Freud did write of "our predisposition to bisexuality" in his "Postcript to Fragment of an Analysis of a Case of Hysteria," SE Vol. 7, p. 114 and elsewhere.
38 R. Balsam, "Thoughts on mothers, daughters, their bodies and showing off," paper presented at the Psychoanalytic Association of New York, December 8, 2003. In an e-mail communication to me dated October 16, 2004, Dr. Balsam made several stimulating comments about the need for a concept of female libido that would be equal to male libido. Many of her references in that communication provided the basis for the present discussion.
39 Personal e-mail communication to L.O. dated October 21, 2004.
40 This point was made by Peter Dunn, in his e-mail of October 18, 2004. I am grateful to Dr. Dunn for his clarification of aspects of Freud's thinking on libido and for bringing to my attention *Basic Psychoanalytic Concepts on the Libido Theory*, Vol. I, ed. H. Nagera, London, The Hampstead Clinic Library, 1969; rpt. Maresfield Reprints, 1981.

41 Kristeva, "From symbols to flesh: the polymorphous destiny of narration," p. 773.
42 Interestingly, though, Cixous denies any affiliation (beyond friendship) with the French psychoanalyst while affirming, rather, a deep allegiance to Freud. Her reversals of Freudian theory (in *Portrait de Dora*, for instance, where the excess of hysteria is celebrated as a positive dimension of the feminine) are criticisms, but also declarations of fealty to the man she calls "a real hero" and, playfully, her uncle: "Freud oui: comme je le dis toujours for fun c'est mon oncle. [. . .] un vrai héros." (Freud yes: as I always say for fun he's my uncle [. . .] a real hero." *Entretien avec Hélène Cixous*, F.-Y. Jeannet, Paris, Galilée, 2005.
43 Cf. M. Calle-Gruber: "To write, to paint is: never to see the end; attempt after attempt, to begin again, to begin *oneself* again. By which the work is infinite desire. The desire to work." "Afterword," *The Hélène Cixous Reader*, ed. S. Sellers, London, Routledge, 1994, p. 212.
44 H. Cixous, "Coming to writing," *"Coming to Writing" and Other Essays*, ed. D. Jenson, trans. Sarah Cornell et al., Cambridge, Harvard University Press, 1991, pp. 56–58.
45 See Josephine Donovan, "Feminist style criticism," in *Images of Women in Fiction*, ed. S. Koppelman Cornillon, Bowling Green, OH, Bowling Green University Popular Press, 1972, pp. 343–345. It should be noted, however, that my use of the term "female consciousness" differs entirely from that to which Donovan refers in her essay.
46 Balsam, R. (2001) "Integrating male and female elements in a woman's gender identity," *Journal of the American Psychoanalytic Association* 49(4), 1338 and 1357.
47 For a close analysis of the term, see Hoffman, L. (1996) "Freud and feminine subjectivity," *Journal of the American Psychoanalytic Association* 44 (suppl.), 23–44.
48 S. LeVay, *The Sexual Brain*, Cambridge, MIT Press, 1993, pp. 28–29 and M. Solms and O. Turnbull, *The Brain and the Inner World*, New York, Other Press, 2002, pp. 223 and 227.
49 Solms and Turnbull, *The Brain and the Inner World*, p. 231. This is not to imply, however, that social values are not also profoundly influential or that biology is the sole determinant of cognitive and behavioral differences between the sexes. For an eloquent discussion of the interplay of biological and social causation, see L. Rogers "What causes sex differences" in *Sexing the Brain*, NewYork, Columbia University Press, 2001, pp. 23–46.
50 D. D. Kelly, "Sexual differentiation of the nervous system," *Principles of Neural Science*, eds E. R. Kandel and J. H. Schwartz, 2nd edn, NewYork, Elsevier, 1985, p. 778.
51 Cf. Solms and Turnbull, *The Brain and the Inner World*, pp. 228–229. With regard to the size differential of the corpus callosum, while most studies confirm this, there is some conflicting evidence. See, for example, Bishop, K. M. and Wahlsten, D. (1997) "Sex differences in the human corpus callosum: myth or reality?", *Neuroscience and Biobehaviorial Reviews* 21, 581–601. Similarly, with regard to claims of superior spatial abilities in men, Lesley Rogers cites a review of the relevant literature on sex differences that yielded conflicting results, *Sexing the Brain*, p. 84.
52 See, for instance, Rabinowitz, T. et al. (2002) "Structure of the cerebral cortex in men and women," *Journal Neuropathology and Experimental Neurology* 61(1), 46–57, and Schlaepfer, T. E. et al. (1995) "Structural differences in the cerebral cortex of healthy female and male subjects: a magnetic resonance imaging study," *Psychiatry Research* 61(3), 129–135. Other studies reaching the same conclusions are far too numerous to name.
53 Solms and Turnbull, *The Brain and the Inner World*, p. 64.
54 Solms and Turnbull, *The Brain and the Inner World*, p. 91.

55 Solms and Turnbull, *The Brain and the Inner World*, p. 91.
56 E. Showalter, "Feminist criticism in the wilderness," p. 250.
57 D. Morris, *The Biology of Art*, London, Methuen, 1962, pp. 159–167.
58 G. Rose, *The Power of Form*, Madison, CT, International Universities Press, 1980, p. 200.
59 H. Shevrin, "The unconscious: theory and findings," paper presented at the neuro-psychoanalysis meeting of July 2003, at the New York University Medical Center in New York. I am exceedingly grateful to Dr. Shevrin for making his work available to me prior to publication.
60 See P. Blos, "Modifications in the traditional psychoanalytic theory of female adolescent development," in *Adolescent Psychiatry*, eds S.C. Feinstein et al., Chicago: University of Chicago Press, 1980, p. 12.
61 J. LeDoux, *The Emotional Brain*, New York, Simon & Schuster, 1996, p. 282.
62 Solms and Turnbull, *The Brain and the Inner World*, pp. 82–83. I wish to acknowledge Oliver Turnbull's clarification, in a succession of e-mails from June 2004, of some of the most complex aspects of the representational system.
63 Decety, J. and Sommerville, J. A. (2003), "Shared representations between self and other: a social cognitive neuroscience view," *TRENDS in Cognitive Sciences* 7(12), 527–533.
64 A. Modell, *The Private Self*, Cambridge: Harvard University Press, 1993, p. 49.
65 S. Freud (1915) "Instincts and Their Vicissitudes," SE Vol. 14, pp. 122–123. "Drive" is today considered closer to Freud's use of the German *Trieb* than "instinct." The other components are aim (*Ziel*), object (*Objekt*), and source (*Quelle*): with aim denoting satisfaction; object meaning that which allows drive to achieve its aim; and source being the somatic origin.
66 J. Panksepp, *Affective Neuroscience*, New York and Oxford, Oxford University Press, 1998, p. 168.
67 H. Shevrin, "The psychoanalytic theory of drive in the light of recent neuroscience findings and theories," paper presented at the Psychoanalytic Association of New York, September 15, 2003.
68 R. Balsam, "Integrating male and female elements in a woman's gender identity," p. 1338.
69 Irigaray, *Thinking the Difference*, pp. 20, 21, and 31.
70 Rogers, *Sexing the Brain*, pp. 12–13.
71 For a succinct overview of the neuroscientific evidence of drive, see Solms, M. (May 2004) "Freud returns," *Newsweek* 290(5), 82–89.
72 Interview with Gary Koepke, in *Louise Bourgeois: Destruction of the Father Reconstruction of the Father: Writings and Interviews 1923–1997*, eds M.-L. Bernadac and H.-U. Obrist, Cambridge, MA, MIT Press, 1998, p. 309.
73 J. Gorovoy and D. Tilkin, "There's No Place Like Home," *Louise Bourgeois: Memory and Architecture*, Museo Nacional Centro de Arte Reina Sofía, Madrid, November 16, 1999–February 14, 2000, p. 15.
74 *Louise Bourgeois: Destruction of the Father Reconstruction of the Father*, p.101.
75 Cited in *Louise Bourgeois: The Locus of Memory, Works 1982–1993*, eds C. Kotik, T. Sultan and C. Leigh, NewYork, Brooklyn Museum in association with Harry N. Abrams, Inc., 1994, pp. 25 and 13.
76 J. Chicago, *Beyond the Flower: The Autobiography of a Feminist Artist*, New York, Penguin, 1996, p. 39.
77 Panksepp, J. and Bernatzky, G. (2002) "Emotional sounds and the brain: the neuro-affective foundations of musical appreciation," *Behavioral Processes* 60, 142–143.
78 See, for instance, Gaab, N. Keenan, J. P. and Schlaug, G. (2003) "The effects of gender on the neural substrates of pitch memory," *Journal of Cognitive Neuroscience* 15(6), 1–11.

79 Panksepp, *Affective Neuroscience*, p. 183.

3 Psychic boundaries in the work of Samuel Beckett

1 N. Holland, *Your Mind on Media*, available on-line at http://www.clas.ufl.edu/users/nnh/, October 10, 2004.
2 Phelan, P. (2004) "Lessons in blindness from Samuel Beckett," *PMLA* 119(5), 1280.
3 Shainberg, L. (1987) "Exorcising Beckett," *Paris Review*, fall, 102.
4 These include several articles and a book by psychoanalyst Didier Anzieu, *Beckett et le Psychanalyste*, Paris, Mentha-Archimbaud, 1992; Phil Baker's *Beckett and the Mythology of Psychoanalysis*, London, Macmillan, 1997; J. D. O'Hara's *Samuel Beckett's Hidden Drives*, Gainesville, University Press of Florida, 1997; *The World of Samuel Beckett*, ed. J. H. Smith, Baltimore, Johns Hopkins University Press, 1991. Though it has not yet been noted, and it may or may not be significant, one of Beckett's titles even bears the surname of a member of the Kulpe School of Psychology, Henry Watt, with whom Beckett was familiar from his readings in the field.
5 The notes are housed in the Beckett archives of the Trinity College Dublin library.
6 Samuel Beckett to Tom MacGreevy, undated letter, but James Knowlson dates it to 23 September 1935. Cited by Knowlson, *Damed to Fame*, New York, Simon & Schuster, 1996, pp. 197–198.
7 Just how influential this treatment was with regard to his writing, though, is not clear. Some, like psychoanalysts Didier Anzieu and Bennett Simon, make claims for a mutual influence between Bion and Beckett on their respective work. Personally, I remain more skeptical. For an in-depth discussion of the question of Bion's impact on Beckett's work, see Oppenheim, L. (2001) "A preoccupation with object-representation: the Beckett–Bion case revisited," *International Journal of Psychoanalysis* 82(4), 767–784.
8 In the introduction to the *Grove Companion*, Stan Gontarski tells us that Robert Burton's *Anatomy of Melancholy* was particularly admired by Beckett and that he could quote easily from his three-volume edition of it (New York, Grove Press, 2004, p. vi).
9 Beckett, *Murphy*, New York, Grove Press, 1957, p. 168.
10 See A. Piette, "Beckett, early neuropsychology and memory loss: Beckett's reading of Clarapede, Janet and Korsakoff," *Beckett in the 1990s*, eds M. Buning and L. Oppenheim, Amsterdam, Rodopi, 1993, pp. 46 and 41.
11 B. Simon, "The fragmented self, the reproduction of the self, and reproduction in Beckett and in the Theater of the Absurd," *The World of Samuel Beckett*, ed. J. Smith, 1991, p. 158.
12 Beckett, *Stirrings Still*, New York, Blue Moon Books and London, John Calder, 1989, p. 1.
13 The term is Ruby Cohn's. See her essay, "Ghosting Through Beckett," *Beckett in the 1990s*, eds M. Buning and L. Oppenheim, pp. 1–11.
14 Cf. M. Bryden, J. Garforth and P. Mills, *Beckett at Reading Catalogue of the Beckett Manuscript Collection at The University of Reading*, Reading, Whiteknights Press and the Beckett International Foundation, 1998, p. 83.
15 S. Beckett, *The Unnamable*, New York, Grove Press, 1958, pp. 71 and 19.
16 E. Brater, *Beyond Minimalism*, New York, Oxford University Press, 1987, p. 172.
17 J. Knowlson, *Damned to Fame*, New York: Simon & Schuster, 1996, p. 589.
18 S. Gilman, *Disease and Representation*, Ithaca, Cornell University Press, 1988, p. 2.
19 Winnicott, D. W. (1974) "Fear of breakdown," *International Journal of Psycho-Analysis*; rpt. *Psychoanalytic Explorations*, eds C. Winnicott et al., London, Karnac, 1989, pp. 89–90.

20 Knowlson, p. 383.
21 A. Flaherty, *The Midnight Disease: The Drive to Write, Writer's Block, and the Creative Brain*, Boston and New York, Houghton Mifflin, 2004, pp. 119–123.
22 Knowlson, p. 544.
23 Knowlson, pp. 172 and 174. I am grateful to Bernard Meehan, Keeper of Manuscripts of the Trinity College Dublin library, for early access to Beckett's notes.
24 S. Beckett, *Not I, The Collected Shorter Plays of Samuel Beckett*, New York, Grove Press, 1984, pp. 216 and 215.
25 B. Whitelaw, *Who He?*, New York, St. Martin's Press, 1995, pp. 116 and 130.
26 S. Beckett, *Not I, The Collected Shorter Plays of Samuel Beckett*, New York, Grove Press, 1984, p. 216.
27 A. Damasio, *The Feeling of What Happens*, San Diego, New York, and London, Harcourt, 1999, p.145.
28 See Holland's "The willing suspension of disbelief: a neuro-psychoanalytic view," in *PsyArt: A Hyperlink Journal for the Psychological Study of the Arts*, article 020919. Available http://www.clas.ufl.edu/ipsa/journal/2003/hollan06.htm, December 31, 2003.
29 Flaherty, pp. 42 and 206–209.
30 See Oppenheim, L. (2001) "A preoccupation with object representation: the Beckett–Bion case revisited," pp. 769–770.
31 Cf. Anzieu, D. (1983) "Un soi disjoint, une voix liante: l'écriture narrative de Samuel Beckett," *Nouvelle Revue de Psychanalyse* 28, 81.
32 H. P. Abbott, *Beckett Writing Beckett: The Author in the Autograph*, Ithaca, Cornell University Press, 1996, p. 14. Abbott's thesis in this important book is based on a distinction between autography, all self-writing, and autobiography, a subset of it that is the narrative of one's life (see p. 2). My own concept of Beckett's artistic purpose as a means of writing a unified self into existence is in full accord with Abbott's vision, though our interpretive aims differ.
33 R. Schafer, *Tradition and Change in Psychoanalysis*, London, Karnac, 1997, p. 97.
34 Winnicott, personal letter housed in the archives of the British Psychoanalytic Society.
35 In Freudian drive theory, which neuroscience is now able to validate with modern imaging devices, excitation in the body is what impels the mind to work. Charles Brenner has stressed the point that the term "somatopsychic" is tautologous for this very reason. See Brenner, *The Mind in Conflict*, New York, International Universities Press, 1982, pp. 20, 23, and 25.
36 Cf. Freud, "Instincts and Their Vicissitudes," SE Vol. 14, p. 122. Although Freud's reference in this paper was to instinctual stimuli produced within the body, insofar as the perception of external stimuli is also an organic process, the notion of what Freud calls a "psychic representative" remains the same. At a meeting of the American Psychoanalytic Association (January 2003), Howard Shevrin called attention to this distinction between representation as re-presentation and representation in the sense members of congress represent us.
37 I owe this explanation to J. D. Nasio, *Hysteria from Freud to Lacan*, ed. and trans. S. Fairfield, New York, Other Press, 1998; French edition 1990, pp. 13–31.
38 Freud (1988) "Hysteria," SE Vol. 1, pp. 57 and 49.
39 *Not I*, pp. 217 and 218.
40 See, for example, Turnbull, O., Jones, K. and Reed-Screen, J. (2002) "Implicit awareness of deficit in anosognosia: an emotion-based account of denial of deficit," *Neuro-Psychoanalysis* 4, 69–86.
41 Damasio, *The Feeling of What Happens*, p. 112.
42 Most of this list comes from Abbott, *Beckett Writing Beckett*, pp. 165–166.
43 Sidney Feshbach offers a highly intelligent consideration of this tension in "Unswamping a backwater: on Samuel Beckett's film," *Samuel Beckett and the Arts*, ed. L. Oppenheim, New York and London, Garland, 1999, pp. 333–363.

44 See Feshbach, p. 343.
45 I am grateful to Eugene Kaplan, M.D., for his clarification in a personal communication of the criteria of the diagnosis of alexithymia based on J. C. Nemiah and P. E. Sifneos, "Affect and fantasy in patients with psychosomatic disorders," in O.W. Hill, ed. *Modern Trends in Psychosomatic Medicine 2*, London, Butterworths, 1970, pp. 26–34.
46 S. Beckett, letter to Axel Kaun, *Disjecta*, ed. R. Cohn, New York, Grove Press, 1984, p. 172.
47 See Schafer, p. 81.
48 Cf. McMullan, A. (2001) "Virtual subjects: performance, technology and the body in Beckett's late theatre," *Journal of Beckett Studies* 10, 165–172.
49 H. P. Abbott, "Egregious omissions: Samuel Beckett and the theory and practice of narrative gaps," *Palgrave Advances in Beckett Studies*, ed. L. Oppenheim, London and New York, Palgrave Macmillan, 2004, pp. 20 and 10.
50 Whitelaw, *Billie Whitelaw . . . Who He?*, p. 120.
51 Whitelaw, p. 125.
52 E. Brater, *Why Beckett*, London, Thames and Hudson, 1989, p. 85; G. Buttner, *Samuel Beckett's Novel "Watt"*, trans. J. P. Dolan, Philadelphia, University of Pennsylvania Press, 1984, p. xiii.
53 G. Hauck, *Reductionism in Drama and the Theatre: The Case of Samuel Beckett*, Potomac, MD, Scripta Humanistica, 1992, p. 206, n.17.
54 M. Esslin, "Teaching it how it is: Beckett and the mass media," *The World of Samuel Beckett*, ed. J. H. Smith, p. 211.
55 A. Modell, *Imagination and the Meaningful Brain*, Cambridge, MA, MIT Press, 2003, p. 27.
56 Esslin, p. 208.
57 Brater, *Beyond Minimalism*, p. 23.
58 Whitelaw, p. 118.
59 Janet Baird, a neuroscientist and psychiatrist, has intelligently demonstrated how schema theory may function as a "common language and conceptual framework" of neuroscience and psychoanalysis to allow for a "more fertile collaboration" between the two disciplines. It is her explanation of the evolution of schema "beyond the a priori cognitive structures envisioned by Kant" to the Piagetian conceptions of assimilation and accommodation that serves as the basis for the following discussion. I am grateful to Dr. Baird for allowing me to read her forthcoming papers, "Toward Building a Unified Theory of Mind. I: Schema Theory" and "Toward Building a Unified Theory of Mind. II: Reframing Psychoanalytic Concepts from a Schema Theory Perspective" and for our many fruitful conversations.
60 P. L. Wachtel, "Transference, schema, and assimilation: the relevance of Piaget to the psychoanalytic theory of transference," http://www.cyberpsych.org/sepi/wachtel.htm, available July 3, 2003, n.p.
61 A. Damasio, *Descartes' Error*, New York, Avon, 1994, pp. 173–174 and 177.
62 S. Pinker, *The Blank Slate: The Modern Denial of Human Nature*, New York, Viking, p. 417.
63 Wachtel, "Transference, schema, and assimilation: the relevance of Piaget to the psychoanalytic theory of transference," n.p.
64 I take my inspiration here from Wachtel's discussion of the arousal of schemata in analysis.
65 Modell, *The Private Self*, Cambridge, MA, Harvard University Press, 1993, p. 175.
66 Modell, *The Private Self*, pp. 48–49.
67 J. Baird, "Toward building a unified theory of mind. II: Reframing psychoanalytic concepts from a schema theory perspective," p. 8.

68 L. Hunt, "The novel and the origins of human rights: the intersection of history, psychology and literature," paper presented at Fordham University, New York City, February 19, 2003.
69 See J. A. Seitz, "The embodied self," paper presented at the 13th annual meeting of the Jean Piaget Society, June 3, 2000, http:www.york.cuny.edu/seitz/montreal.htm, available March 13, 2003.
70 G. Rose, *The Power of Form*, Madison, CT, International Universities Press, 1980, p. 200.
71 Cf. J. R. Keller, *Samuel Beckett and the Primacy of Love*, Manchester, Manchester University Press, 2002, p. 19.
72 *No Author Better Served: The Correspondence of Samuel Beckett and Alan Schneider*, ed. M. Harmon, Cambridge, MA, Harvard University Press, 1998, p. 283.
73 Beckett was said by Alan Schneider to have written this, or something comparable. See L. Oppenheim, *Directing Beckett*, Ann Arbor, University of Michigan Press, 1994, p. 10.

4 Paul Klee's late style

1 See M. Franciscono, "Klees Krankheit und seine Bilder des Todes," *Paul Klee: Das Schaffen im Todesjahr*, eds S. Frey, J. Helfenstein, and W. Kersten, Berne, Kunstmuseum, 1990, p. 13. I am very grateful to Franciscono for supplying me with the original English version of his essay.
2 M. Franciscono, *Paul Klee: His Work and Thought*, Chicago, University of Chicago Press, 1991, p. 289.
3 Franciscono, "Klees Krankheit und seine Bilder des Todes," p. 13. It should be noted that the critic does very briefly take up these two questions in the essay, if not in the above named book.
4 Franciscono, "Klees Krankheit und seine Bilder des Todes," p. 20.
5 R. Kudielka, *Paul Klee: The Nature of Creation*, London, Hayward Gallery, 2002, pp. 161–162.
6 A. Kagan, "Klee's development," *Paul Klee at the Guggenheim Museum*, New York, Guggenheim Museum, 1993, p. 46.
7 P. Klee, *The Thinking Eye*, ed. J. Spiller, trans. R. Manheim, New York, George Wittenborn, 1961, p. 17.
8 J. S. Pierce, *Paul Klee and Primitive Art*, New York and London, Garland, 1976, pp. 139–146.
9 W. Haftmann, *The Mind and Work of Paul Klee*, New York, Frederick A. Praeger, 1967, pp. 197–199.
10 M. Luprecht, *Of Angels, Things, and Death: Paul Klee's Last Painting in Context*, New York, Peter Lang, 1999, p. 61.
11 E. Dreifuss-Kattan, *Beyond Words and Time: Mourning and Art. A Psychoanalytic Exploration*, forthcoming. I am grateful to Dr. Dreifuss-Kattan for sharing material from her book with me prior to its publication.
12 Franciscono, *Paul Klee: His Work and Thought*, p. 320.
13 S. Abrams, paper presented at the Psychoanalytic Association of New York meeting of February 9, 2004.
14 J. McDougall, "Creativity and sexuality," in *Spectrum of Psychoanalysis: Essays in Honor of Martin S. Bergmann*, eds A. Kramer Richards and A. D. Richards, Madison, CT, International Universities Press, p. 374.
15 See, for instance, Wolf, G. (1999) "*Endure!*: how Paul Klee's illness influenced his art," *The Lancet*, p. 1517.

16 Personal e-mail communication to L. O. of January 31, 2004. All additional citations from Dr. Benedek are from this or another e-mail of February 3, 2004. I am extremely appreciative of Dr. Benedek's having made this information and other materials available to me.

17 G. Castenholz, *Die progressive systemische Sklerose: Analyse und Geschichte unter besonderer Berücksichtigung der Krankheit des Malers Paul Klee*, Marburg, Verlag Görich and Weierschäuser GmbH, 2000, pp. 136–139.

18 This is reported by Dr. Hans Suter in the medical report "Vom Leiden gezeichnet – und dennoch" in Blackwell Wissenschafts-Verlag GmbH Berlin, Deutscher Schmerzkongress 1998, Nr. 31/22, 1998, pp. 20–21.

19 On p. 1118 of Osler's *The Principles and Practice of Medicine*, 9th edn, New York, Appleton, 1920, we read: "Thyroid feeding should be tried thoroughly in the diffuse form. In one case the disease appeared to be arrested; the patient took the extract for seven years. In a second case, after a year the face became softer and there was permanent improvement." The quotation appears in R. L. Sutton and R. L. Sutton, Jr., *Diseases of the Skin*, St. Louis, C. V. Mosby, 1939, p. 488. In addition to thyroid, "posterior pituitary extract, ovarian extract, and probably others received small trials in those years," Benedek has said. "But these were more indicative of therapeutic desperation than underlying medical hypotheses."

20 I owe much of this information to Benedek to whom, once again, I am grateful for his many personal communications.

21 See Beerman, H. and Stokes, J. H. (1949) "The treatment of scleroderma," *American Journal of the Medical Sciences* 217, 453–461.

22 F. Klee, *Paul Klee*, trans. R. and C. Winston, New York, George Braziller, 1962, p. 71.

23 For what he himself admits is a purely speculative connection between external stress and Klee's illness, see M. Reiner, "Dämmerblüten – Versuch einer Pathographie Paul Klees," in the exhibition catalogue of the Mendrisio Museum of Art, *Paul Klee – Ultimo decennio 1930–1940*, Mendrisio, 1990, pp. 35–38, cited in Castenholz, p. 143. For Morscher's discussion of the psychosomatic pathogenesis of Klee's scleroderma, see Morscher, C. (1994) "Paul Klee une die Hypothese der morphischen Resonanz," *PPmP Psychotherapie Psychosomatik Medizinische Psychologie* 44, 200–206.

24 Klee, *The Diaries of Paul Klee 1898–1918*, ed. F. Klee, Berkeley and Los Angeles, University of California Press, 1964, entry no. 675, p. 185. I am grateful to Marcel Franciscono for supplying me with the precise date of this entry: July 1905.

25 Arlow, J. (1969) "Unconscious fantasy and disturbances of conscious experience," *Psychoanalytic Quarterly* 38, 21.

26 Klee, *The Diaries*, entry no. 638, pp. 176–177.

27 Arlow, J., "Unconscious fantasy and disturbances of conscious experience," p. 5.

28 Cited by M. Vishny, "Paul Klee's self-images," *Psychoanalytic Perspectives on Art*, ed. M. M. Gedo, Hillsdale, NJ, Analytic Press, 1985, p. 137.

29 Vishny, p. 137.

30 Klee, *The Diaries*, entry no. 517, p. 144.

31 Vishny, p. 147. Although Vishny refers to this work as *Lost in Thought*, *Absorption* is the official title.

32 Klee, *The Diaries*, entry no. 1008, pp. 344–345.

33 Klee, *The Thinking Eye*, p. 105.

34 Klee, *The Thinking Eye*, p. 79.

35 J. Spiller, preface to *The Thinking Eye*, p. 17.

36 Franciscono, *Paul Klee His Work and Thought*, p. 262.

37 I owe this brief review of erotic imagery to Vishny, pp. 147–148.

38 Klee, cited by Spiller in the preface to *The Thinking Eye*, p. 20.

39 Klee, *The Diaries*, entry no. 633, p. 176.

40 Klee, *The Diaries*, entry no. 538, p. 147.
41 Vishny, pp. 137–138 and Klee, *The Diaries*, entry no. 610, p. 172.
42 See, in particular, Vishny, p. 140 and p. 165–166.
43 Ferraro, F. (2003) "Psychic bisexuality and creativity," *International Journal of Psychoanalysis* 84, 1453–1454.
44 Klee, *The Diaries*, entry nos. 943, 944, 57, and 505; pp. 310, 312, 16, and 141.
45 Luprecht, *Of Angels, Things, and Death: Paul Klee's Last Painting in Context*, pp. 62 and 82.
46 See Luprecht, p. 83. Luprecht also notes, with regard to *Daemon*, that "Klee has seemingly followed the etymology of the word, which derives from 'daimonai' meaning 'divide.'"
47 Luprecht, p. 86.
48 Klee, *The Diaries*, entry no. 538, p. 147.
49 Franciscono, *Paul Klee: His Work and Thought*, p. 283.
50 Franciscono, *Paul Klee: His Work and Thought*, pp. 193–194.
51 Luprecht, p. 84.
52 Vishny, p. 150.
53 Franciscono, *Paul Klee: His Work and Thought*, p. 300.
54 Dreifuss-Kattan, n.d., n.p.
55 See Franciscono's intelligent interpretation of the works on this list in *Paul Klee: His Work and Thought*, pp. 308–322.
56 These citations are found in the following entries of *The Diaries:* nos. 411/412, 873, 170, 421, 899, 611, and 411/412; pp. 119, 244, 55, 122, 260, 172, and 119 respectively.
57 Brody, MS. (2001) "Paul Klee: art, potential space and the transitional process", *Psychoanalytic Review* 88, 374–375.
58 "Le fantasme d'une surface de peau commune à la mère et à l'enfant" (English translation mine). Cited by Angela Moorjani in "Beckett et le Moi-Peau: Au-delà du fétichisme matriciel," in *L'Affect dans l'Oeuvre Beckettienne*, eds M. Engelberts et al., Rodopi, Amsterdam, 2000, p. 63. I owe this definition to Moorjani's essay as well.
59 See Ferraro, p. 1454.
60 Klee, *The Diaries*, entry no. 425, p. 124.
61 Klee, *The Diaries*, entry nos. 840, 899, 857 and 425; pp. 231, 260, 236–237 and 123–124.
62 A. Temkin, "Klee and the Avant-Garde 1912–1940," *Paul Klee*, ed. C. Lanchner, New York, Museum of Modern Art, 1987, p. 31.
63 Brenner, C. (2002) "Reflections on psychoanalysis," *Journal of Psychoanalysis* 11, 33. Cf. Brenner's statement: "Every sensory stimulus produces physical changes. Unless you believe that there is a spirit that's apart from the body, which I don't, for reasons I believe are compelling ones – unless you believe in a non-corporeal spirit, the conclusion is inescapable that every sensory stimulus normally produces physical changes in the brain." Personal e-mail communication to L.O. dated March 25, 2004. See also Fred Levin's explanation of brain function in *Psyche and Brain: The Biology of Talking Cures*, Madison, CT, International Universities Press, 2003, p. 214.
64 Cited by Sander Gilman in *Disease and Representation*, Ithaca, Cornell University Press, 1988, p. 1. I am also grateful to Luba Kessler for her insights into the ways in which disease produces change in internal representations.
65 For the relation between stress and memory function, see J. LeDoux, *The Emotional Brain*, New York, Simon & Schuster, 1996, pp. 242–245.
66 See A. Flaherty's *The Midnight Disease: The Drive to Write, Writer's Block, and the Creative Brain*, Boston and New York, Houghton Mifflin, 2004, specifically

pp. 23, 26, 42, and 75. (Flaherty discusses several writers in the context of hypergraphia; Lewis Carroll, for instance, who probably had temporal lobe epilepsy and who wrote 98,721 letters between his late twenties and the time of his death at age 65.) This material on epilepsy and scleroderma is also drawn from an e-mail communication by Flaherty to L.O. of April 30, 2004. Snyder's work was discussed in an interview with him on CNN's "Anderson Cooper 360" on May 19, 2004.

67 Solms and Turnbull, *The Brain and the Inner World*, New York, Other Press, 2002, p. 109.

68 See LeDoux, *The Emotional Brain*, pp. 112–114.

69 J. J. Ratey, *A User's Guide to the Brain*, New York, Random House, 2002, p. 248.

70 Howard Shevrin, in conversation with the author, January 23, 2003.

71 "Another technique for fending off suffering is the employment of the displacements of libido which our mental apparatus permits of and through which its function gains so much in flexibility. The task here is that of shifting aims in such a way that they cannot come up against frustration from the external world. In this, sublimation of the instincts lends its assistance. One gains the most if one can sufficiently heighten the yield of pleasure from the sources of psychical and intellectual work. When that is so, fate can do little against one. A satisfaction of this kind, such as an artist's joy in creating, in giving his phantasies body, or a scientist's in solving problems or discovering truths, has a special quality which we shall certainly one day be able to characterize in metapsychological terms." S. Freud, "Civilization and Its Discontents," SE Vol. 21, p. 79.

72 V. S. Ramachandran, "The neurological basis of artistic universals," http://www.interdisciplines.org/artcog/papers/9/3/printable/paper, available January 13, 2003.

73 P. Klee, *The Thinking Eye*, p. 76. Cited by B. Riley in "Making visible," *Paul Klee: The Nature of Creation, Works 1914–1940*, London, Hayward Galleries, 2002, p. 18.

74 Riley, "Making visible," pp. 18 and 19.

75 Klee, *The Thinking Eye*, p. 454. Cited by Riley, p. 19.

76 See Locher P. et al. (1998) "The role of balance as an organizing design principle underlying adults' compositional strategies for creating visual displays," *Acta Psychologica* 99, 141–161; (1999) "An empirical evaluation of the visual rightness theory of pictorial composition," *Acta Psychologica* 103, 261–280; (2001) "An empirical investigation of the role of balance in the creation of visual designs by adults," *Empirical Studies of the Arts* 19, 213–227.

77 H. Shevrin, "The experimental investigation of unconscious conflict, unconscious affect, and unconscious signal anxiety," *Investigating Phenomenal Consciousness: New Methodolgies and Maps*, ed. M. Velmans, Amsterdam and Philadelphia, John Benjamins, 2000, p. 62.

78 Shevrin, "The experimental investigation of unconscious conflict, unconscious affect, and unconscious signal anxiety," p. 61.

79 Haftmann, pp. 200–201. Readers will see this work referred to variously as "Harmonized strife" or "Harmonized battle." "Harmonized struggle," however, is the title used by the Klee Foundation in Berne.

80 The two works are in the private collection of Christoph A. Bürgi to whom I am very grateful for granting me access and for our conversations about Klee's relationship to the Bürgi family.

81 Klee, cited by J.-L. Ferrier in *Paul Klee*, trans. M. Imrie, Paris, Terrail Editions, 1998, p. 201.

82 Geelhaar's thinking on the angels appears in Luprecht, p. 87; Boehm's interpretation is found in Gottfried Boehm, "'Strebend noch Gesicht' – Hinweise zum

zeichnerischen Spätwerk Paul Klee," *Paul Klee: Späte Zeichnungen von 1939*, Museum Folkwang Essen, 1989, p. 164.

83 Kudielka, p. 163.

84 In a paper presented at the New York Psychoanalytic Society on January 27, 2004, Gilbert Rose rightly noted: "Great art succeeds not only in renewing the sense of wholeness but in enhancing it, for the aesthetic experience is one of illumination and transcendence."

85 F. Klee, *Paul Klee*, p. 137.

86 W. Grohmann, *Paul Klee*, New York, Harry N. Abrams, n.d., pp. 154 and 156.

87 Kudielka, p. 162.

88 F. Klee, *Paul Klee*, p. 72.

89 Freud, *Beyond the Pleasure Principle*, SE Vol. 18, p. 9. The citation from Freud's lecture appears in James Strachey's introduction to *Studies on Hysteria*, SE Vol. 2, p. xx, note 1.

90 J. Panksepp, *Affective Neuroscience*, New York and Oxford, Oxford University Press, p. 145.

91 Temkin, 35.

92 See, especially, pp. 288–301 in Franciscono's *Paul Klee: His Work and Thought* where these affinities are outlined.

5 The shape of process: Martha Graham's journey into self

1 See Kosslyn, S. M. et al. (1999). "The role of area 17 in visual imagery: convergent evidence from PET and rTMS," *Science* 284; Ganis, G. et al. (2000) "Transcranial magnetic stimulation of primary motor cortex affects mental rotation," *Cerebral Cortex* 10, 175–180. I am very grateful to Julian P. Keenan for bringing these studies, and others referenced in this chapter, to my attention.

2 S. Beckett, *Endgame*, New York, Grove Press, 1958, pp. 1 and 84; *Play, The Collected Shorter Plays of Samuel Beckett*, New York, Grove Press, 1984, p. 147.

3 S. Langer, *Philosophy in a New Key*, Cambridge, MA, Harvard University Press, 1942; cited by Nettleton, S. (2004) "Music and internal experience," *Journal of the British Association of Psychotherapists* 42, 12.

4 This point was made by Sarah Nettleton in "Music and internal experience," p. 16.

5 F. Sparshott, *Off the Ground: First Steps to a Philosophical Consideration of the Dance*, Princeton, Princeton University Press, 1988, p. 375.

6 Francis Sparshott discusses this notion of the dancer's transposed state of being in *Off the Ground: First Steps to a Philosopical Consideration of the Dance*, see, principally, pp. 204–207 and 346.

7 Cited by Terese Capulcilli in an interview with Robert Tracy, *Goddess: Martha Graham's Dancers Remember*, New York, Limelight Editions, 1997, p. 307.

8 Interview with Nan Robertson, *New York Times*, October 2, 1988.

9 See A. de Mille, *Martha: The Life and Work of Martha Graham*, New York, Random House, 1991, p. 140. It might also be noted that one of Graham's earliest dances, "Project in Movement for a Divine Comedy" (1930), was performed in complete silence. This is the only time in her career that she would use no music at all.

10 The letters referred to here are dated April 26 (no year given); June 28, 1959; July 18, 1951; and July 12, 1959. They are from container 2, Frances Wickes papers, Manuscript Division, Library of Congress, Washington, DC. The letters of June 28, 1959, and July 12, 1959, are from container 63, Muriel Rukeyser Papers, Manuscript Division, Library of Congress, Washington, DC.

11 Letter from Martha Graham to Frances Wickes dated August 4, 1953, from container 2, Frances Wickes papers, Manuscript Division, Library of Congress, Washington, DC.
12 Interview with Matt Turney by Robert Tracy in *Goddess: Martha Graham's Dancers Remember*, p. 208.
13 G. Rose, *Between Couch and Piano*, London, Routledge, 2004, pp. 86 and 130.
14 Nettleton, "Music and internal experience," pp. 9–10.
15 D. Epstein, "On affect and musical motion," *Psychoanalytic Explorations in Music*, eds S. Feder et al., Madison, CT, International Universities Press, 1993, p. 99.
16 See, for example, C. C. Pratt, *Music and the Language of Emotion*. Washington, DC, US Library of Congress, 1952, p. 17; cited by Pinchas Noy, "How music conveys emotion," *Psychoanalytic Explorations in Music*, p. 127. Possible evolutionary benefits of sound are also discussed by Panksepp, J. and Bernatzky, G. (2002) "Emotional sounds and the brain: the neuro-affective foundations of musical appreciation," *Behavioural Processes* 60, see especially p. 136.
17 A. Damasio, *The Feeling of What Happens*, New York, Harcourt, 1999, pp. 39–40 and 51.
18 Panksepp and Bernatzky, "Emotional sounds and the brain: the neuro-affective foundations of musical appreciation," pp. 135–136.
19 See Rose, *Between Couch and Piano*, pp. 49 and 137. Rose, however, speaks of an externalization of body ego that he seems to acquaint with self-recognition. I believe this tends to confuse the necessary distinction between ego and self.
20 The results of the first study referred to here were reported in Schlaug, G. et al. (1995) "Increased corpus callosum size in musicians," *Neuropsycholgia* 33, 1047–1055; the second, conducted by Thomas Ebert and colleagues, is cited by L. R. Squire and E. Kandel, *Memory: From Mind to Molecules*, New York, Henry Holt, 1999, p. 199; the studies on the planum temporale are discussed in Keenan, J. P. et al. (2001) "Absolute pitch and planum temporale," *NeuroImage* 14, 1402–1408; and the fourth, "Differences in white matter architecture between musicians and non-musicians: a diffusion tensor imaging study," appeared in *Neuroscience Letters* 321, 2002, pp. 57–60.
21 Panksepp and Bernatzky, "Emotional sounds and the brain: the neuro-affective foundations of musical appreciation," p. 137.
22 J. Panksepp, *Affective Neuroscience*, New York, Oxford University Press, 1998, p. 309.
23 See J. Ratey, *A User's Guide to the Brain*, New York, Random House, 2002, pp. 151, 162, and 174.
24 Panksepp and Bernatzky, "Emotional sounds and the brain: the neuro-affective foundations of musical appreciation," p. 140.
25 M. Sheets-Johnstone, *The Phenomenology of Dance*, New York, Arno Press, 1980.
26 See B. Mittelmann (1954) "Motility in infants, children, and adults: patterning and psychodynamics," *The Psychoanalytic Study of the Child* IX, New York, International Universities Press, pp. 142–177.
27 Damasio, *The Feeling of What Happens*, p. 146.
28 M. Sheets-Johnstone, *The Primacy of Movement*, Amsterdam, John Benjamins, 1999, p. 442.
29 These quotations come from interviews conducted by Robert Tracy and appear in *Goddess: Martha Graham's Dancers Remember*, pp. 56, 127, 141, 305, 306, 309.
30 Paul Taylor, interviewed by Robert Tracy in *Goddess: Martha Graham's Dancers Remember*, p. 238.
31 Gus Solomons Jr., interviewed by Robert Tracy in *Goddess: Martha Graham's Dancers Remember*, p. 279.

32 Cited by R. Tracy as the epigram to *Goddess: Martha Graham's Dancers Remember* (n.p.).
33 S. Langer, *Feeling and Form*, New York, Charles Scribner's Sons, 1953, p. 127.
34 Hodes, S. (1996) "Graham's technique," *Ballet Review* 24, 89.
35 Flaherty points this out in *The Midnight Disease*, New York, Houghton Mifflin, 2004, p. 253.
36 Cited by A. J. Helpern in "The evolution of Martha Graham's technique," doctoral dissertation, New York University, 1981, p. 9.
37 Pearl Lang, cited by A. de Mille in *Martha: The Life and Work of Martha Graham*, p. 251.
38 This letter is housed in the archives of Jacob's Pillow, the celebrated dance center in Becket, Massachusetts.
39 E. Or, "Body and mind: the yoga roots of Martha Graham's 'Contraction' and 'Release,' " *Border Crossings: Dance and Boundaries in Societies, Politics, Gender, Education, and Technology*, Riverside, University of California, 1995, p. 205.
40 M. Graham, "A modern dancer's primer for action," *Dance: A Basic Educational Technique*, ed. F. R. Rogers, New York, Dance Horizons, 1980, rpt. from 1941, p. 179.
41 Sparshott, *Off the Ground: First Steps to a Philosopical Consideration of the Dance*, pp. 349–350.
42 M. Graham, *Blood Memory*, New York, Doubleday, 1991, p. 13.
43 This biographical information appears throughout the early chapters of A. de Mille's *Martha: The Life and Work of Martha Graham.*
44 de Mille, *Martha: The Life and Work of Martha Graham*, p. 250.
45 S. and R. Larsen, *A Fire in the Mind: The Life of Joseph Campbell*, New York, Doubleday, 1991, p. 106. The role of mythology in Jung's break with Freud often goes unrecognized. As Martin Bergmann has recently pointed out, it was not psychic pathology as much as the cosmic versus personal significance of mythology, and particularly the function of incest within it, that was at the center of that controversy. See Bergmann's astute analysis of the question in "Rethinking dissidence and change in the history of psychoanalysis," *Understanding Dissidence and Controversy in the History of Psychoanalysis*, New York, Other Press, 2004, pp. 14–23.
46 Cited by Larsen, *A Fire in the Mind: The Life of Joseph Campbell*, p. 248 and further explicated on p. 267.
47 Lang interview in Tracy, *Goddess: Martha Graham's Dancers Remember*, p. 88.
48 Larsen, *A Fire in the Mind: The Life of Joseph Campbell*, p. 520.
49 Cohan interview in Tracy, *Goddess: Martha Graham's Dancers Remember*, p. 141.
50 Telephone interview of Dr. George Hogle with L. O., August 2, 2004, and e-mail correspondence of the same date.
51 This is Rukeyser's son's term and explanation of the relationship as ascertained in a telephone interview by L.O. with him on August 20, 2004.
52 McGehee interview in Tracy, *Goddess: Martha Graham's Dancers Remember*, p. 129; Lang interview with L. O., August 19, 2004.
53 Taped interview of Bertram Ross by Agnes de Mille, November 21, 1983, located at the New York Public Library for the Performing Arts at Lincoln Center.
54 Telephone interview with the author, July 2004.
55 The typescript of Wickes paper, "Creative awareness," presented at the Cosmopolitan Club on March 30, 1948, is in the papers of Muriel Rukeyser, container I: 66, Manuscript Division, Library of Congress, Washington, DC. The unused notes for "The creative process" are in container 4. All references to the Graham letters are as cited previously.

56 I take these examples from Graham's autobiography, *Blood Memory*, p. 251, but well remember them and a host of others from my days as a Graham-trained dancer.
57 According to Agnes de Mille, Wickes was instrumental in arranging for Graham to meet Jung during a 1954 company tour in Europe (*Martha: The Life and Work of Martha Graham*, p. 316). From the correspondence one also detects Wickes' involvement in the referral of Graham's sister for treatment with Werner Engel, then the president of the New York Association of Analytical Psychology, though her role in this remains uncertain.
58 With regard to Graham's reading in Jung and the literary critics, see E. Or, "Martha Graham's 'Night Journey': a study of the portrayal of Jocasta as the archetypal heroine," MFA thesis submitted to York University, Toronto, 1987, p. 47; S. Shelton, "Jungian roots in Martha Graham's dance imagery," in *Proceedings: Dance History Scholars Sixth Annual Conference*, Ohio State University, 1983, p. 121.
59 I owe this formulation to Marni Thomas, who danced with the company from 1958 to 1968. Telephone interview with the author August 4, 2004.
60 D. McDonagh, *Martha Graham: A Biography*, New York, Praeger, 1973, p. 188; E. Stodelle, *Deep Song: The Dance Story of Martha Graham*, New York, Macmillan, 1984, p. 140; T. Tobias, cited by de Mille in *Martha: The Life and Work of Martha Graham*, p. 269; Stodelle, p. 139.
61 *The Notebooks of Martha Graham*, New York, Harcourt Brace Jovanovich, 1973, p. 190.
62 Graham's notations for the solo appear on pp. 162–164 of *The Notebooks of Martha Graham*. The partial program note appears in Stodelle, *Deep Song*, p. 143.
63 This paragraph owes much to the excellent analysis of Jung's interpretations of the night sea journey by J. Jacobi in *Complex/Archetype/Symbol in the Psychology of C.G. Jung*, New York, Pantheon, 1959, pp. 179–189.
64 Or, *Martha Graham's "Night Journey,"* p. iv.
65 *Notebooks*, p. 206.
66 In the second chapter of her thesis, Or discusses in detail the sources of both the epic nature and the divine quality of Graham's Greek heroines.
67 de Mille, *Martha: The Life and Work of Martha Graham*, p. 281.
68 Lyman interview with Tracy, *Martha Graham's Dancers Remember*, p. 291.
69 I am grateful to Alice Flaherty for directing me to the work of Michael Merzenich and others at the University of California at San Francisco whose studies further confirm this.
70 See Meglin, J. A. and Woollacott, M. H. (1991–92) "The neural choreography underlying a pirouette-arabesque," *Kinesiology and Medicine for D.A.N.C.E.* 14, 96.
71 See T. Feinberg, *Altered Egos: How the Brain Creates the Self*, New York, Oxford University Press, 2001, pp. 117–118.
72 Stodelle, p. 138.
73 Alvin Ailey cited by J. Dunning, *Alvin Ailey: A Life in Dance*, Reading, MA, Addison-Wesley, 1996, p. 123. The Dunning quotation is from the same source.
74 Walter Terry cited by Stodelle in *Deep Song*, p. 258; John Martin cited by Anna Kisselgoff in *The New York Times*, April 2, 1991, p. 1.
75 Graham, *Blood Memory*, p. 249.

Epilogue

1 Cited by Kaplan, D. (1988) "The psychoanalysis of art: some ends, some means," *Journal of the American Psychoanalytic Society* 36, 266. Kaplan's thinking in this

paper on the significance of analogy as an applied psychoanalytic method are congruent with my own.

2 Berman, E. (2003) "Reader and story, viewer and film: on transference and interpretation," *IJPA* 84, 127.

3 Both Emanuel Berman and Shoshana Felman offer interesting discussions on transference and countertransference in art. See, in particular, pp. 122–123 and 127 in Berman (2003) and pp. 30–1 and 165–183 in Felman (2003).

4 Kant, *The Critique of Pure Reason*, cited by J. Baird, "Toward Building a Unified Theory of Mind. I: Schema Theory," forthcoming publication.

5 Solms, M. (2004) "Freud returns," *Scientific American* 290(5), 88.

6 Kandel, E. R. (1999) "Biology and the future of psychoanalysis: a new intellectual framework for psychiatry revisited," *American Journal of Psychiatry* 156, 520.

7 See Solms's excellent synthesis of the neuroscientific substantiation of Freud's pleasure principle and other theories in "Freud returns," pp. 82–89.

Bibliography

Abbott, H. P. (1996). *Beckett Writing Beckett: The Author in the Autograph*. Ithaca: Cornell University Press.

Aichele, K. P. (2002). *Paul Klee's Pictorial Writing*. Cambridge: Cambridge University Press.

Aiken, N. (1998). *The Biological Origins of Art*. Westport, CT: Praeger.

Almond, R. (1999). Psychoanalytic process and literary narrative: transference and countertransference: *Jane Eyre*. *Psychoanalysis and Culture at the Millennium*. Ginsburg, N. and R. (eds). New Haven: Yale University Press, 117–148.

Anderson, R. (ed.) (1992). *Clinical Lectures on Klein and Bion*. London: Routledge.

Anzieu, D. (1981). *Le Corps de l'Oeuvre: Essais Psychanalytiques sur le Travail Créateur*. Paris: Gallimard.

—— (1983). Un soi disjoint, une voix liante: l'écriture narrative de Samuel Beckett. *Nouvelle Revue de Psychanalyse* 28, 71–85.

—— (1986). *Freud's Self-Analysis*. Madison, CT: International Universities Press.

—— (1998). *Beckett*. Paris: Gallimard.

Arlow, J. (1969). Unconscious fantasy and disturbances of conscious experience. *Psychoanalytic Quarterly* 38, 1, 1–27.

Bachant, J. L. and Adler, E. (1997). Transference: co-constructed or brought to the interaction? *Journal of theAmerican Psychoanalytic Association* 45, 4, 1097–1120.

Bair, D. (2003). *Jung: A Biography*. Boston: Little, Brown.

Baird, J. (forthcoming). Toward building a unified theory of mind. I: Schema theory.

—— (forthcoming). Toward building a unified theory of mind. II: Reframing psychoanalytic concepts from a schema theory perspective.

Balsam, R. (2001). Integrating male and female elements in a woman's gender identity. *Journal of the American Psychoanalytic Association* 49, 4, 1335–1360.

—— (2003) Thoughts on mothers, daughters, their bodies and showing off. Paper presented at the Psychoanalytic Association of New York, December 8.

Balter, L. (1999). On the aesthetic illusion. *Journal of the American Psychoanalytic Association* 47, 4, 1293–1333.

Beckett, S. (1958). *The Unnamable*. New York: Grove Press.

—— (1973). *Not I*. In *The Collected Shorter Plays of Samuel Beckett*. New York: Grove Press, 1984, 213–223.

—— (1989). *Stirrings Still*. NewYork: Blue Moon Books, London: John Calder.

Beerman, H. and Stokes, J. (1949). The treatment of scleroderma. *American Journal of the Medical Sciences* 217, 453–461.

Beres, D. (1957). Communication in psychanalysis and in the creative process: a parallel. *Journal of the American Psychoanalytic Association* 5, 3, 408–423.

—— (1959). The contribution of psycho-analysis to the biography of the artist: a commentary on methodology. *International Journal of Psycho-Analysis* 40, 26–37.

Bergmann, M. S. (2000). *The Hartmann Era*. New York: Other Press.

Bergmann, M. V. (1994). Creative work, work inhibitions, and their relation to internal objects. *The Spectrum of Psychoanalysis: Essays in Honor of Martin S. Bergmann*. Richards, R. K. and Richards, A. D. (eds). Madison, CT: International Universities Press, 353–371.

Berman, E. (2003). Reader and story, viewer and film: on transference and interpretation, *International Journal of Psycho-Analysis* 84, 1, 119–129.

Bion, W. (1965). *Transformations*. London: Karnac.

—— (1967). *Second Thoughts*. London: Karnac.

—— (1970). *Attention and Interpretation*. London: Karnac.

Blos, P. (1980). Modifications in the traditional psychoanalytic theory of female adolescent development. *Adolescent Psychiatry*, S. C. Feinstein et al. (eds). Chicago: University of Chicago Press, 8–24.

Boehlich, W. (ed.) (1990). *The Letters of Sigmund Freud to Eduard Silberstein 1871–1881*. Cambridge, MA: Harvard University Press.

Boehm, G. (1989). "Strebend noch Gesicht" – Hinweise zum zeichnerischen Spätwerk Paul Klees. *Paul Klee: Späte Zeichnungen von 1939*. Franz, E. (ed.). Essen: Museum Folkwang Essen, 157–164.

Bollas, C. (1978). The aesthetic moment and the search for transformation. *The Annual of Psychoanalysis* 6, 385–394.

Brater, E. (1987). *Beyond Minimalism*. New York: Oxford University Press.

Brenner, C. (2004). Creativity and psychodynamics. *Psychoanalytic Quarterly* 73, 2, 511–515.

Burke, K. (1978). (Nonsymbolic) motion/(symbolic) action. *Psychoanalysis, Creativity, and Literature*, Roland, A. (ed.). New York: Columbia University Press, 117–143.

Burnside, F. (1991). Intellectuality versus emotionality: a comparison of modern dance techniques. *Ballet International* 14, 9, 20–23.

Bywaters, E. G. L. (1987). Paul Klee: the effect of scleroderma on his painting. *Art, History and Antiquity of Rheumatic Diseases*. Appelboom, T. (ed.). Brussels: Elsevier, 49–50.

Calle, M. (ed.) (1996). *On the Feminine*. McGann, C. (trans.). Atlantic Highlands, NJ: Humanities Press.

Campbell, P. and Kear, A. (2001). *Psychoanalysis and Performance*. London and New York: Routledge.

Canestri, J. (2000). Notes on linguistic activity and psychoanalysis. *Changing Ideas in a Changing World*. Sandler, J., Michels, R. and Fonagy, P. (eds). London: Karnac, 197–205.

Castenholz, G. (2000). *Die progressive systemische Sklerose: Analyse und Geschichte unter besonderer Berücksichtigung der Krankheit des Malers Paul Klee*. Marburg: Verlag Görich and Weierschäuser GmbH.

Chicago, J. (1985). *The Birth Project*. NewYork: Doubleday.

—— (1996). *Beyond the Flower: The Autobiography of a Feminist Artist*. New York: Penguin.

Chicago J. and Lucie-Smith, E. (1999). *Women and Art: Contested Territory*. New York: Watson-Guptil.

Chodorow, N. (1989). *Feminism and Psychoanalytic Theory*. Oxford: Blackwell.

Cixous, H. (1976). The laugh of the Medusa. *Signs*; rpt. *New French Feminisms*, Marks, E. and de Courtivron, I. (eds). Amherst: University of Massachusetts Press, 1980, 245–264.

—— (1991). *"Coming to Writing" and other Essays*. Cambridge: Harvard University Press.

—— (1994). *The Hélène Cixous Reader*. Sellers, S. (ed.). London: Routledge.

Coen, S. J. (1994). *Between Author and Reader*. New York: Columbia University Press.

Comte, P. (1991). *Paul Klee*. Marshall, C. (trans.). Woodstock, NY: Overlook Press.

Compton, A. (2000). Current views on psychoanalytic practice. *Changing Ideas in a Changing World*, 25–31.

Conley, V. A. (1984). *Writing the Feminine*. Lincoln: University of Nebraska Press.

—— (1992). The feminine and ecology. *On the Feminine*. Calle, M. (ed.), McGann, C. (trans.). Atlantic Highlands, NJ: Humanities Press, 1996, 38–45.

Cooper, A. (2000). The changing psychoanalytic model of the mind. *Whose Freud?: The Place of Psychoanalysis in Contemporary Culture*, Brooks, P. and Woloch, A. (eds). New Haven: Yale University Press, 275–280.

Cornillon, S. K. (ed.) (2002). *Images of Women in Fiction*. Bowling Green, OH: Bowling Green University Popular Press.

Crick, F. and Koch, C. (2002). Consciousness and neuroscience. <http://artsci.wustl.edu/~jprinz/consciousness/crick-koch-cc-97.html> (accessed May 2, 2002).

Damasio, A. (1994). *Descartes' Error*. New York: Avon Books.

—— (1999). *The Feeling of What Happens*. New York: Harcourt.

Danuser, B. (2000). Von den Gefahren des Künstlerberufs: Paul Klee und die Sklerodermie. Newsletter 3. Ausgabe, November. Institut für Hygiene und Arbeitsphysiologie, 17–20.

Da Silva, G. (2002). The emergence of thinking: Bion as the link between Freud and the neurosciences. <http://www.sicap.it/~merciai/papers/silva.htm> (accessed April 12, 2002).

Davidson, D. (2000). On truth. *Whose Freud?: The Place of Psychoanalysis in Contemporary Culture*. Brooks, P. and Woloch, A. (eds). New Haven: Yale University Press, 300–303.

Decety, J. and Sommerville, J. A. (2003). Shared representations between self and other: a social cognitive neuroscience view. *TRENDS in Cognitive Sciences* 7, 12, 527–533.

De Mille, A. (1991). *Martha: The Life and Work of Martha Graham*. New York: Random House.

Dierkens, J. (1987). New psychological approach to illness and creativity. *Art, History and Antiquity of Rheumatic Diseases*. Appelboom, T. (ed.). Brussels: Elsevier, 51–54.

Donovan, J. (ed.) (1975). *Feminist Literary Criticism*. Lexington: University Press of Kentucky.

Dreifuss-Kattan, E. (forthcoming). *Beyond Words and Time: Mourning and Art*.

Duparc, F. (1996). *André Green*. Paris: Presses Universitaires de France.

Eagleton, M. (ed.) (1996). *Feminist Literary Theory*, 2nd edn. Oxford: Blackwell.

Ehrenberg, D. B. (1992). *The Intimate Edge: Extending the Reach of Psychoanalytic Interaction*. New York: Norton.

Eissler, K. R. (1967). Psychopathology and creativity. *American Imago* 24, 35–79.

Everts, E.W. (1980). Physiological imperatives. *Dance: A Basic Educational Technique*, Rogers, F. R. (ed.). New York: Dance Horizons, 115–147.

Feder, S. (1990). *Psychoanalytic Explorations in Music*. Monograph 3. Madison, CT: International Universities Press.

Feder, S. et al. (eds) (1993). *Psychoanalytic Explorations in Music*. Madison, CT: International Universities Press.

Feinberg, T. (2001). *Altered Egos: How the Brain Creates the Self*. Oxford and New York: Oxford University Press.

Felman, S. (1993). *What Does a Woman Want? Reading and Sexual Difference*. Baltimore: Johns Hopkins University Press.

—— (2003). *Writing and Madness*. Palo Alto: Stanford University Press.

Ferraro, F. (2003). Psychic bisexuality and creativity. *International Journal of Psycho-Analysis* 84, 6, 1451–1467.

Ferrier, J.-L. (1998). *Paul Klee*. Imrie, M. (trans.). Paris: Terrail.

Flaherty, A.W. (2004a). *The Midnight Disease: The Drive to Write, Writer's Block, and the Creative Brain*. Boston and New York: Houghton Mifflin.

—— (2004b). Mood and creative state influences on temporal perception: how the brain minds the time. Paper presented at the International Psychoanalytical Biennial Meeting, New Orleans, March 11.

Forrest, D. V. (2000). "Freud's neuromental model: analytic structures and local habitations. *Whose Freud?: The Place of Psychoanalysis in Contemporary Culture*. Brooks, P. and Woloch, A. (eds). New Haven: Yale University Press, 255–266.

Forrester, J. (2000). What kind of truth? *Whose Freud?: The Place of Psychoanalysis in Contemporary Culture*. Brooks, P. and Woloch, A. (eds). New Haven: Yale University Press. 311–323.

Franciscono, M. (1990). Klees Krankheit und seine Bilder des Todes. *Paul Klee: Das Schaffen im Todesjahr*. Frey, S. Helfenstein, J. and Kersten, W. (eds). Wechsler, M. (trans.). Berne: Kunstmuseum, 13–25.

—— (1991). *Paul Klee: His Work and Thought*. Chicago: University of Chicago Press.

Freedman, N. (1994). More on transformation: enactments in psychoanalytic space. *The Spectrum of Psychoanalysis: Essays in Honor of Martin S. Bergmann*, Richards, R. K. and Richards, A. D. (eds). Madison, CT: International Universities Press. 93–110.

Freedman, N. and Lavender, J. (1997). On receiving the patient's transference: the symbolizing and desymbolizing countertransference. *Journal of the American Psychoanalytic Association* 45, 1, 79–103.

Freedman, R. (1998). *Martha Graham: A Dancer's Life*. New York: Clarion Books.

Freud, S. (1894). The Neuro-Psychoses of Defence, SE 3, 45–61.

—— (1905). Three Essays on Sexuality, SE 7, 125–245.

—— (1910). Leonardo da Vinci and a Memory of His Childhood, SE 11, 57–137.

—— (1914). Remembering, Repeating and Working-Through. SE 12, 147–156.

—— (1915). Instincts and their Vicissitudes. SE 14, 117–140.

—— (1923). *The Ego and the Id*. SE 19, 3–66.

—— (1933). Femininity. SE 22, 112–135.

Frey, S. and Helfenstein, J. (2000). *Paul Klee Rediscovered: Works from the Bürgi Collection*. London: Merrell.

Friedman, L. (1997). Introduction to panels: does the face of analytic treatment show its character? *Journal of the American Psychoanalytic Association* 45, 4, 1225–1229.

—— (2000). Are minds objects or dramas? *Changing Conceptions of Psychoanalysis: The Legacy of Merton M. Gill*, Silverman, D. K. and Wolitzky, D. L. (eds). Hillsdale, NJ: Analytic Press, 145–170.

Gaab, N. et al. (2003). The effects of gender on the neural substrates of pitch memory. *Journal of Cognitive Neuroscience* 15, 6, 1–11.

Gabbard, G. (2000). The integration of psychoanalytic and neuroscientific thought in the realm of personality. *Changing Ideas in a Changing World*, 155–162.

Gallop, J. (1998). *Thinking Through the Body*. New York: Columbia University Press.

Gamwell, L. (1999). A century of silence: abstraction and withdrawal in modern art. *Psychoanalysis and Culture at the Millennium*. Ginsburg, N. and Ginsburg, R. (eds). New Haven: Yale University Press, 219–238.

Gardiner, J. K. (1982). On female identity and writing by women. *Writing and Sexual Difference*. Abel, E. (ed.). Chicago: University of Chicago Press, 177–191.

Gardner, H. (1993). *Creating Minds*. New York: Basic Books.

Gay, P. (1989). *The Freud Reader*. New York and London: Norton.

—— (1998). *Freud: A Life for Our Time*. New York and London: Norton.

—— (2000). Against post-modernism. *Changing Ideas in a Changing World*, 247–254.

Gay, V. P. (1992). *Freud on Sublimation*. Albany: State University of New York.

Gedo, J. E. (1996a). *The Artist and the Emotional World: Creativity and Personality*. New York: Columbia University Press.

—— (1996b). *The Languages of Psychoanalysis*. Hillsdale, NJ: Analytic Press.

—— (1997). Reflections on metapsychology, theoretical coherence, hermeneutics, and biology. *Journal of the American Psychoanalytic Association* 45, 3, 779–806.

Glover, N. *Psychoanalytic Aesthetics: The British School*. <http://www. human-nature.com/free-associations/glover/> (accessed January 31, 2001).

Goldberg, A. (1997). Three forms of meaning and their psychoanalytic significance. *Journal of the American Psychoanalytic Association* 45, 2, 491–506.

Gombrich, E. H. (1954). Psycho-analysis and the history of art. *International Journal of Psycho-Analysis* 35, 401–411.

Gorovoy, J. and Tilkin, D. (eds) (2000). There's no place like home. *Louise Bourgeois: Memory and Architecture*. Madrid: Museo Nacional Centro de Arte Reina Sofía.

Graham, M. (1973). *The Notebooks of Martha Graham*. New York: Harcourt Brace Jovanovich.

—— (1980). A modern dancer's primer for action. *Dance: A Basic Educational Technique*. Rogers, F. R. (ed.). New York: Dance Horizons, 178–187.

—— (1991). *Blood Memory*. New York: Doubleday.

Green, A. (1978). The double and the absent. *Psychoanalysis, Creativity, and Literature*, 271–292.

—— (1992). *La Déliaison: psychanalyse, anthropologie et littérature*. Paris: Hachette.

—— (1993). *Le Travail du Négatif*. Paris: Les Editions de Minuit.

—— (1994). *Un Psychanalyste Engagé*. Paris: Hachette.

—— (1999). *The Fabric of Affect in the Psychoanalytic Discourse*. London: Routledge.

—— (2000). *La Diachronie en Psychanalyse*. Paris: Les Editions de Minuit.

Greenacre, P. (1957). The childhood of the artist: libidinal phase development and giftedness. *Psychoanalytic Study of the Child* 12, 47–72.

—— (1959). Play in relation to creative imagination. *Psychoanalytic Study of the Child* 14, 61–80.

—— (1960). Woman as artist. *Psychoanalytic Quarterly* 29, 208–227.

Grohmann, W. (n.d.). *Paul Klee*. New York: Harry N. Abrams.

Haftmann, W. (1967). *The Mind and Work of Paul Klee*. New York: Frederick A. Praeger.

Hall, C. S. and Nordby, V. J. (1973). *A Primer of Jungian Psychology*. New York: Taplinger.

Hartmann, H. (1955). Notes on the theory of sublimation. *Psychoanalytic Study of the Child* 10, 9–29.

Hawkins, A. M. (1964). *Creating through Dance*. Englewood Cliffs, NJ: Prentice-Hall.

Haxthausen, C. (1990). Zur "Bildsprache" des Spätwerkes. *Paul Klee: Das Schaffen im Todesjahr*. Frey, S. Helfenstein, J. and Kersten, W. (eds). Berne: Kunstmuseum, 27–36.

Helpern, A. (1991). The technique of Martha Graham. *Studies in Dance History* 2, 2.

Hodes, S. (1996). Graham's technique. *Ballet Review* 24, 1, 87–91.

Hoffman, L. (1996). Freud and feminine subjectivity, *Journal of the American Psychoanalytic Association* 44 (suppl.), 23–44.

—— (1999). Passions in girls and women: toward a bridge between critical relational theory of gender and modern conflict theory, *Journal of the American Psychoanalytic Association* 47, 4, 1145–1168.

Holland, N. (2003). The willing suspension of disbelief: a neuro-psychoanalytic view. *PsyArt: A Hyperlink Journal for the Psychological Study of the Arts*, article 020919. <http://www.clas.ufl.edu/ipsa/journal/2003/hollan06.htm> (accessed December 31, 2003).

—— (2004). What is creativity? *Your Mind On Media*. <http://www.clas.ufl.edu/users/nnh/> (accessed March 15, 2005).

Horosko, M. (ed.) (1991). *Martha Graham: The Evolution of Her Dance Theory and Training 1926–1991*. Chicago: A Cappella Books.

Humphrey, D. (1980). My approach to the modern dance. *Dance: A Basic Educational Technique*. Rogers, F. R. (ed.). New York: Dance Horizons, 188–192.

Hunt, L. (2003). The novel and the origins of human rights: the intersection of history, psychology and literature. Paper presented at Fordham University, New York City, February 19, 2003.

Irigaray, L. (1977). *Ce sexe qui n'en est pas un*. Paris: Les Editions de Minuit.

—— (1991). *Philosophy in the Feminine*. London: Routledge.

—— (1994). *Thinking the Difference*, Montin, K. (trans.). New York: Routledge.

Jacobi, J. (1959). *Complex/Archetype/Symbol in the Psychology C. G. Jung*. Manheim, R. (trans.). New York: Pantheon.

Jacobs, T. J. (2000a). On insight and engagement. *Changing Ideas in a Changing World*, 3–10.

—— (2000b). The one-person-two-person controversy: a view from the future. *Changing Conceptions of Psychoanalysis: The Legacy of Merton M. Gill*, 172–187.

Johnson, D. H. (1990). A Martha Graham dance technique class: symbols in the semiotic. *Journal for the Anthropological Study of Human Movement* 6, 1, 1–20.

Jones, S. (ed.) (1991). *Writing the Woman Artist*. Philadelphia: University of Pennsylvania Press.

Kagan, A. (1993). Klee's development. *Paul Klee at the Guggenheim Museum*. New York: Guggenheim Museum.

Kandel, E. (1998). A new intellectual framework for psychiatry. *American Journal of Psychiatry* 155, 4, 457–468.

—— (1999). Biology and the future of psychoanalysis: a new intellectual framework for psychiatry revisited. *American Journal of Psychiatry* 156, 4, 505–524.

Kandel, E. and Schwartz, J. H. (eds) (1985). *Principles of Neural Science*, 2nd edn. New York: Elsevier.

Kaplan, D. (1988). The psychoanalysis of art: some ends, some means. *Journal of the American Psychoanalytic Society* 36, 2, 259–293.

Kaufman, L. (ed.) (1989). *Gender and Theory: Dialogues on Feminist Criticism*. Oxford: Blackwell.

Kealiinohomoku, J. W. (1977). Hopi social dance as a means for maintaining homeostasis. *Journal for the Association of Graduate Dance Ethnologists* 1, 1, 1–11.

Keenan, J. P. et al. (2001). Absolute pitch and planum temporale. *NeuroImage 14*, 1402–1408.

Kennard, G. (2002). The uses of paradox: brain function and the arts. *PsyArt: A Hyperlink Journal for Psychological Study of the Arts*, article 010214. <http://www.clas.ufl.edu/ipsa/journal/articles/psyart2001/kennar01.htm> (accessed April 12, 2002).

Klee, F. (1962). *Paul Klee*. Winston, R. and C. (trans). New York: George Braziller.

Klee, P. (1948). *Paul Klee on Modern Art*. Findlay, P. (trans.). London: Faber and Faber.

—— (1964a). *The Diaries of Paul Klee 1898–1918*. Klee, F. (ed.). Berkeley and Los Angeles: University of California Press.

—— (1964b). *The Thinking Eye*. New York: George Wittenborn.

Klein, M. (1930). The importance of symbol-formation in the development of the ego. *International Journal of Psycho-Analysis* 11, 24–39.

Kleinschmidt, H. J. (1967). The angry act: the role of aggression in creativity. *American Imago* 24, 98–127.

Knowlson, J. (1996). *Damned to Fame: The Life of Samuel Beckett*. New York: Simon & Schuster.

Koepke, G. (1998). Interview. *Louise Bourgeois: Destruction of the Father Reconstruction of the Father: Writings and Interviews 1923–1997*. Bernadac, M.-L. and Obrist, H.-U. (eds). Cambridge, MA: MIT Press.

Kohon, G. (ed.) (1999). *The Dead Mother: The Work of André Green*. London and New York: Routledge.

Kolodny, S. (2000). *The Captive Muse: On Creativity and Its Inhibition*. Madison, CT: Psychosocial Press.

Kosslyn, S. M. et al. (1999). The role of area 17 in visual imagery: convergent evidence from PET and rTMS. *Science* 284, 167–170.

Kotik, C. et al. (eds) (1994). *Louise Bourgeois: The Locus of Memory, Works 1982–1993*. New York: Brooklyn Museum in association with Harry N. Abrams.

Kris, E. (1952). *Psychoanalytic Explorations in Art*. New York: Schocken.

—— (1955). Neutralization and sublimation: observations on young children. *Psychoanalytic Study of the Child* 10, 30–46.

Kristeva, J. (1980). *Desire in Language*. Roudiez, L. S. (ed.), Gora, T., Jardine, A. and Roudiez, L. S. (trans.). New York: Columbia University Press.

—— (1986). *The Kristeva Reader*. Moi, T. (ed.). New York: Columbia University Press.

—— (1994). Freudian models of language: a conversation. <http://www.psychomedia.it/jep/number3–4/kristeng.htm> (accessed June 12, 2002).
—— (2000). From symbols to flesh: the polymorphous destiny of narration. *International Journal of Psycho-Analysis* 81, 771.
Kudielka, R. (2002). *Paul Klee: The Nature of Creation*. London: Hayward Gallery.
Lakoff, G. and Johnson, M. (1999). *Philosophy in the Flesh*. New York: Basic Books.
Lanchner, C. (ed.) (1987). *Paul Klee*. New York: Museum of Modern Art.
Langer, S. K. (1953). *Feeling and Form*. New York: Charles Scribner's Sons.
Larsen, S. and R. (1991). *A Fire in the Mind: The Life of Joseph Campbell*. New York: Doubleday.
Lear, J. (2000). Truth in psychoanalysis. *Whose Freud?: The Place of Psychoanalysis in Contemporary Culture*. Brooks, P. and Woloch, A. (eds). New Haven: Yale University Press, 304–310.
Le Doux, J. (1996). *The Emotional Brain*. New York: Simon & Schuster.
LeVay, S. (1993). *The Sexual Brain*. Cambridge, MA: MIT Press.
Levin, F. M. (1997). Integrating some mind and brain views of transference: the phenomena. *Journal of the American Psychoanalytic Association* 45, 4, 1121–1151.
Levine, M. P. (ed.) (2000). *The Analytic Freud*. London and New York: Routledge.
Locher, P. J. (1996). The contribution of eye-movement research to an understanding of the nature of pictorial balance perception: an overview of the literature. *Empirical Studies of the Arts* 14, 2, 143–163.
Loewald, H. W. (1975). Psychoanalysis as an art and the fantasy character of the psychoanalytic situation. *Journal of the American Psychoanalytic Association* 23, 277–299.
—— (1988). *Sublimation: Inquiries into Theoretical Psychoanalysis*. New Haven: Yale University Press.
—— (2000a). *The Essential Loewald: Collected Papers and Monographs*. Hagerstown, MD: University Publishing Group.
—— (2000b). *Sublimation: Inquiries into Theoretical Psychoanalysis, The Essential Loewald: Collected Papers and Monographs*, Hagerstown, MD: University Publishing Group.
Luprecht, M. (1999). *Of Angels, Things, and Death*. New York: Peter Lang.
Luria, A. R. (1973). *The Working Brain*. New York: Basic Books.
McDonagh, D. (1973). *Martha Graham: A Biography*. New York: Praeger.
McDougall, J. (1994). Creativity and sexuality. *The Spectrum of Psychoanalysis: Essays in Honor of Martin S. Bergmann*, Richards, R. K. and Richards, A. D. (eds). Madison, CT: International Universities Press, 373–390.
Mahler, M. S. (1972). On the first three subphases of the separation–individuation process. *International Journal of Psycho-Analysis*, 53, 333–338. Rpt. in *Essential Papers on Object Relations*, Buckley, P. (ed.). New York: New York University Press, 1986. 222–232.
Mahony, P. (1987). *Psychoanalysis and Discourse*. London: Tavistock.
Makari, G. J. (1997). Current conceptions of neutrality and abstinence. *Journal of the American Psychoanalytic Association* 45, 4, 1231–1239.
Manning, S. A. (1991). The mythologization of the female: Mary Wigman and Martha Graham. A comparison. *Ballet International* 14, 9, 10–15.
Marks, E. and de Courtivron, I. (1980). *New French Feminisms*. Amherst: University of Massachusetts Press.

Masson, J. M. (1980). *The Oceanic Feeling: The Origins of Religious Sentiment in Ancient India*. Dordrecht: D. Reidel.

Mayes, L. C. and Cohen, D. J. (1992). The development of a capacity for imagination in early childhood. *Psychoanalytic Study of the Child* 47, 23–47.

Meglin, J. A. and Woollacott, M. (1991/92). The neural choreography underlying a pirouette-arabesque. *Kinesiology and Medicine for D.A.N.C.E.* 4, 1, 95–105.

Mills, J. (2000). Hegel on projective identification: implications for Klein, Bion, and beyond. *Psychoanalytic Review* 87, 6, 841–874.

Milner, M. (1952). Aspects of symbolism in comprehension of the not-self. *International Journal of Psycho-Analysis* 33, 181–195.

—— (1987). *The Suppressed Madness of Sane Men*. London: Routledge.

Minogue, V. (1981). *Nathalie Sarraute and the War of the Words*. Edinburgh: Edinburgh University Press.

Mitchell, S. (1993). *Hope and Dread in Psychoanalysis*. New York: Basic Books.

Mittelmann, B. (1954). Motility in infants, children, and adults. *Psychoanalytic Study of the Child* 9, 142–177.

Modell, A. (1993). *A Private Self*. Cambridge: Harvard University Press.

—— (2002). *Imagination and the Meaningful Brain*. Cambridge, MA: MIT Press.

Moi, T. (ed.) (1987). *French Feminist Thought*. Cambridge, MA: Blackwell.

—— (1999). *What is a Woman?* Oxford: Oxford University Press.

—— (2000). Is anatomy destiny: Freud and biological determinism. *Whose Freud? The Place of Psychoanalysis in Contemporary Culture*. Brooks, P. and Woloch, A. (eds). New Haven: Yale University Press, 71–92.

Moorjani, A. (1996). Translating theory and feminism(s) from the French. *Contemporary Literature* 37, 4, 671–692.

Morris, D. (1962). *The Biology of Art*. London: Methuen.

Morscher, C. (1994). Paul Klee und die Hypothese der morphischen Resonanz. *PPmP Psychotherapie Psychosomatik Medizinische Psychologie* 44, 200–206.

Nasio, J. D. (1998). *Hysteria from Freud to Lacan*. Fairfield, S. (ed. and trans.). New York: Other Press. (French edition 1990.)

Nersessian, E. (2000). The role of curiosity in psychoanalysis: changes in my technique in the past fifteen years. *Changing Ideas in a Changing World*, 103–109.

Nettleton, S. (2004). Music and internal experience. *Journal of the British Association of Psychotherapists* 42, 1, 1–19.

Neubauer, P. (1994). Without a sense of time. *The Spectrum of Psychoanalysis: Essays in Honor of Martin S. Bergmann*, Richards, R. K. and Richards, A. D. (eds). Madison, CT: International Universities Press. 81–91.

Neubauer, P. and Neubauer, A. (1996). *Nature's Thumbprint: The New Genetics of Personality*. New York: Columbia University Press.

Niederland, W. G. (1967). Clinical aspects of creativity. *American Imago* 24, 6–34.

—— (1976). Psychoanalytic approaches to artistic creativity. *Psychoanalytic Quarterly* 45, 185–212.

Oppenheim, L. (ed.) (1986). *Three Decades of the French New Novel*. Urbana: University of Illinois Press.

—— (1990). Female Subjectivity in *Not I* and *Rockaby*. *Women in Beckett*, Ben-Zvi, L. (ed.). Urbana: University of Illinois Press.

—— (ed.) (1994). *Directing Beckett*. Ann Arbor: University of Michigan Press.

—— (2000). *The Painted Word: Samuel Beckett's Dialogue With Art*. Ann Arbor: University of Michigan Press.

—— (2001). A preoccupation with object representation: the Beckett–Bion case revisited. *International Journal of Psycho-Analysis* 82, 4, 767–784.

—— (ed.) (2004). *Palgrave Advances in Samuel Beckett Studies*. London and New York: Palgrave Macmillan.

Or, E. (1995). Body and mind: the yoga roots of Martha Graham's "Contraction" and "Release." *Border Crossings: Dance and Boundaries in Society, Politics, Gender, Education, and Technology*, 203–213.

Oremland, J. (1997). *The Origins and Psychodynamics of Creativity: A Psychoanalytic Perspective*. Madison, CT: International Universities Press.

Pally, R. (2000). *The Mind–Brain Relationship*. London: Karnac.

Paniagua, C. (1997). Negative acting in. *Journal of the American Psychoanalytic Association* 45, 4, 1209–1223.

Panksepp, J. (1998). *Affective Neuroscience*. New York and Oxford: Oxford University Press.

Panksepp, J. and Bernatzky, G. (2002). Emotional sounds and the brain: the neuro-affective foundations of musical appreciation. *Behavioral Processes* 60, 133–155.

Parsons, M. (2000). *The Dove that Returns, The Dove that Vanishes*. London: Routledge.

Phelan, P. (2004). Lessons in blindness from Samuel Beckett. *PMLA* 119, 5, 1279–1287.

Pierce, J. S. (1976). *Paul Klee and Primitive Art*. New York: Garland.

Piette, A. (1993). Beckett, early neuropsychology and memory loss: Beckett's reading of Clarapede, Janet and Korsakoff. *Beckett in the 1990s*, Buning, M. and Oppenheim, L. (eds). Amsterdam: Rodopi, 41–48.

Poland, W. S. (1996). *Melting the Darkness: The Dyad and Principles of Clinical Practice*. Northvale, NJ : Jason Aronson.

Ramachandran, V. S. (1998). *Phantoms in the Brain*. New York: William Morrow.

—— (2003). The neurological basis of artistic universals. <http://www.interdisciplines.org/artcog/papers/9/3/printable/paper>. (accessed January 13, 2003).

Ratey, J. J. (2002). *A User's Guide to the Brain*. New York: Random House.

Read, H. (1951). Psycho-analysis and the problem of aesthetic value. *International Journal of Psycho-Analysis* 32, 73–82.

Reiser, M. F. (1996). Relationship of psychoanalysis to neuroscience. *Textbook of Psychoanalysis*. Nersessian, E. and Kopff, R. (eds). Washington, DC and London: American Psychiatric Press, 605–633.

—— (2000). Can psychoanalysis and cognitive-emotional neuroscience collaborate in remodeling our concept of mind–brain? *Whose Freud? The Place of Psychoanalysis in Contemporary Culture*. Brooks, P. and Woloch A. (eds). New Haven: Yale University Press, 248–254.

Ricoeur, P. (1970). *Freud and Philosophy: An Essay on Interpretation*. New Haven: Yale University Press.

Riley, B. (2002). Making visible. *Paul Klee: The Nature of Creation*. London: Hayward Gallery.

Rogers, L. (2001). *Sexing the Brain*. New York: Columbia University Press.

Rose, G. J. (1980). *The Power of Form*. Madison, CT: International Universities Press.

—— (1987). *Trauma and Mastery in Life and Art*. Madison, CT: International Universities Press.

—— (1991). Abstract art and emotion: expressive form and the sense of wholeness. *Journal of the American Psychoanalytic Association* 39, 131–156.

—— (1994). From dreams to creative vision: toward affect theory. *The Spectrum of Psychoanalysis: Essays in Honor of Martin S. Bergmann*, Richards, R. K. and Richards, A. D. (eds). Madison, CT: International Universities Press, 337–352.

—— (1996). *Necessary Illusion: Art as Witness*. Madison, CT: International Universities Press.

—— (2002). The artist as child: roots of human creativity. Paper presented at Lucy Daniels Foundation Conference on Creativity, New York City, April 27.

—— (2004). *Between Couch and Piano*. Hove and New York: Brunner-Routledge.

Rothenberg, A. (1978). The unconscious and creativity. *Psychoanalysis, Creativity, and Literature*, 144–161.

St. Denis, R. (1980). Dance as spiritual expression. *Dance: A Basic Educational Technique*, Rogers, F. R. (ed.). New York: Dance Horizons.

Schafer, R. (1968). *Aspects of Internalization*. New York: International Universities Press.

—— (1992). *Retelling a Life: Narrative and Dialogue in Psychoanalysis*. Basic Books.

—— (1997). *Tradition and Change in Psychoanalysis*. London: Karnac

Schneider Brody, M. (2001). Paul Klee: art, potential space and the transitional process. *Psychoanalytic Review* 88, 369–392.

Schore, A. N. (1997a). Interdisciplinary developmental research as a source of clinical models. *The Neurobiological and Developmental Basis for Psychotherapeutic Intervention*. Moskowitz, M. et al. (eds). Northvale, NJ, and London: Jason Aronson.

—— (1997b). A century after Freud's Project: is a rapprochement between psychoanalysis and neurobiology at hand? *Journal of the American Psychoanalytic Association* 45, 3, 807–840.

—— (2001). Effects of a secure attachment relationship on right brain development, affect regulation, and infant mental health. *Infant Mental Health Journal* 22, 1–2, 7–66.

—— (2002). Dysregulation of the right brain: a fundamental mechanism of traumatic attachment and the psychopathogenesis of post-traumatic stress disorder. *Australian and New Zealand Journal of Psychiatry* 36, 9–30.

Schwaber, P. (1999). The enigmatic Jewishness of Leopold Bloom. *Psychoanalysis and Culture at the Millennium*, 149–192.

Segal, H. (1952). A psycho-analytical approach to aesthetics. *International Journal of Psycho-Analysis* 33, 196–207.

—— (1991). *Dream, Phantasy and Art*. London: Routledge.

Sellers, S. (ed.) (1994). *The Hélène Cixous Reader*. London: Routledge.

Shapiro, T. (2000). Words, ideas, and psychoanalysis. *Changing Ideas in a Changing World*, 189–195.

Sharpe, E. F. (1930). Certain aspects of sublimation and delusion. *International Journal of Psycho-Analysis* 11, 12–23.

—— (1935). Similar and divergent unconscious determinants underlying the sublimation of pure art and pure science. *International Journal of Psycho-Analysis* 16, 186–202.

—— (1950). Psycho-physical problems revealed in language: an examination of metaphor. *Collected Papers on Psychoanalysis*. London: Hogarth.

Sheets-Johnstone, M. (1980). *The Phenomenology of Dance*. New York: Arno Press.

—— (ed.) (1984). *Illuminating Dance: Philosophical Explorations*. London and Toronto: Associated University Presses.

—— (1999). *The Primacy of Movement*. Amsterdam and Philadelphia: John Benjamins.

Shelton, S. (1983). Jungian roots of Martha Graham's dance imagery. *Proceedings: Dance History Scholars Sixth Annual Conference*. Ohio: Ohio State University, 119–132.

Shevrin, H. (2003a). The psychoanalytic theory of drive in the light of recent neuroscience findings and theories. Paper presented at the Psychoanalytic Association of New York, September 15.

—— (2003b). The unconscious: theory and findings. Paper presented at the 4th Annual International Neuro-Psychoanalysis Congress, New York University School of Medicine, July.

—— (2000c). *The Experimental Investigation of Unconscious Conflict, Unconscious Affect, and Unconscious Signal Anxiety. Investigating Phenomenal Consciousness: New Methodologies and Maps*. Velmans, M. (ed.). Amsterdam and Philadelphia: John Benjamins, 33–65.

Showalter, E. (1985). *Feminist Criticism: Women, Literature and Theory*. New York: Pantheon.

Shulman R. G. and Rothman, D. L. (2000). Freud's theory of the mental and modern functional imaging experiments. *Changing Ideas in a Changing World*, 163–169.

Simon, B. (1991). The fragmented self, the reproduction of the self, and reproduction in Beckett and in the Theater of the Absurd. *The World of Samuel Beckett*. Smith, J. (ed.). Baltimore: Johns Hopkins University Press, 157–180.

Simonton, D. K. (2003). Scientific creativity as constrained stochastic behavior: the integration of product, person, and process perspectives. *Psychological Bulletin* 129, 475–494.

Skura, M. A. (1981). *The Literary Use of the Psychoanalytic Process*. New Haven: Yale University Press.

Slochower, H. (1967). Genius, psychopathology and creativity. *American Imago* 24.

Smith, H. F. (1997). Creative misreading: why we talk past each other. *Journal of the American Psychoanalytic Association* 45, 2, 335–357.

Solms, K. K. and Solms, M. (2000). *Clinical Studies in Neuro-Psychoanalysis*. Madison, CT: International Universities Press.

Solms, M. (1997a). What is consciousness? *Journal of the American Psychoanalytic Association* 45, 3, 681–703.

—— (1997b). Review of *Affect Regulation and the Origin of the Self* by Allan Schore. *Journal of the American Psychoanalytic Association* 45, 3, 964–969.

—— (2004). Freud returns. *Scientific American* 290, 5, 82–89.

Solms, M. and Turnbull, O. (2002). *The Brain and the Inner World*. New York: Other Press.

Sparshott, F. (1988). *Off the Ground: First Steps to a Philosophical Consideration of the Dance*. Princeton: Princeton University Press.

Spector, J. J. (1972). *The Aesthetics of Freud: A Study in Psychoanalysis and Art*. New York: Praeger.

Spitz, E. H. (1985). *Art and Psyche*. New Haven: Yale University Press.

Squire, L. R. and Kandel, E. R. (eds) (1999). *Memory: From Mind to Molecules*. New York: Henry Holt.

Stevens, C. (1999). *L'Ecriture Solaire d'Hélène Cixous*. Amsterdam: Rodopi.

Stodelle, E. (1984). *Deep Song: The Dance Story of Martha Graham*. New York: Macmillan.

Suter, H. (1998). Zur Krankheit von Paul Klee: Vom Leiden gezeichnet – und dennoch. Berlin: Blackwell Wissenschafts-Verlag GmbH. *Deutscher Schmerzkongress* 31, 22, 20–21.

Temkin, A. (1987). Klee and the Avant-Garde 1912–1940. *Paul Klee*. Lanchner, C. (ed.). New York: Museum of Modern Art.

Tracy, R. (1997). *Goddess: Martha Graham's Dancers Remember*. New York: Limelight.

Trosman, H. (1990). Transformations of unconscious fantasy in art. *Journal of the American Psychoanalytic Association* 38, 47–59.

—— (1996). *Contemporary Psychoanalysis and Masterworks of Art and Film*. New York and London: New York University Press.

Tuckett, D. (2000). Theoretical pluralism and the construction of psychoanalytic Knowledge. *Changing Ideas in a Changing World*, 237–246.

Turnbull, O. (2001). Cognitive neuropsychology comes of age. *Cortex* 37, 445–450.

Turnbull, O. et al. (2002). Implicit awareness of deficit in anosognosia: an emotion-based account of denial of deficit. *Neuro-psychoanalysis* 4, 69–86.

Van der Kolk, B.A. (2000). Trauma, neuroscience, and the etiology of hysteria: an exploration of the relevance of Breuer and Freud's 1893 article in light of modern neuroscience. *Journal of the American Academy of Psychoanalysis* 28, 2, 237–262.

Van Rossum-Guyon, F. (1997). *Le Coeur Critique: Butor, Simon, Kristeva, Cixous*. Amsterdam: Rodopi.

Vermorel, H. and Vermorel, M. (1993). *Sigmund Freud et Romain Rolland: Correspondance 1923–1936*. Paris: Presses Universitaires de France.

Vishny, M. (1985). Paul Klee's Self-Images. *Psychoanalytic Perspectives on Art*, Vol. I. Gedo, M. M. (ed.). Hillsdale, NJ: Analytic Press, 133–168.

Wachtel, P. L. (2003). Transference, schema, and assimilation: the relevance of Piaget to the psychoanalytic theory of transference. <http://www.cyberpsych.org/sepi/wachtel.htm>. (accessed March 7 2003).

Whitebook, J. (1994). Sublimation – a frontier concept. *The Spectrum of Psychoanalysis: Essays in Honor of Martin S. Bergmann*, Richards, R. K. and Richards, A. D. (eds). Madison, CT: International Universities Press, 321–336.

Whitelaw, B. (1995). *Who He?* New York: St. Martin's Press.

Williams, D. (1991). *Ten Lectures on Theories of the Dance*. Metuchen, NJ: Scarecrow Press.

Wilson, E. O. (1998). *Consilience: The Unity of Knowledge*. New York: Alfred A. Knopf.

Winer, J. A. (1999). Unconscious fantasy in *Jane Eyre* and *Ulysses*: Comment on Almond and Schwaber. *Psychoanalysis and Culture at the Millennium*, 193–215.

Winnicott, D. W. (1961). Psycho-analysis and science: friends or relations? Paper presented to Oxford University Scientific Society, May 19.

—— (1966). The location of cultural experience. *International Journal of Psycho-Analysis* 48, 368–372.

—— (1970). Applied theory. Paper presented May 12, 1970; reprinted as "The place of the monarchy" in *Home is Where We Start From*. Winnicott, C. et al. (eds). New York: Norton. 260–268.

—— (1971). *Playing and Reality*. London: Routledge.

—— (1989a). Basis for self in body. *Psycho-Analytic Explorations*, Winnicott, C. et al. (eds). London: Karnac.
—— (1989b). Fear of breakdown. *Psycho-Analytic Explorations* Winnicott C. et al. (eds) London: Karnac.
Witford, M. (1991). *Luce Irigaray: Philosophy in the Feminine*. London: Routledge.
Wolf, E. S. (1978). The disconnected self. *Psychoanalysis, Creativity, and Literature*. Roland, A. (ed.). New York: Columbia University Press, 103–114.
Wolf, G. (1999). *Endure!*: how Paul Klee's illness influenced his art. *The Lancet* 353, 1516–1518.
Wolheim, R. (2000). Psychoanalytic theory and kinds of truth. *Whose Freud?: The Place of Psychoanalysis in Contemporary Culture*. Brooks, P. and Woloch, A. (eds). New Haven: Yale University Press, 296–299.
Wolstein, B. (1959). *Counter-Transference*. New York: Grune and Stratton.
Woodson, J. C. and Gorski, R. A. (1999). Structural differences in the mammalian brain: reconsidering the male/female dichotomy. *Sexual Differentiation of the Brain*. Matsumoto, A. (ed.). Boca Raton: CRC Press, 229–255.
Wright, E. (1998). *Psychoanalytic Criticism: A Reappraisal*. New York: Routledge.
Young-Bruehl, E. (1988). *Anna Freud: A Biography*. New York and London: Norton.
—— (1990). *Freud on Women: A Reader*. New York and London: Norton.
—— (1991). *Creative Characters*. New York: Routledge.
Zeki, S. (1999). *Inner Vision: An Exploration of Art and the Brain*. Oxford: Oxford University Press.

Index